W9-DIJ-952

Voices
from the
Earth
A Year in the Life of a Garden

The Queen Must Die . . and other affairs of bees and men
The Darkening Land
The Poisons in Your Food
The Pink Slip (with Ed Wallace)

Voices from the Earth

A Year in the Life of a Garden

WILLIAM LONGGOOD

W·W·NORTON & COMPANY·NEW YORK·LONDON

The text of this book is composed in 10/13 Janson,
with the display set in Zaph Chancery Light.
Composition and manufacturing by The Maple-Vail Book Manufacturing
Group.

First Edition.

Library of Congress Cataloging-in-Publication Data
Longgood, William F. (William Frank), 1917–
Voices from the earth : a year in the life of a garden / William Longgood.
        p.   cm.
            1. Gardening.   I. Title.
            SB455.L63   1991

635—dc20   90–38610

ISBN 0-393-02950-6

W.W. Norton & Company, Inc., 500 Fifth Avenue, New York, N.Y. 10110
W.W. Norton & Company, Ltd., 10 Coptic Street, London WC1A 1PU

1 2 3 4 5 6 7 8 9 0

For Peggy

My sometimes gardening companion
and always life companion

It amuses and astonishes me to be here now, at this point in my life, in a garden, behind me the years as a New York newspaperman, an observer and recorder of the violence and idiosyncrasies of the city, its triumphs, civic disasters and private tragedies, the monstrous inequities of life, the stuff of news. In those days I wrote much about the disadvantaged and luckless, the losers, many of whom rejected society and others rejected by it.

I found failure more interesting than success. There is only one way to succeed, usually involving the accumulation of money, which means power, and in the end, I suppose, excessive amounts of money are largely meaningless except as a way of keeping score, tangible proof of how you are doing in the game. But there are many ways to fail. I recall Jerry the Scot, a bum. I asked him how he landed on the Bowery. Jerry, sober for once, smiled and replied, "I came to see the sights and stayed to be one of them."

All of it now long behind me, the unfairness, the sorrows and terrible things I wrote about that were my livelihood. Now I sit amidst tranquility, watching the sun set, listening to birds, the conversations of insects, observing things grow, living out a self-indulgent and fading life of contentment. Time blurs all in this idyllic and unlikely setting. I could never have planned this odd turn of the road. Fate makes sport of our efforts to anticipate our lives. Indeed, I may be the garden counterpart of Jerry the Scot. I, too, came to see the sights and stayed to be one of them.

There is a wide range between an optimum garden and one that is adequate. Even a poor garden will usually produce something. A gardener, regardless how unskilled, indifferent, disorganized, or discombobulated, has one thing in his favor: Every seed wants to reproduce itself. It bears this command within its gene structure.

I have seen some pitiful gardens and in the midst of weeds, neglect, and poor soil, a stunted tomato plant bears demoralized fruit, a spunky little cabbage tries to head, a tattered row of onions, like sagging troops mauled in battle, stands at forlorn attention, proud of a game fight for survival. Some vegetables, like some people born in adversity, rise above hardship, while others succumb.

Every garden, good, bad, or indifferent, proud or demoralized, has the same thing going for it: the life force.

A garden, according to one inspired writer, is concerned with economic realities that go deeper than money. What are these realities? They are probably found in the variety of needs that a garden fulfills, individual requirements of body and soul. A garden is a way of life, a way of thinking, a way of looking at life.

For the overly industrious or driven, a garden may offer peace and relaxation. For the heartsick or stricken it is a refuge of solace. For the lazy or indolent it is a quiet place to putter and nap. For the thinking person it may be conducive to more profound thoughts or to the simplification of life's complexities. For the simpleton it is a cheerful place to be simple. For the insightful, a mecca of insights. For the weary, a place to rest and recharge spent energies. For those who treasure privacy, what offers more solitude than a garden?

For the convalescent it is a place to heal. For those wounded or bruised in the daily competitive battle to earn a living, it is a place to unwind or compose private fictions to counter realities that besiege the fortress of sanity. For the conniving and unscrupulous, it is a place to plot new strategies and schemes to outwit the unwary. For those faint of heart, it may lend its own quiet courage and resolution. The slothful or indifferent might not garden successfully by the purest standards but may fulfill their own uncritical needs in their own way. One may garden out of habit or momentum, from fad or for reasons unknown. One gardener, asked why he gardened, replied, "Why not garden?" Why not, indeed?

A garden is what you make of it. It bears your fingerprints and personality rising out of your character. The return of fresh vegetables may be one of the less important reasons for having a garden. They may be more bonus than the real, underlying reason for gardening. Whatever you put into a garden, you take from it. A garden is much like a marriage or any strong relationship: The more you give, the more you take. That is the only true measure of the economy of a garden.

More than anything else, a garden is a portal, a passage into another world, one of your own thoughts and your own making; it is whatever you want it to be and you are what you want to be. Try to give that a monetary value.

To own a bit of ground, to scratch it with a hoe, to plant seeds, and watch the renewal of life—this is the commonest delight of the race, the most satisfactory thing a man can do.

—Charles Dudley Warner

Voices
from the
Earth

A Year in the Life of a Garden

Accuse not Nature! she hath done her part;
Do thou but thine.
                                    —John Milton

It seems presumptuous to write still another gardening book. Surely, by now, nothing remains to be said or written that has not already been repeated countless times. And yet, each year new gardening books appear like the flowers of spring. In common they urge that the peas be planted as early in the season as the ground can be worked, a fertile soil is essential to good crop production, mulching conserves moisture and discourages weeds, and planting potatoes in or near fresh manure promotes scab.

This is valuable and useful information for the neophyte gardener and his experienced counterpart who may, perhaps, have to be reminded occasionally not to neglect the first principles of successful growing. But I leave that to others.

This is not a book *on* gardening. It is *about* gardening and gardens. There is a difference. It is not intended as how-to, although there may be helpful suggestions for those new to gardening. The intent here is to explore facets of gardening that are often neglected or overlooked altogether.

It is less concerned with how deep to plant the peas than with their exquisite beauty when the ripe pod is split open and nestled therein are perfect, shiny green nuggets, snug in their elongated nest, usually eight in number but not always, each an approximate replica of its predecessor, each attached to the womb shell by tiny umbilical cords like, well, so many peas in a pod.

Most remarkable of all is the miracle we take for granted: that one tiny seed can reproduce a huge plant in infinite succession, each new generation heir of its forebears, all alike and yet each different, each a repository of future generations in a continuing evolutionary genetic chain. Each seed represents a minuscule part of the life process.

In these pages will be found the vagaries and treacheries of weather, the perversity of the seasons, the complexity and cleverness of insects, the continuing cycle of life and death, compost and immortality, the sights, sounds, and aromas of gardens, the throb of a foghorn through morning mist that hangs over the plants like a wandering, misplaced sea.

It is also concerned with the netherworld of invisible soil organisms and other creatures that make life possible, the mysteries of unidentified plant diseases, seeds that do not germinate, seedlings that refuse to grow, plants that fail to reproduce for no known rational reason, gardening triumphs and disasters, visitors, volunteers, intractable weeds, wind, water, the mystique of manure, merging seasons, how plants defend themselves, the foibles and ingenuity of animals and my fellow gardeners, and my own lapses, failures, and small successes.

Managed and manipulated though it is, remote from wildness or unspoiled nature, a garden is the closest many people get to a relatively natural setting in this urbanized and industrialized age. I wrote this book primarily for myself but hope that some of the pleasures I found in its preparation will rub off on those who are non-gardeners, and that my experiences can be shared with the experienced as well as would-be gardeners who never quite make it out to the garden. Most of all this is intended as an exploration of that part of nature that is a garden.

I ask indulgence and forgiveness for any errors that betray my efforts and intentions. In the research for factual writing there are often conflicting figures and "facts" to choose from. One authority states that dragonflies fly at 60 miles an hour; another claims 35 as their top speed. I have never timed a dragonfly in flight and am at the mercy of my sources. Error may be an unlucky choice of available data.

To the discerning reader it may seem that at times the subject matter wanders from the topic of gardening, like a wayward butternut squash leaping the fence to escape the confines of its place of origin to reproduce amidst contaminated brush and weeds in the free world beyond, in effect proclaiming, like New Hampshire license plates, "Live Free or Die!"

Reader, do not be misled by these apparent infractions of sound writing technique. At all times I, the steward and overseer of this subject plot, biographer of its adventures, misadventures, and vicissitudes, have gardening firmly in mind.

One more caveat: This is, as noted, a factual work, but at times I take the liberty of engaging in fanciful speculation and ask that such passages be read in that spirit. Not too literal, please. Gardens do inspire fancies.

My present garden, the third I have tended in more than three decades as a gardener, is located on the outer reaches of Cape Cod, a narrow peninsula jutting some sixty-five miles into the sea; it lies about midpoint between the Atlantic, a half mile to the east, and Cape Cod Bay to the west.

Approximately sixty by ninety feet, the tract is irregular in shape to accommodate several scrub pines that I did not have the heart to cut down, to the garden's detriment. The plot is flat, about thirty feet in front of the southern exposure of the house, adjacent to the Cape Cod National Seashore to the east. The garden is surrounded on three sides by the gallant little pines, averaging some twenty feet in height, a wind-whipped but resolute wall of evergreens.

Seashore gardening is different from gardening inland. It is especially difficult because of the almost constant high winds that occasionally reach gale force, and the character of the soil. I have to start from scratch with "dead" yellow sand and contend with the erratic weather patterns of the sea.

The plot had only recently been cleared of a dense growth of pines, by my labor, when we built the house, and there remained a booby trap of buried stumps and roots, waiting to snag shovel and tiller. There was also a solid mat of bearberry, a tenacious ground cover known in these parts as "hog cranberry," with roots that had to be chopped out, inch by inch, with mattock, ax, and shovel; some of the roots were thicker than a man's wrist. The soil, as such, was acid from many years' accumulation of pine needles and compacted by a bulldozer used in building the house. You must pay your dues to garden on Cape Cod.

My experience with this and a previous seashore garden is that it takes about five years of hard work to convert ordinary sand into reasonably usable soil. Rit, who thinks bigger than I, had a bulldozer scoop out a couple feet of sand and filled it with topsoil brought from off Cape. Instant garden! Every pepper probably cost $50. Ken, more frugally, brought his own soil from a garden he kept in Westchester County, New York, a couple barrels at a time.

In the early years here I was graced with almost unlimited quantities of seaweed and thatch from the sea for soil building and mulch; a fairly benign climate except for spring, which is more calendar title than fact; and neighbors who kept horses and were glad to get rid of the manure, which I moved, load by load, in my old Jeep pickup.

The soil now is almost black with organic matter. I even find an occasional earthworm, a modest thrill which must set gardeners apart from other people.

> *How deeply seated in the human heart is the liking*
> *for gardens and gardening.*
> —Alexander Smith

On a day in July when the heat had lulled time itself to sleep, I was handpicking potato beetles and they were eluding me by hiding under the plant leaves. I tired of turning each leaf to search for the wily bugs and their secret egg clusters. Impulsively I flopped down on my back in the path between rows so I could look up at the undersides of the leaves.

Abruptly and unexpectedly I confronted a world new to me. There is a great difference between looking up at a garden instead of looking down. The familiar had suddenly become the unfamiliar. I was seeing the garden, *my* garden, from a potato bug's point of view. It was no longer my garden; it belonged to the potato bugs. The sky was intensely blue above the green garland of plants. Veins in the leaves made a lacy skeleton against the brilliant sunlight.

I forgot my mission and lay quietly, staring up through the thick foliage. It was a miniature jungle. I was in a tropical rain forest, the canopy arching overhead and populated by its real inhabitants. The damp soil under the mulch, my mattress and pillow, released a sweet earthy fragrance. A daddy longlegs rested motionless on a leaf, presumably waiting for breakfast or lunch to come by, depending on what time a daddy longlegs begins its working day.

Other creatures came and went, walking, hopping, crawling, scooting along, and flying: moths, butterflies, grasshoppers, ants, centipedes, spiders, ladybugs, sowbugs, a slug, and scores of resident potato beetles, all strolling along in their own way as if promenading in a private park endowed by a philanthropist for their pleasure. Was this, then, what my efforts really came to—creating a small, verdant world for other life forms, a hunting preserve, a vegetative mall, and these were the "shoppers" making their rounds?

For the first time I was aware of the real life of the garden. For the first time I was part of it and not there as manager or steward. I had no desire to kill any of the creatures I shared this habitat with, not even those intent on destroying the results of my labors for their personal gain. For the moment we were all equals. Were not their endeavors and efforts at survival as important to them as mine to me? They were simply obeying the first law of life: LOOK OUT FOR NUMBER ONE! Any deviation is divinity.

I was content to lie still and observe my companions, my fellow species, their encounters and relationships. Each seemed intent on its own mission or destination. They were not the least concerned with me or even interested in my unaccustomed presence and unorthodox posture. So much for me, the owner and overseer of this fertile little patch of land. Suddenly I was an interloper in a world I had arranged, if not created.

Eventually I got up and went about my business of dispatching the potato beetles, their larvae and eggs, but the experience of lying on my back and looking up instead of down had unsettled me. I had glimpsed something profound and unfamiliar that I did not really understand; it was as if I, a stranger to science, had looked through a microscope at an ordinary drop of pond water and seen strange forms swimming and darting about. For the first time I realized that there was, right in front of me, a whole cosmos that I have been looking at for years but never really seen. It was disturbing because it threatened a perspective that went far beyond the garden itself.

A garden, like a drop of pond water, is a whole universe in microcosm. It provides sustenance for body and spirit alike. A vegetable garden hardly seems a likely place to find cosmic truths, but they are there, waiting to be uncovered. A garden also holds the commonplace: toil, sweat, success, and failure. A garden is a kind of combined private chapel, workplace, and supermarket.

As a result of my horizontal encounter with the potato bugs and other garden creatures, I resolved to devote a year of my life to the garden, not a small investment considering my age and the number of years left me. I would study it intensively, trying to learn such lessons as it had to teach, much as Thoreau went to Walden Pond to learn the lessons of nature, solitude, and contemplation. In my own modest way I would keep a running account of my experiences. I would record random thoughts, observations, and such insights as I could manage, as well as noting various gardening techniques and practices as seemed noteworthy, while keeping an eye on the weather and the seasons.

The most ambitious and significant part of my proposed project was the intention to take the plants and creatures in the garden on their own terms. I would try to see them in a new and unfiltered light, casting aside as much of my conditioning, prejudice, and bias as I could manage. I wanted to see what was really in front of me that I had missed because I was pro- grammed to see or hear something else. We see primarily that which is in our heads rather than in front of our eyes.

I also wanted time to think and reflect, to confront the real- ity of my own life, to make terms with my advancing age. I would, in effect, try to gain a new and fresh perspective, risk examining up close that which I have seen or known only from a distance. The journal kept during that year, on a dozen yel- low pads, provided most of the materiel for this book, but I also cheat by borrowing from the past.

For almost twenty years I worked as a newspaperman in New York City. The paper collapsed in the mid-sixties and I was reincarnated as a text editor in a book factory in midtown Manhattan. From a noisy, sweaty newsroom filled with relics and ghosts of the past, I found myself in an air-conditioned, carpeted, antiseptic high-rise. After years of freely roaming the metropolis I was suddenly leashed and deskbound, a transition I was able to make only by repeatedly taking time to walk around the block and suck in great gulps of polluted air.

My office was on the thirty-fifth floor. Wind updrafts did strange things. Snow often whirled up instead of down. The building had sealed windows and artificial climate control. We knew no seasons. Fluorescent lights were our sun and moon. Deep carpeting stilled the sounds of footsteps and voices. Canned music filtered the silence of stainless-steel cages that hurtled us up and down.

We were all properly dressed, wore plastic faces, called strangers by their first names, and did what was expected of us. Twice monthly I received a check that went directly into my bank account and was spent without my ever seeing or touching the fruit of my labor. We lived by a reality made up largely of symbols, abstractions, and commercial myths. I had a choice: Adapt or flee. I fled.

I reclaimed my own reality in a garden. A gardener plants peas, digs holes for tomatoes, mulches, picks beans, harvests potatoes, fertilizes and turns soil, puts his garden to bed in the fall, and awakens it in the spring. These various tasks must follow a fairly fixed timetable that gives substance, coherence, and continuity. They add meaning to the days. There is little theory or abstraction in a load of manure or a rampant slug bent on plant destruction or self-destruction in a saucer trap of stale beer.

Most gardeners I know would recoil from the suggestion that gardening is therapy, but they must know in their hearts that it helps heal that part of the brain or soul that this materialistic, competitive, noisy culture tends to unravel or destroy altogether. It is an antidote for the way many must earn their living. A garden must be the final refuge from progress and its relentless toll on "civilized" man.

Gardening is, most of all, a stabilizing influence, a silent voice of sanity and purposeful endeavor in a world that often seems mad and without meaning, and our daily labors to earn bread and cake appear pointless and futile. We all have a need to reestablish our own ties with the earth and the economy of existence. I particularly like what an English gardener, a professor of literature, had to say on that score: "By growing what you eat, you keep in touch with economic realities which lie deeper than money."

Gardening itself is basically simple: Scratch the earth, plant a seed, and rain and sun will germinate the dormant life within and make it grow. That happens so often and predictably that we forget it is a miracle. In this world of distorted values and jaded senses we call the most trivial events miracles and see genuine miracles only as ordinary events.

In a single handful of earth live millions of microorganisms, invisible to the naked eye and yet essential to our existence. The pyramid of life above the earth's surface is supported by the base of microscopic life below. Our civilization and survival depend on those unseen specks of organic matter. They are the beginning of our food supply, the air we breathe, the clothing we wear, our art and science, the thoughts we think, the dreams we dream. Is that not miracle enough for anyone?

That, after all, is the real business of a garden: miracles.

Spring

Spring would not be spring without bird songs.
—Francis M. Chapman

As I transplant the tender young onion seedlings in rows marked by taut string between markers, a mockingbird serenades me from the chimney top. What a virtuoso he is. What joy he proclaims! What ecstasy inspires this rapturous outburst? Or is he calling to his mate, perhaps recounting some heroic venture or proclaiming the prowess in his noble little breast?

I am his only audience, the sole beneficiary of this melodic tribute to the rebirth of life. Each spring he, or maybe his descendants, announces a new season, another miracle of renewal and being. The sun is almost hot. The bees seem puzzled by the incongruous green I plant, attracted by the color yet repelled by the smell. I stop planting and sit on the ground, hands still, so I will not frighten away the performer. In this instant the mockingbird and I share a fleeting moment of existence, the thrill of a new spring day.

We often hear the mockingbird sing outside our bedroom

window during the night, so the nest must be nearby. Mockingbirds are prone to serenade on moonlit nights until their eggs hatch, according to my bird book. Is this pride in authorship, pure joy, or warning enemies and interlopers to stay away? The song is so exuberant that it leaves no doubt the musician is celebrating the culmination of his life mission.

Does our little singer know that each year we have fewer songbirds? Is he trying to make up for their absence? The destruction of tropical rain forests in Latin America and once-great forests in the United States is said to be bringing about a sharp decline in the number of song birds that go there to winter and breed; especially hard hit are the colorful warblers and vireos.

This widespread destruction is already affecting world climate and may have profound environmental repercussions, according to those who study such depressing matters. "The tropical deforestation represents the greatest blow to life on earth in all our history," observed an ecologist.

Everything seems at risk nowadays. It must take some doing to be an optimist. My poor little onion seedlings and others to follow must be ready to withstand assault by acid rain, the greenhouse effect, ultraviolet rays penetrating a diminished ozone layer, gene manipulation, deteriorating weather, the unforeseen consequences of shifting earth plates, and all manner of environmental depredations. A young onion, like the rest of us, has something to think about in these perilous times.

The various threats to the environment and life itself do not seem to effect the mockingbird singing so valiantly atop the chimney. At least not yet. It is not a migrating bird but usually remains in the same area year-round, although it may move about a bit; it is said to be extending its range northward, for whatever hope that holds.

Surely the mockingbird does not feel at risk. His song is unadulterated happiness, the distilled essence of joy in life. The onion seedlings and I can take a lesson from this intrepid troubadour: Live in the moment; do not think about the future and its perils.

I read recently about a woman who, after years of depression over the declining environment, put such cares aside and found new pleasure in daily living, concentrating on savoring "those rare moments of grace in an indifferent universe," sound advice for all of us who think too much about the unraveling state of the world.

The soil is still cold and damp as I transplant the tender young onion seedlings. They are the first crop to go into the earth this spring, after being started in flats inside, grown to respectable size under lights, and moved to the garden coldframe to "harden." I have been waiting for a warm day to plant them. This, finally, is the day. I have looked forward to it all winter, the first real day of spring. "The mysterious force of spring rules," just as the Russian poet Fet observed.

It has been a severe winter. Usually we have little or no spring on Cape Cod and each warm day is treasured. The sun is almost hot, the air soft, even balmy. We burst forth from chilled houses to greet the sun, eager as crocuses and daffodils that await rebirth in the warming earth. I listen for the official announcement from spring peepers. The bees are out, investigating what I am up to: they are intensely curious about any new garden activity.

The onion seedlings have splendid roots and thick stems. I kept cutting the tops, "trimming their hair," so new growth would go into the roots. The decapitated shoots release a pungent onion smell, showing no malice for their mistreatment, reminding me of a man I once wrote about who lived in a treehouse in a New Jersey woods.

He was far gone in cancer and kept falling down, rolling over and bouncing up without interrupting his cheerfulness or flow of speech. He claimed that flowers are the most forgiving things in nature because they return good for evil. "Crush them and they give back their fragrance," he said during one of his acrobatic mishaps. Onions must share the same philosophy but the response is less agreeable. I guess all of us give what we have to give, the result depending on whether we are flowers or onions.

I used to plant only onion sets but it was a bother. The robins insisted on thinking they were worms and pulled them out of the earth so they had to be replaced each day until the hairlike roots took hold or the robins gave up. I experimented by growing my own onions from seeds and found that the bulbs kept better than those from bought sets. I do not know why this is so; possibly there is an analogy to children and young animals and developing roots should not be disturbed too soon.

It is exhilarating to be back in the garden after the long, harsh winter of confinement. I especially enjoy thrusting my hands into the cool, moist earth. It gives me a sense of achievement, of being close to life's origins. There is a feeling of hope, even optimism, although optimism does not come easily to me; it makes me uneasy, as if I am tempting the gods.

Because of my innate skepticism I tend to plant too many seeds in flats and am invariably amazed when almost all germinate. Each year I think it cannot possibly happen again, but it always does, with only the occasional reassuring failure to support my skepticism.

Each new and unexpected success brings dilemma. I cannot find it in my heart or hands to thin or cut the excess seedlings, so over Peggy's opposition I spend hours transplanting them. Then what to do with so many plants? Are they not succulent and beautiful? Do they not deserve their chance at life? Into the garden they all go, and invariably we end up with a tangle of excess plants and more produce than we can use or give away.

Each year I resolve not to let it happen again. Each year I am caught anew in the same trap of my own making. By now I accept this failing of mine. Gardening, I have learned, is often governed less by sound technique and rational procedure than by the flaws and shortcomings of the gardener, admittedly a dreary and discouraging admission for a gardening book.

Later I will plant onion seeds for a late fall crop and will have a devilishly hard time finding space for them. But that is in the future. I know I am putting in too many onions and picture the overcrowding at season's end but do nothing to prevent it. My thoughts are of the earth. I consider the biblical phrase, "For dust thou art, and unto dust shalt thou return." Some scientists now theorize that life began not in the ocean, as is commonly believed, but in the dust of earth, just as the Bible claims. Scientific theory can take odd turns and make strange allies.

As I transplant the onions on this warm day, serenaded by the mockingbird, it does not seem to make a great difference whether we began in the saline ocean, in the dust of the earth, through cosmic bombardment, or in the Garden of Eden. It is a glorious spring day, the first of the year. The new gardening season lies ahead, with its successes, failures, and surprises yet to unfold. That alone matters and cheers me, one of those "rare moments of grace in an indifferent universe." Soon I must plant the peas. I am already late.

See, Winter comes to rule the varied year.
—James Thomson

The peas are planted, the onion transplants have taken root, and the cold frame is full of seedlings being acclimated to the weather. I thought winter was over. Instead, I look out at snow rather than spring greenery. For the last three days the temperature has been below freezing. On this sixth day of April snow is falling. Several inches cover the garden, drifts pile against the fence, wind drives the tumbling flakes horizontally. This is a nor'easter, rare at this time of year, a setback for spring.

It is odd to look out at the garden covered with white. Only the fencing the peas will grow on, the stakes supporting it, and sticks marking the rows of onions thrust out of the snow. Manure and bales of straw look like cakes with frosted icing. Snow is mounded on the birdbath in the middle of the garden, mocking the season. Suddenly we are back to winter, but the work of spring goes on under the snow as multitudes of organisms continue their labors in the soil preparing for the return of more gentle weather.

That God once loved a garden
We learn from Holy writ.
And seeing gardens in the spring
I well can credit it. . .
    —Winifred Mary Letts

*S*pring, skittish spring, has reasserted itself. The snow has melted. The robins are back. Bees are out. A chipmunk slithered through the fence and a rabbit dug under it. As the season moves along there will be a progression of other visitors, all on the same mission.

A garden is gregarious by nature, so to speak. It attracts expected and unexpected visitors alike. If the days are not filled with high drama that would raise the blood pressure of a city person, there are quiet pleasures and satisfactions for grubbers in the dirt. A garden is itself a kind of companion for those who tend to live in themselves; little time is left for loneliness or reflections on the more efficient uses of time.

I begin the day with an inspection tour to see how my realm

fared the night. I enjoy the smells and bracing exuberance of morning, the fresh aromas that rise from the earth and its new growth. Dew glistens on the crisp leaves of young cabbage plants. Tomatoes and peppers, still prisoners of the open cold frame, stand tall, refreshed by the night's vapors. Herbs tantalize with their blend of scents. Night mist yields to the sun's gathering warmth.

A pair of robins, mates I suppose, as one appears swollen with eggs, hurl mulch about in search of worms and other bird delicacies. The resident mockingbird is already serenading the return of spring and a new day. Crows bicker and complain out of sight beyond the screen of twisted pines; crows always seem out of sorts.

Lily, our Siamese, keeps an eye on the robins at the far end of the garden but accompanies me as I make rounds. She wants to be fed. If hungry, she rubs against my legs. If the situation is desperate, she stands on my feet. Lily spends much time with me in the garden, occasionally taking off on some private cat business and turning up as abruptly as she vanished.

The sun gains warmth and more bees appear, not to pollinate plants but to congregate around a pail of brackish water. The bees prefer this rank brew to the birdbath of prescribed fresh water near the hives. My bees will have none of the sterile presumption of fresh water the rules call for, a shingle slanted in to keep them from drowning; they prefer the open and dangerous pails of water in the garden.

This means time lost flying to and from the hives. Seaweed and manure had been in the pails, which I reasoned gave the water a bit of zip or tang they preferred. Then why not put a pail of the rich brew near the hives to save flying time? I would teach them a thing or two about efficiency overlooked in their programming.

I placed brackish water near the hives but the bees rejected it as they had fresh water in the birdbath. They continue to gather around the pails in the garden. Bees and cats are alike: An idea is no good unless it is their own. Both are excellent garden companions.

I interrupt the morning inspection tour to get a hoe from the toolshed. The door must be kept closed to exclude Lily. A mouse lives in the toolshed and Lily is eager to get in and redress the balance of nature. Numerous mouse families have been raised in the toolshed; they seem to prefer the existing precarious arrangement to finding new quarters.

Last summer a small rabbit broke security and sneaked into the garden, remaining for weeks, living and hiding among thick leaves of rhubarb along the fence. Lily, surprisingly, showed no interest in the rabbit and I was unable to catch it. The rabbit seemed to do little damage so we coexisted.

Now and then a neighboring dog, ignoring the local leash law, leaps the fence and exuberantly uproots a few plants. Dogs are more clever getting in than out, and usually I have to open the gate to escort them out, making me a co-conspirator in their surreptitious freedom.

Michelob, a cat who lives nearby, often skulks in weeds outside the garden, hoping to ambush Lily. A raccoon visits the compost bin at night, an untidy diner who leaves a mess behind. Many mornings I am greeted by the lingering aroma of a nocturnal skunk who came to dine on grubs in the manure pile.

Birds are frequent visitors, making a fine splashing in the birdbath. Mourning doves always travel in pairs, waddling as if their feet hurt. There are flashes of yellow, blue, and red as orioles, jays, and cardinals zip by in season.

An occasional hawk soars majestically against the sky on thermal updrafts, wheeling and suddenly diving, and everything on earth goes suddenly still. A hawk is said to be able to spot a mouse a mile away, although that may be stretching it a bit. Hawks are incredibly swift and agile in flight, suggesting more spirit of sky than flesh of earth, surely one of nature's masterpieces.

A merlin, better known as a pigeon hawk, was observed catching in flight a swallow, itself one of the swiftest flyers. The local naturalist who reported the incident said the swallow gave a terrible cry as it was seized in the rapacious talons and then went silent, as if accepting its doom.

A garden symbolizes the world. For the combatants it is a lethal arena but also a pastoral scene of mutuality, a theater of the absurd, an unfolding of creation which I watch from my ringside seat, so engrossed in the ongoing dramas, tragedies, comedies, triumphs, and mockeries that it does not occur to me to want for other diversion, amusement, or companionship.

The early spring garden is the most beautiful of all, brilliant green vegetation against brown soil, rectangular beds separated by mulched paths, the rows in neat alignment. All is in early-season order. But soon, as the days get longer and hotter, order will be overwhelmed by riotous growth, plants spilling over their given boundaries as the tyranny and triumph of production begin.

This early spring garden has a geometrical appearance as if laid out with mathematical precision. This is deception. My gardens invariably are shaped more by whim than design. I tend to plant closer than usually recommended, a modified form of "French intensive planting," crowding the plants so the canopy of foliage gets full sunlight while casting shade that discourages weeds and loss of soil moisture, an economy often practiced by nature in her own gardens.

Morning inspection gives way to a multitude of chores. The mood of the garden changes as the day advances. Night's lingering fragrance is inhaled by the sun. The harmonies about me vary. A delicate breeze stirs new plants. There is the subtle rhythm of insects. Birds call to one another, sing love songs, and proclaim territorial aspirations. Small creatures stir unseen among the encroaching weeds outside the garden.

Shifting patterns of shadow and shade accompany the great driving force of the sun. Plants draw into themselves to withstand the midday heat. Roots strike deeper into the earth in search of liquid food. New life emerges as eggs are laid and hatch. Insects and their larvae share the feast I provide. Activity increases as the heat intensifies.

Newcomers arrive to try the accommodations. Resident bugs depart in search of new hospitality, a kind of ongoing upward mobility. There is constant coming and going; we have our own sociology.

The sun reaches its zenith and retreats. New fragrances rise. The wind reverses direction to blow off the water, now bearing the salt tang of the sea. Delicately tinted clouds hover against the horizon. The sun loses force and shadows gather among the rolling hills and hollows to the east. Daylight fades in a burst of brilliant colors, dissolving into an afterglow of elegant pastels.

How much have the plants gained this day in their secret journey to maturity? How much life was lost? How much added? Who is ahead? Who is behind? Who advanced and who fell back? Who or what controls the great wheel of equilibrium? Is some new arrangement or order in the affairs of other species being worked out here beyond sight and understanding? Some things are better sensed than understood.

I go to the toolshed to put away the hoe used to cultivate the onions. Mouse, startled by my appearance, takes cover behind a shovel on the floor, her tail sticking out. The foolish creature thinks that if she cannot see me, then I cannot see her, a rather common problem up and down the line, I suspect. I shut the door and leave mouse to her dangerous illusion and deliberations.

Before closing the gate for the night I pause for a final look around the garden. Nothing apparent has changed in my small fiefdom this day. I have little tangible result to show for my labors. The great mysteries that govern this and every garden remain as profound and untouched as when I began my morning inspection in that glory of nature, the early spring garden.

> *Oh, Adam was a gardener, and God*
> *who made him sees*
> *That half a proper gardener's work is*
> *done upon his knees.*
> —Rudyard Kipling

Planting peas is one of the annual rites of spring. Conventional wisdom holds that peas should go in "as soon as the soil can be worked." This generally means when frost is out of the ground and a handful of earth can be squeezed into a soft, moist ball. Many gardeners traditionally plant peas on St. Patrick's Day, but hereabouts March 17 is pushing your luck. Spring, as noted, comes late to Cape Cod, if at all, because of the chilly ocean waters. Usually we go almost directly from winter into summer.

I generally wait to plant until about April 1, as I did this year, but even this was too soon. The ground was still so cold and damp that the seeds rotted in the ground and had to be replanted. Instead of getting a jump on the season, I was late. The early bird may get the worm but it may not be accompanied by early peas.

It is always touch and go with peas. They, along with lettuce and spinach, are the first crops planted directly in the garden, so I like to get them in as soon as possible. I am impatient after the long winter, eager to plunge my hands into the soil and see something green emerge from the earth. Often I plant too early.

Peas are more than a harbinger of spring. They are tasty, rich in vitamins A, B, and C, and enjoy a distinguished history, probably originating in central Asia, as they are considered the oldest cultivated plants. Pea remains have been found dating back five thousand years to the Bronze Age, leaving us to speculate on whether that distant ancestor cooked his peas in a primitive bronze pot or ate them raw, seeds only or shells and all.

Did he have a problem with seeds rotting in the cool earth? He was at least spared being chided that he would not have the problem if he ordered seeds treated with a fungicide. Once we received treated pea seeds by mistake. I tried to wash off the garish purple coating, without success. The few I planted performed no better than untreated seeds.

The only extra care I give pea seeds is planting them with a natural and innocent inoculant, a bacterial culture that is supposed to promote fertility, my concession to progress. I have never been able to test the efficacy of the inoculant but take it on faith, just as we do most progress.

Peas, once planted, require little attention. They are largely self-fertilizing and self-pollinating, although some insect pollination does take place. The exquisite blossoms are a spring favorite of the bees. Being legumes, peas have this wonderful little trick of adding nitrogen to the soil instead of having to be fed like most plants.

The self-fertilization of legumes is a complex process, usually dismissed with a cryptic line or two. I puzzled over it a long time before finding a detailed explanation. The roots, it seems, form little wartlike nodules which release a substance that attracts certain soil bacteria called rhizobia. Millions of these microscopic organisms invade the nodules which swell to accommodate the vast population of callers. The clever bacteria take gaseous nitrogen from the air and convert it into a form usable by the plant which, in turn, feeds the rhizobia sugar (made from carbohydrates produced by photosynthesis) for energy to multiply and do their remarkable job.

Bacteria feed plant; plant feeds bacteria. Nitrogen stimulates plant growth, the new leaves producing more sugar for the roots to expand, form more nodules, and attract more rhizobia. In the end, when the plant dies, the bacteria remain behind to fertilize the soil with their nitrogen-rich bodies, adding up to two hundred pounds of vital growth-producing nitrogen per acre. The inoculant I use is supposed to excite the rhizobia to even greater achievements.

The symbiotic relationship between plant and bacteria is more complex than the bare-bones outline offered here. Only certain bacteria will live in certain nodules, which exude substances that keep unwelcome bacteria away. Soil teems with different kinds of bacteria, many of them specialists in one job or another. These bacteria are attacked by specialist killer phages, smaller than the microscopic bacteria they prey upon, which will eat only certain bacteria; it is a highly specialized world down there.

Bacteria and phages are always at war. Were it not for the censoring phages, we are told, the bacteria would multiply until their bulk exceeded that of the earth, overwhelming all other life. So we are indebted to the phages which, in turn, have their own enemies that keep them in line. First bacteria have the upper hand, then the phages, and that is the way it goes. What takes place is wonderfully intricate and was worked out millions of years ago, an essential part of the drama we glibly refer to as "the delicate balance of nature"—less delicate, really, than precarious, less balanced than in constant turmoil.

Such matters were never mentioned and probably never considered by my mentor, Farmer Bagley, who knew intuitively what most of us have to learn. He did urge me to plant early, noting that peas like cool weather and fade quickly once heat sets in. I also mulch soon after the young plants appear in order to keep their "feet" cool and damp, just as Farmer Bagley advised.

The book calls for planting peas about an inch apart and thinning to two or three inches. This seems wasteful to me and suggests a lack of confidence in the peas, if not the life force itself. I plant about two inches apart and do no thinning. The peas seem to appreciate this expression of faith; at least they respond favorably enough so we usually have a satisfactory crop.

The weather is invariably chilly when I plant, cold and damp, and my knees are soon soaked, as Kipling must have anticipated when he consigned us gardeners to half our time on our knees. The seed bed has been prepared in advance by turning under manure and compost to provide food and habitat for the myriad underground work forces.

The bed is further enriched with wood ashes to "sweeten" the soil and make certain nutrients available to the plants. I also add ground phosphate rock for phosphorus, and green sand containing potash and trace minerals from the (New Jersey) sea deposits whence it came. Bacteria will supply nitrogen as soon as the first leaves appear and issue their commands.

Working together, the various elements provide vigorous tissue growth, promote photosynthesis, and inspire strong roots and fruit development. They put the soil in good heart, able to support healthy disease-resistant growth, mysteriously capable of transforming inert matter into the stuff of life. The book recommends the use of bonemeal and dried blood fertilizers but both are animal products, as well as expensive. I do not use them.

When ready to bear, the plants get a jolt of manure tea, a potent brew made by steeping a porous bag filled with manure in a barrel of water, a garden equivalent of fast food. Manure tea is particularly useful when a quick nitrogen fix is called for. It must be used judiciously on peas and other fruit-forming produce or it excites new growth that goes into foliage instead of pods or fruit. Overfertilized plants may be beautiful but are otherwise useless, like people whose energies are devoted so completely to their appearance that there is no other development.

Peas can be temperamental and should not be grown in the

same space in successive years. Usually I follow this injunction. One year I tested it inadvertently by replanting it in the same bed as the previous year and had a poor crop, an unintentional experiment never repeated for scientific validation.

I plant a row of peas on each side of two sections of forty-inch-high galvanized fencing. The peas usually reach the top and lop over. Once we planted a dwarf variety, using dead brush and branches for support, as recommended in a garden column, and harvested more scratches from the dry wood than peas from the vines.

For planting peas and beans I devised a homemade labor- and time-saving contraption, a narrow two-foot board with two dozen quarter-inch doll pins glued into drilled holes two inches apart, each pin two inches long and pointed. Pushed against the earth the device makes twenty-four evenly spaced holes in a straight line. Depth depends on how firmly the board is pressed down.

Simply pop a pea or bean into each hole, firm the earth, and the rest is up to nature. Not exactly high tech but handy enough. I do not anticipate the need for a patent. In truth, I rarely use the thing, preferring to punch individual holes with my finger or an improvised dibble. The pleasure in inventions is primarily in the inventing, not the use. Often they are a bother. I have learned to be wary of most labor- and time-saving short-cuts, especially those I devise.

In about fifty-five days, if all goes well, we will be eating peas. With luck the weather is fairly warm by then. The swollen pods hang gracefully from the vines, exquisitely shaped, a brilliant green, almost invisible against the rich foliage. Peas are ideally picked before fully mature to assure tenderness and greater production. The more heavily and the earlier they are harvested, the harder they try to reproduce themselves and the more futile their attempt. A garden exists largely by duping nature. That is our particular trick.

Peas are among the first returns of the spring garden. The initial picking is particularly tender and sweet, a special treat eaten raw, right off the vines before the sugar turns to starch. If spring has a taste it is in peas. Edible spring! When I grew up in the Midwest, my mother prepared new peas and new potatoes in a white sauce, a taste memory that lingers. They probably were never as delicious as I recall, but taste may be one of the many treacheries of memory.

The vines produce steadily over a couple of weeks, providing a continuing supply of peas for the table and enough for freezing and friends, the ideal balance. Almost at once, it seems, the vines are exhausted and turn yellow, as if suddenly realizing that their time is up, and I recall, almost with shock, that we are practically into summer.

Pods left on the vines to mature and dry for next year's seeds gradually shrivel, turn brown, and become brittle. At last nature has her way. The pods are taken into the house for further drying and then shelled, and the seeds made ready for winter storage. Freezing them first in a moisture-proof container for twenty-four hours will kill any weevils under the skins, according to a report I read. I learned this only recently; until then I never knew it was a problem. Is a problem not recognized still a problem?

Unlike other seeds, the report advised, peas and beans should not be stored in airtight jars but kept loosely in cloth or burlap so they can "breathe," an idiosyncrasy apparently limited to stored legumes.

Dead and dying pea vines that cling to the fencing while the seed pods are drying are a melancholy and incongruous sight among early summer's new growth. As soon as the pods are removed, the shriveled vines are dispatched to the compost bin, and the wire fence is rolled up and set outside the garden until next spring.

In a few weeks fall spinach will be planted in the nitrogen-enriched bed where the peas made their valiant stand, and already I am thinking about where to plant next year's crop of peas, whose seeds have not yet even made it into winter quarters where they can breathe.

Heaven is not reached at a single bound.
—Josiah Gilbert Holland

Periodically, about this time of year, I am tempted to keep chickens to complement the garden. It is a springtime project and the notion occurred to me again today after I read an article on how to build a henhouse. I even have a folder containing such plans and will probably add this one to my collection, although undoubtedly I will never build a henhouse or keep chickens. It is one of those fantasies I keep toying with.

Keeping a small flock seems a good idea, theoretically. It is a lovely sensation to walk into a henhouse at dusk and hear the residents clucking softly as they discuss the day's events and boast of their accomplishments.

I know several people who keep a few chickens more or less successfully, although most seem primarily concerned with the economic advantages rather than the peripheral benefits. The idea appeals to me because it fits in with my inclination to live as self-sufficiently as possible in a dependency-oriented culture. Hens would provide a steady supply of fresh, inexpensive, uncontaminated eggs, and manure fertilizer that is rich in nitrogen and an excellent soil conditioner.

Chicken manure has become very expensive and hard to come by at any price. I used to buy it by the pickup load at a local farm a few years ago and the grateful seller helped me load the truck. No more. The best I can do now is buy an occasional bag from a neighbor who keeps a few chickens and sells the manure for almost what the feed costs. A few years ago I drove forty miles to clean out two abandoned henhouses and paid the owner $10. An amused friend said I got a "shitty deal." I thought it a bargain.

Along with providing eggs and manure, chickens are excellent for getting rid of garden pests when allowed to range freely. They may do a bit of damage with their scratching and pecking, but in days past no respectable kitchen garden was without chickens. The primary disadvantage is that, like all domestic animals, chickens require constant care. Their keeper is, in effect, also their prisoner; the best of symbiotic relationships has drawbacks.

That alone does not stop me. The main deterrent is the threat of emotional entanglements that I do not care to deal with. It is not easy to feed and care for creatures every day and not develop a certain bond or attachment to them. I learned long ago that it is unwise to get emotionally involved with animals when the parting is likely to be premature or bloody.

I still carry vivid childhood memories of visiting a Kansas farm and seeing a pig I had fed shot and quivering in its death agony, of chickens having their necks wrung or placidly leaving their heads where Aunt Dora placed them on a chopping block and *zing!* down came the ax, the decapitated body flopping wildly about spurting blood from its severed neck, the dismembered head on the red earth nearby, unseeing eyes staring intently at the body's frenzied death dance.

Intimate relationships with domestic animals come about insidiously. Usually they begin by giving the creature a name and feeding it every day. Dependency is one of the strongest bonds in any relationship, working for and against nurturer and nurtured alike. People who are not professional farmers or dedicated homesteaders, or who lack the necessary detachment, often fail to consider the deeper implications and ultimate end when they casually acquire animals. The backlash may come later, in different degrees, depending on the person and their view of life.

Take Dorothy and Farmer Bagley. . .

Dorothy, like Farmer Bagley, was a friend of ours when we lived in New Jersey before moving to Cape Cod. She was a spinster, well off, lived on an estate, and maintained as tidy a garden as ever I have seen. Brick paths were bordered with flowers. Each planting was properly tagged, position dictated by size, growing requirements, and aesthetics. Dorothy was artist and gardener, a not unusual pairing. You knew much about her, as you do most gardeners, by looking at her garden. Everything was in order.

Dorothy decided to keep chickens and went about it in her methodical way. She hired a skilled carpenter who built the finest chicken coop imaginable, a Kubla Khan of chicken coops. It was designed by Dorothy and was functional as well as a work of art. It had a sun parlor, day room, custom-built laying nests, protected run for rainy days, and storage room for feed and bedding. The henhouse was near the garden so the chickens could have a steady diet of fresh produce and comfrey grown especially for them. They were fed vitamins and the finest natural rations. Each had a name and identity. Dorothy personally cleaned the henhouse, changed the bedding, collected eggs, and discussed things with her charges.

She was horrified by modern commercial practices of raising poultry on factory farms. Such hens live and die without ever knowing the blessed sensation of darkness, never touch or scratch earth, taste a juicy insect, know a rooster's companionship, the feel of warm eggs in a nest under their downy feathers. Most live and die without hearing the cluck of a baby chick from their bodies. They lay by artificial light around the clock in tiers of elevated wire cages with conveyor belts that feed them automatically and remove their eggs and wastes; their diet is laced with growth hormones, antibiotics, appetite enhancers, and God knows what else to promote fast growth and quick profits.

Commercial hens are never summoned to dawn by the triumphant crowing of a rooster, one of my earliest and fondest memories. In those days many people, even in cities, kept a few chickens. The crowing of a rooster at dawn was an accepted neighborhood sound. That was long ago. Today commercial chickens may be the most exploited and ill-used creatures on earth, outside of animal-testing and research laboratories, destined, after they cease to lay, for a labeled can or plastic bag in a supermarket. It takes a tough man, indeed, to raise tender chickens, just as the ad proclaims.

Dorothy's pampered hens must have appreciated their good fortune. In the early days the association worked out fine. She was ecstatic. The chickens responded to her care and expectations by laying heroically. There were so many eggs that she sold or gave them away.

This probably helped assuage some of the guilt she lived with because of her affluence and the universal poverty and suffering that caused her much distress. The chickens must have considered themselves so many hen princesses. Dorothy even bought them a rooster to assure their happiness and biological fulfillment.

This felicitous relationship had to end, as all idyllic life must end, dreams fade, and fantasies betray. Eventually the chickens aged and ceased to lay. Most hens, at this point, are converted into soup or salads. Not Dorothy's flock. She could not bear the thought of killing them. That would be barbaric, she explained. Like eating old friends. Each of the dozen hens represented a personal commitment.

When Dorothy entered the henhouse to gather eggs or care for her charges, they carried on, cackling and clucking contentedly, rustling about her feet as if they considered her one of them and she was paying a social call.

The problem could have been resolved easily enough by selling the hens or giving them to her neighbor Farmer Bagley, who had originally provided the chicks. He did not share her compunctions about eating the fowl and pigs he raised. Giving the chickens to him, Dorothy said, would have been almost the same as killing them herself—even worse, because it represented a shirking of moral responsibility. Things like that were part of the psychic anguish Dorothy lived with; she was victim of her own good heart, like most kind-hearted people.

Eventually she found her own solution. Instead of killing or disposing of the chickens she retired them. The palatial coop became, in effect, a nursing home and then hospice for geriatric hens. Dorothy was chicken-hearted in every sense of the word.

When we departed New Jersey the chickens had grown to a phenomenally old age for their kind. Dorothy was still conscientiously looking after them in their dotage, still feeding them vitamins, choice bought rations, comfrey, and fresh organic produce from the tidy garden. She bought eggs for her own use.

Although Farmer Bagley did not flinch from eating flesh he raised, he had his own Achilles' heel where animals were concerned. He was a big man with broad shoulders, ruddy complexion, fiery red hair, and long fiery sideburns that made him look deceptively fierce. His manner was gruff but he was one of the most gentle men I ever knew, especially with animals and children. His matched team of bays were the pride of his life.

The bays, whose names I no longer remember, were kept in a rundown stable—all of his buildings were rundown—but their stalls were cleaned daily. They were given fresh bedding, groomed regularly, and fed the best grains and hay, along with apples, lumps of sugar, and ears of corn from the fields, such as remained of his modest holdings.

"They're my friends," he would say of the bays, giving them a tidbit from his pocket, scratching their necks, and making sure they were not tormented by flies. The bays were never overworked and wore protective netting in the fields. While plowing or cultivating he would talk to them as if they were humans. It was touching to see that big, ferocious-looking man's affection and tenderness for his horses and the shepherd dog, Rory, who was always at his heels.

In most matters Farmer Bagley was practical, even Spartan in self-denial. He must have felt uneasy over his sentimental relationship with the bays. I do not know what happened but he either decided or was convinced by someone that it was foolish and uneconomical to maintain the team for the limited use he made of it; a tractor would make more sense.

Farmer Bagley impetuously sold the team to an Amish farmer in Pennsylvania for money to buy a sensible tractor. The night of the sale he lay in bed full of remorse and misery. Suddenly, at midnight, he leaped up, frightening his wife, and phoned the Amish farmer that the deal was off; he had to have the horses back at once. At dawn he left to reclaim them and by nightfall they were back in their old stable. Farmer Bagley never again considered getting rid of the bays. He still had them when we moved.

Later, we heard, the farm was sold and carved into lots for expensive houses in what had become an exclusive neighborhood of corporate executives. I do not know what happened to the bays or Rory, the shepherd dog. Farmer Bagley, we were told, had moved out of the state. My source did not know where he went or if he continued to farm. Dorothy still lives where she did. By now, I assume, the geriatric chickens have gone to their reward, as they say, although it probably could not touch their earthly paradise.

When I consider taking on chickens, I think of Dorothy and Farmer Bagley and continue to buy chicken manure by the bag and grumble about the outrageous price. The neighbor who supplies me seems to have no problem about what to do with overage hens and roosters, and I try not to dwell on the hypocrisy of my position and the advantages of keeping a few chickens.

"There is a place for everything
In earth, or sky, or sea,
Where it may find its proper use,
And of advantage be,"
Quoth Augustine, the saint.
—Benjamin B. Warfield

Several years ago I awakened on a chilly spring night exclaiming, "Oh my God! I forgot the zucchini." Peggy sat up, startled, muttered something uncivil, and went back to sleep. Minutes later I was in the garden, in robe and slippers, pulling a tarp over the cold frame containing the zucchini, considering the absurdity of my situation, and thinking, I'm really losing my marbles.

Gardening is full of pitfalls and pratfalls but quitting a warm bed on a chilly night to cover tender zucchini plants is one the gardening books do not mention. And just as well. I got into this bind with the zucchini by chance. Many years ago I tried to force it in early spring as an experiment. The plants were grown in the house and transplanted to a cold frame in the garden around May 1.

This violates garden orthodoxy. Zucchini is notoriously cold sensitive. The most risky step is going directly from warmth under lights into cool soil. For several days I let the sun beat on the closed cold frame to warm the earth. Even then the transfer is a shock; the plants seem to cringe as their rootballs are slipped into the cool ground.

The cold frame must be opened, or vented, during the day

to prevent heat buildup that can cook plants, and closed at night to keep out cold. Even this is not protection enough at first and the entire cold frame is covered with a tarp at night. This morning / night routine of opening and closing the cold frame can go on for days or even weeks until the weather warms and the plants are on their own.

Our last official frost date is April 23 but often the weather does not respect this calendar optimism. Tardy frost or cold may cut down fragile plants that are not protected, chilling the ardor of overly zealous gardeners; I have had my ardor chilled often enough.

Most years, if the weather behaves, we have fresh zucchini by mid-June, and once even earlier but that was a freak. It is not that I am so fond of zucchini or eager to get a leg up on my fellow gardeners zucchiniwise. I am not on the fast track in the garden or elsewhere. Somehow the original experiment got out of hand and became an annual contest to see if I can outwit the weather, then evolved into routine or ritual, probably the way most vices get started.

The weather seems to enjoy this seasonal confrontation as much as I and does its best to catch me unaware. More often than I like to admit, it succeeds. But each spring I am back for another round, and so is the weather.

I went outside this morning to vent the cold frame protecting the young zucchini, and there, on top of the plastic cover, was a squash bug waiting for the restaurant to open. It was a startling sight. He or she, most likely she, was far ahead of schedule, as optimistic as I in putting out the plants this soon.

Squash bugs usually do not arrive until July, and here it is barely the start of June. I never saw one this early. Is it an omen of what is to come or merely a single individual out of sync or confused? Every species seems to have its nonconformists and eccentrics. Is it reconnoitering or ready for serious business? I had not planned to write about squash bugs until later, after they arrived in invasion strength, but this overachiever forces my hand, just as I force the zucchini.

The squash-bug story is worth telling. Not because of their menace but for their staying power and dedication, qualities not to be dismissed lightly in this volatile world of quick changes, passing fads, and failed commitments. Squash bugs, in some vague and indefinable respect, may even be considered admirable, although they also may challenge the concept of reverence for life. I wonder if Dr. Albert Schweitzer and St. Augustine ever had to deal with rampant squash bugs.

Squash bugs do not have an especially exciting life history or genealogy to take pride in. About all they have going for them is their fecundity, tenacity, and a foul odor they release when distraught. They are related to the well-named stinkbugs and are often called stinkbugs themselves, an entomological error but not a libel.

Squash bugs are one of the most difficult insects to control. They have ravenous appetites, breed maniacally, and lay their eggs on the undersides of leaves where they are hard to find.

Squash bugs are fatalistic; they make little effort to escape when threatened but this may be due to excessive confidence in their disagreeable smell to protect them from danger. Overconfidence is the undoing of many species.

My primary complaint against squash bugs is that there is no spirit of live and let live in them as there is in some garden pests of lesser consequence. And yet, it ill becomes me to be too harsh on them. They are, after all, my fellow vegetarians.

Squash bugs are not celebrities or glamour figures of the insect world like, say, Japanese beetles or gypsy moths which, under certain conditions, become media events. Squash bugs have fewer pretentions, more modest aspirations, and less mobility. They maintain a low profile outside the garden and tend strictly to business, keeping the old mouthparts to the squash leaves, in pursuit of their life mission, which is to keep squash and gardeners from getting the upper hand.

Adult squash bugs measure slightly over a half inch, are brownish-black in tone, and wear on their backs a shield design suggesting a coat of arms. They are quite striking in appearance, even distinguished, prejudice aside and certain personality shortcomings overlooked. Traditionally they appear about the time squash vines start to run, around mid-July hereabouts. I assume the one I encountered in early June was drawn from its winter quarters prematurely by the lure of new zucchini but this is surmise. Who knows what goes on in a squash bug's head or genes?

Females lay their eggs in clusters, in a symmetrical pattern somewhat suggestive of a triangle of racked pool balls, on the leaf underside where veins form angles. This is probably a survival tactic worked out over the milleniums and not some impromptu compulsion. The newly laid eggs, one to three dozen per lot, are a shiny yellowish gold which fades after a few hours to a more subdued brownish tone, making them even harder to detect. Squash bugs obviously have given this much thought.

The eggs hatch in about two weeks, and after a rainy spell, seem fairly to explode in number; suddenly there are multitudes of tiny juicy nymphs, miniature replicas of their parents, with grayish bodies and rather elegant black legs. The young are a clannish lot, the nymph siblings remaining together as they feed on the leaf where they hatched, then moving to a new leaf that is also devoured. The more they eat, the fewer leaves remain for food and nursery, a kind of progressive habitat destruction. Success is their ultimate undoing, which is not unique to squash bugs.

Quick work is made of an entire plant, the bugs employing their syringe-like mouthparts to suck juices out of leaves while injecting a caustic fluid that makes the foliage curl and die, turning black and barren as if hit by heavy frost. After killing the plant the relentless hordes attack the fruit, puncturing the skin and causing rot. When every zucchini is wiped out they may, in desperation, go after pumpkins and other cucurbits, even cucumbers, or attempt other dietary innovations.

Is this simple insect gluttony or some deeper life truth in operation? The English novelist Samuel Butler could have had squash bugs in mind when he observed that there is "a universal desire on the part of every organism to live beyond its income." I pass this along for whatever it is worth but decline to see squash bugs as bearers of deeper truths or a metaphor for universal self-destruction. Every summer they appear anew, like supplicants at a bank seeking a new line of credit. If they do convey a deeper truth it is no substitute for the zucchini they wipe out. Try making zucchini bread with deeper truths.

Squash bugs, in pursuit of their life work, mature in about four weeks, molting five times along the way. Adults have wings and after polishing off one garden take off to another. They seem to possess an unerring instinct for where to go, much like Willie Sutton, who, asked why he robbed banks, replied, "That's where the money is." Squash bugs could as well say about gardens, "That's where the zucchini is."

I indicated earlier that squash bugs display considerable savoir faire when threatened, but under serious attack they drop to the ground to hide in the mulch, working their way back to the tops of plants when driven by lust. They are easiest to catch when too preoccupied with sex to sense danger, which, again, is not unique to their kind.

Adults do not mate the season they reach maturity but sleep away the winter, taking shelter under a board or garden trash, emerging in the spring to mate and start laying eggs, a cycle repeated year after year. The gardener's objective is to break the cycle, wiping them out if possible, a kind of garden genocide. Without using violent poisons this is most unlikely.

I have tried almost every recommended means of harassment without much success. Repellent flowers have not repelled, wood ashes and lime have failed to discourage, rototilling after frost did not expose the sleepers to winter's lethal blasts. Some gardeners report success placing a shingle on the ground to entice them to congregate under it during off-duty hours for mass destruction. My particular line of bugs appears too brainy to be taken in by so simplistic a ruse.

Squash bugs have a few natural enemies. Birds will have no part of them because of their smell. Assassin bugs, their cannibalistic relatives, have no prejudices about smell but are rarely around. When desperate I resort to a mild form of chemical warfare, dusting the assault force with rotenone, probably the least toxic garden pesticide, so mild indeed that it makes little impression other than initiating considerable excitement and even panic. Rotenone has no residual value beyond, possibly, causing nervous indigestion.

My only effective defense is handpicking, but I may cause as much damage removing egg patches as the nymphs would do if left alone, and the adults I miss replace the eggs as fast as they are removed. There is another thought: Am I removing the weak, lazy, forlorn, and inept, in effect strengthening the gene pool of the rest, as the wolf is said to strengthen the caribou by wiping out the unfit? Am I an unwitting tool of nature, helping create a new race of super squash bugs?

Handpicking is the one garden task I dislike, dousing the creatures in a can of kerosene or squishing them. Squishing is especially unpleasant. I considered devising a mechanical squisher that was to work on the principle of two blocks of wood on a hinge, a kind of lethal pliers, but it was too gory for my taste. Like my other inventions it never got off the ground.

As the season progresses I fall further behind and the bugs gain in numbers and self-confidence. They no longer bother to hide their eggs under the leaves but deposit them on top in full view, a kind of squash-bug throwing down of the garden gauntlet, a challenge I fail to meet.

They have become immune or indifferent to everything but a smart pinch between thumb and forefinger. I have little stomach for that kind of hand-to-hand, or thumb-to-forefinger, combat, and it is a bother to have a can of kerosene at the ready. The only unresolved issue is who will be first to wipe out the zucchini, the squash bugs or the borers? These latter will be dealt with in their turn.

I am not especially distraught at the loss of the zucchini. They, like the bugs attacking them, are wildly prolific. By the time they go down we have had our fill and exhausted the patience of friends who will eat them. Losing plants to insects is part of the game. I expect it when planting and often put in extra for them. The only thing that "bugs" me is this: What did evolution have in mind for squash bugs, and why? But I guess the same could be asked about me.

The age of miracles is forever here.
—Thomas Carlyle

In my hand I hold a remnant of early spring that found its way into my jacket pocket when I was planting peas several weeks ago. I cannot explain how this solitary seed got into my pocket. Perhaps providence slipped it in to teach me a lesson. I learned about seeds in biology class many years ago, dissecting them and memorizing their various parts and functions, but largely forgot what I learned. There is nothing like memorizing the parts of a miracle to reduce it to the commonplace.

This pea seed, larger than most seeds I plant, has a green coat, is wrinkled, and appears shriveled. Looked at a certain way it has a troubled expression. A magnifying glass does little for it except to enlarge the folds and wrinkles. Under the glass it could be a miniature of earth seen from space. Ridges and hollows suggest mountain ranges, mighty gorges, great seas, plains, rivers, and valleys; smudges of dirt could be the continents.

The most compelling aspect of this seed is that it is of manageable dimension. Most of the great dramas of creation recounted by science are beyond me. This one is within my grasp. I am more attuned to prehistoric man paying homage to the mystery of being at Stonehenge than the scientists at Houston "conquering" space. This wayward little pea is my Stonehenge.

A seed is the basic unit of life, surely one of nature's more inspired inventions; it is to vegetation what the egg is to animal continuity. The pea seed's shriveled husk contains the embryo of a three-foot plant, complete with roots, vines, leaves, and pods, a matrix inherited and passed along, bearing instructions for growth, how and when to climb and cling, when to produce the seed that is its immortality, when to decline and die; life and death are encoded in genes beholden to Earth's chemicals and organisms, sunlight, temperature, weather, and other forces and events of which we have little or no knowledge.

Regardless how the wily seed lands in the soil, the stem will grow up, the roots down. Seeds have many ways of providing food for the new plant until it can care for itself—nutrients surrounding the embryo within, packed in the fruit or nut, arising from special tissues or, as in legumes, cradled in the incipient nurturing leaves themselves.

Within my pea seed the folded winglike cotyledons are swollen with a reservoir of protein, starch, and oil to sustain early growth until photosynthesis and the true leaves take over. The fragile interim leaves send a message to tiny roots to summon bacteria to produce nitrogen to feed the hungry plant tissues aboveground. Soil microbes work mysteriously together to supply essential vitamins.

The leaves, less than 1 / 150th of an inch thick, are miniature chemical factories powered by an energy source 93 million miles away, photons from the sun hurtling against green-leaf chloroplasts at 186,000 miles per second, the speed of light, splitting water and carbon molecules, the porous leaves inhaling carbon from the air and exhaling oxygen. Carbohydrates formed in the process are converted to glucose, the simple sugar that is basic to life, the plant's primary sustenance. Foraging roots deliver mineral salt nutrients in solution from the soil; leaves, stem, and roots work together to sustain delicate new life.

All of this in one small seed, a process that began 200 million years ago when the first seeds were formed. It is profound and amazing, both commonplace and predictable. The seed comes in a packet that sells for about one dollar. Perhaps we have lost the capacity to recognize miracles that we can afford.

Not the least of the wonders of this seed is its individuality, despite its origin in mass production. It looks like its traveling companions but each is unique. Some will attain optimum growth like the splendid pictures in seed catalogues; others will falter, compromise, or fail altogether.

Plants, even offspring of the same parents, can be as unpredictable, temperamental, and perverse as animals. Each seed dictates its own terms but some are more flexible and forgiving than others. Most grow without mishap. Some thrive through adversity. A few take hold, then suddenly fail or sicken and die.

Those that reproduce are usually amazingly prolific. I counted 538 seeds in a medium-sized pumpkin I grew. A single cherry tomato had 105 seeds, an ordinary green pepper, 129. Many seeds—among them celery and carrots—are too small and numerous to count.

Most garden seeds are viable for three to five years but exceptions are onions, parsnips, and parsley, which are generally held to be good for only one year, and beets, cucumbers, eggplants, and tomatoes, which may be good for more than five years. Why do some remain alive longer than others? Is it a caprice of nature or some master plan that governs the days of all living things?

Tales abound of seeds found in the tombs of ancient kings, still usable after thousands of years, but documented proof is said to be lacking. The oldest viable seed known was an Indian lotus found in a drained lake in Manchuria. Carbon testing determined it to be 1,040 years old, minus or plus 210 years, but still capable of diffusing its radiance in a laboratory after a millennium. Is a storied Indian lotus a thousand times more valuable to nature's vegetative economy than a contemporary onion?

The plant that emerges from a seed has a strange story to tell about the likeness of all life. The makeup of a plant and that of a person are remarkably similar; both are composed of the same chemicals, primarily oxygen, carbon, hydrogen, nitrogen, and varying amounts of other elements that are nature's basic formula for life.

Indeed, plants and animals have an almost identical chemical makeup. Plant chlorophyll is known as "green blood," and with good reason, explains James Poling in *Leaves*. He notes that a single molecule of chlorophyll consists of a lone atom of magnesium linked to 136 atoms of nitrogen, carbon, and oxygen. "If you remove the single magnesium atom from the chlorophyll molecule and replace it with just one atom of iron, what you get is essentially a molecule of red blood—and further proof that nature's formula has a common denominator." A scientific truth expressed poetically in the Bible when Isaiah says, "All flesh is grass."

Each step in a plant's development pushes it toward the final goal of reproduction. An internal timetable instructs when to set flower and cast seed, the male anthers opening on invisible command to release hundreds, thousands, or millions of minuscule grains of pollen that are relayed to the female ovary where fertilization takes place, the pollen often "perishable as a snowflake," possibly with a life of only two or three hours in which to strike a target no bigger than the head of a pin, the union of pollen and ovule setting the stage for the ultimate drama—life begetting life.

Is it not a remarkable story? How did evolution alone program such linear intelligence into a mere dab of organic matter? How did nature conceive of seed and egg as the primary mediums of life continuity? Was it all worked out in advance and executed by some guiding force, or did it just take place, largely by chance, bit by bit, each step falling into line and waiting for the next phase to develop or a new idea to take shape? Design or chance? One seems as improbable as the other.

Modern science has explained the how of many mysteries that tormented the ancients but is no closer than they were to understanding the why. We have information, religion, and ritual but have lost our capacity for reverence of the Great Unknown, which Indians called the Great Mystery. What gardening gives us, at best, perhaps, is that which we have lost in ourselves, the mystic tie that bound primitive man to nature. We have been largely desensitized to that which gives life meaning and substance.

For men to live and prosper on a psychic level he must have a sense of earth, a sense of time, a sense of awe. All living things are much alike, utilizing energy through various means, differing primarily in form and expression. We are akin to the composition of the planet that nurtured us, our physical being, like that of Earth, approximately 70 percent water.

The great enigma of life is not resolved in the laboratory where science dismisses any reaching for the unknown as mysticism or "unproved claims," and rightly so, for proof is the essence of science. But there is more to life than science, and some of the most profound life truths may not be provable. We cannot hope to understand that which exceeds our comprehension. How is it that a leaf made up largely of protoplasm, a blend of lifeless compounds, is itself alive, and whence comes that life? That is the ultimate riddle.

Botanists say that we, of this era, live in the age of soil plants because they form the basis of the food chain on which mammals like ourselves depend largely for survival. The small pea that I hold is part of the invisible continuity, an infinitesimal unit of eternity. I gaze not upon a single seed, an object of commerce, but a link in the chain of life.

> To dig and delve in nice clean dirt
> can do a mortal little hurt.
> —John Kendrick Bangs

The old green metal chair is warm on my backside from the sun although it is not yet noon. This is my favorite garden observation post. Here I can see what is going on. I am practically unnoticed by the birds. Robins come within a few feet of where I sit, tossing mulch in pursuit of worms. Bees risk drowning in a standing pail of manure tea. Lily jumps up on my lap and the robins take off.

I notice, without moving, that the parsley needs weeding, the cabbage should be watered, some lettuce is already threatening to bolt, the kale wants thinning, the garlic could use fertilizer. I see a dozen things that need doing that I had not noticed while moving about. The green metal chair is an indispensable piece of equipment. As Farmer Bagley said, "How can you grow anything without a chair? How else you going to see what's going on?"

Farmer Bagley, as my mentor, taught me some gardening techniques but, more important, he imparted a philosophy or attitude toward gardening. The essence of his approach was, perhaps, the importance of a chair, the seat of his philosophy, as it were.

His was an ancient overstuffed easy chair, often water-soaked but still serviceable. In the beginning I had an old wooden chair, which finally collapsed and was replaced by a metal chair from the dump. A little paint and it was good as new, almost on a par with the soil and plants in importance. How could anyone garden without a chair, indeed? "How else you going to see what's going on?"

I knew Farmer Bagley through Dorothy, who got her chickens and rooster from him. The rooster eventually became too macho and began to attack his harem. That upset Dorothy. Any violence distressed her, and she considered the hens her wards. Then the rooster started after Dorothy. She went to Farmer Bagley for advice. As usual, he came right to the point: "That rooster ain't good for nothin' but eatin'."

Of course Dorothy could not bear the thought of eating the rooster. That would be practically cannibalism, "almost like eating a member of your family." A proper moral dilemma! What to do? People with kind hearts are forever facing moral dilemmas. Her ultimate solution was to give the macho rooster to Farmer Bagley and he ate it without second thoughts. Like most practical people, he was able to compartmentalize his life in most respects—sentiment had nothing to do with eating the rooster, a sensible way to reduce conflicts and complications.

Dorothy was the opposite of Farmer Bagley. She was unable to compartmentalize her life. All of the various bins spilled over so the contents intermingled. There were endless conflicts, complexities, and guilt, nothing black or white.

Giving the macho rooster to Farmer Bagley did not simply resolve the dilemma. She suffered agonies of guilt and kept asking herself if she did the right thing. I suppose it could be argued that most of us, most of the time, do what we are comfortable with in resolving moral dilemmas. If that is true, Dorothy and Farmer Bagley were each served in their own way. Only the rooster came out behind, as someone usually does in moral dilemmas, unless it happened to have a death wish.

Dorothy and Farmer Bagley were, as in most other things, opposites in their approach to gardening, except that neither used chemicals. She for principles. He because "it ain't natural." Her garden was exquisitely tidy, a picture out of a garden catalogue, as if each plant had been selected for its team spirit. The garden, I suspect, represented the order she wanted in her life.

In some odd way Dorothy convinced herself that the garden was an economy. Despite her wealth and large estate, she was sure she would end a pauper. She was forever practicing small economies. Most wound up costing a small fortune, like the palatial chicken coop. She loved to point out that the manure from the chickens went into the garden and the garden helped feed the chickens. In her system of economies that exchange not only completed the great cycle but justified the cost of both chickens and garden. All of us have our own little self-deceptions about gardening and other matters. In truth, if one grows vegetables for economy, it often would be cheaper to go to the supermarket. But more about this later.

Farmer Bagley never considered the economics of gardening. For him it was both a practical and spiritual necessity. His head and heart were in the soil. He and his wife had once owned a large amount of land but sold most of it off, bits at a time, to stave off creditors and raise their family. When I knew them, they had only about sixteen acres left and developers were hot after the rest. The offers kept getting higher. They refused to sell. She had been born in the small house and lived there all her life. Her children were born and raised there. She and Farmer Bagley loved the land. Each sale was painful, almost like losing a child. Taxes and expenses kept increasing. The pressure mounted. Their story may be a kind of historical document of the times.

Life was a struggle for the couple. He cut and chopped all of the wood that heated the small house with its dirt cellar and old stove. In the fall he used the team of bays to take local groups on hayrides. He sold vegetables and eggs to neighbors. She canned most of their food for winter and helped in the garden. Periodically he tried to bring order into his life. It was in one of those fanciful spells that he sold the bays to buy a tractor and then, horrified by what he had done, called the deal off in the middle of the night.

Farmer Bagley was, in reality, more gardener than farmer because of the modest size of his operation. In spirit he was still a farmer as he had been before selling off the land. All he wanted in life was to be left alone to farm. In moments of reflection he would talk about the past and the huge crops he grew.

In place of chemicals, he disked into the soil mountains of manure from the horses and chickens which ranged loose and foraged for insects among the crops. He would never have described himself as an organic farmer. He was a "grower." He was what, in my youth in the Midwest, was known as a dirt farmer.

He did not oversee the land or hire help. He was out mucking in the earth himself, never so happy as when out plowing behind the bays, sweating and watching straight black furrows turn up. I walked alongside him, talking and picking up bits of gardening lore and folk wisdom, along with the fumes of a huge black cigar to keep away mosquitoes that strayed from the nearby pond.

Before turning to farming he had a trucking business and it was profitable but he hated it and sold out. "You ride in one of them things all day and you get piles. They almost killed me."

We paused at the rows of tomatoes on the way back to the stable, now followed by a cloud of smoke-defiant mosquitoes. No one else could have grown tomatoes under such conditions, not even in that black, fertile Jersey earth. Every garden manual cautions against letting weeds choke out crops and rob them of nutrients and moisture. His tomatoes were almost smothered by weeds. He pulled the weeds aside and held aloft a gloriously big, red, juicy, unblemished tomato. "Tomatoes like the shade," he cried. "Look how happy they are down there!"

The potatoes were enormous and unflawed, the corn unbelievably sweet, the strawberries the most succulent this side of the Garden of Eden. Farmer Bagley charged only 50¢ a quart for those magnificent berries when others got half again as much and the supermarkets even more. Frequently I urged him to increase the price. "No," he said, "that's all strawberries are worth." It was not principle or morality, as such. It was his own sense of propriety, an inner integrity that ruled his life. He never used the word; it was not in his vocabulary, just in the way he lived.

He was forever in trouble with his neighbors after the developers came in and turned that lovely rural area into a suburban enclave of tidy expensive houses, some of them built on land he once owned. He occasionally moved things here and there and cleaned up a bit but somehow it always looked the same. Then new complaints. This wounded him. "Them people come and buy my vegetables and eggs and then complain about me."

He drove a school bus for a while but quit when ordered to take a TB test. He was indignant. What was in his blood was nobody else's business; it was his blood. The town tried to force him to get rid of the team after neighbors complained about the manure, the only time I ever saw that gentle man really aroused. Fiery red hair wild and sideburns bristling, he charged into the town hall and laid into the town fathers. They backed down against that fury but he knew the game was up. "They're out to get me," he said. He and his wife considered moving to Pennsylvania, among the Amish whose farming methods he admired, but even then the price of a farm was staggering. They stayed on. The pressures kept increasing.

In the end they were driven out. That was after we left Jersey. I still see him sitting in the old overstuffed easy chair at dusk. I am perched on a makeshift seat beside him. About us are the chickens clucking and pecking happily at the earth, innumerable cats stalking mice or bugs, Rory the shepherd at his side, the bays stomping in their rundown shed, all so soon to be gone and replaced by still more expensive tidy houses with neat lawns.

We did not talk much in those moments. There was always lots of silence between us. We sat watching night come on, slapping at the ferocious mosquitoes from the pond, looking out at the fields below. Farmer Bagley said that was the best part of farming: watching things grow.

That is why you need a chair for successful gardening. How else you going to see what's going on?

> *Pray for peace and grace and spiritual food*
> *For wisdom and guidance, for all these are good*
> *But don't forget the potatoes.*
> —John Tyler Petee

Growing potatoes may be the ultimate act of faith in gardening. The plants go about their mysterious business of forming tubers underground, in secrecy and darkness, with no interchange between grower and crop until the harvest. The gardener plants, feeds, waters, cultivates, and then must await the result with no real assurance of success. He is, in his own way, as much in the dark as the developing tubers.

Possibly because of their secret life, a mystique has grown up around potatoes, based largely on legend, superstition, verse, and literature. "Small potatoes" is a common metaphor for inadequacy. The exquisite leaves and flowers have inspired designs in arts and crafts. Potatoes have been shortchanged in aesthetic appreciation; they are ornamental as well as functional. Leaves, flowers, and stems are said to have a narcotic effect, an allegation I have never tried to verify.

The mighty tuber's greatest fame is as a survival food for millions and an article of commerce; it has helped shape world history and individual destinies. But potatoes have another dimension often neglected and overlooked. Many people still believe they have a magical quality. Some carry about a slice of raw potato for rheumatism; others consider them aphrodisiacs. The common spud also has a prominent role in folk medicine and folklore.

By any measure, potatoes are a success story in the grand tradition of a modest beginning and rising above adversity and obstacles to achieve universal acclaim. "Batatas" were first grown by the Incas, stolen by the rapacious conquistadors, and taken to Spain. From there they spread throughout the world, variously propelled by colonization, trade, wars, and ruse, often preventing mass starvation, making personal fortunes, linked to national economies and politics, stabilizing and upsetting governments.

Tubers may have achieved their greatest success in Ireland, which became a one-crop nation as early as the seventeenth century. When black rot wiped out crops in successive years, beginning in 1845, thousands starved and thousands of others fled to the United States and Canada, many refugees bringing little more than a few seed potatoes to plant in the New World and bitter memories of the old.

> Oh, the praties they are small
>   over here, over here
> Oh, the praties, they are small
>   when we dig 'em in the fall,
> And we eat 'em, coats and all
>   Full of fear, full of fear.
>   —Irish Famine Song

Potatoes were first grown in North America in 1719 at Londonderry, New Hampshire, according to one of my references. But after several phone calls I learned that the actual site was in Derry, once part of Londonderry Township, which was largely settled by immigrants from northern Ireland. Lieutenant Paul Lutz of the Derry police, my informant, said, "There used to be a commemorative sign on Route 28 but now it's gone and there's an apartment complex where it was."

Were the folks in Derry proud of their association with potatoes? "Not really," he replied, sounding wistful. "Most people don't even know about it. It's one of those things unfortunately buried in obscurity. It's too bad because it's part of history."

The potatoes I plant bear little resemblence to their distant ancestors the Spanish stole from the Incas, along with enslaving the people, raping the women, taking their gold, and destroying a noble culture. The Spanish "Patata" was scrawny, almost pitiful compared to today's robust spud. The potato lost its innocence about 1870 when Luther Burbank, inspired by Charles Darwin's work in plant development, bred the revolutionary Idaho potato, an immediate worldwide sensation.

Things have moved along swiftly since then. There are now more than eighty varieties that come in assorted sizes, shapes, colors, and textures. The proper measure of a potato, according to experts, is its starch content, which determines cooking quality and flavor. Low starch makes for dryness which is superior for boiling. A potato with a high starch content is considered best for baking and fluffy mashed potatoes. Some consumer advocates would like to see potatoes labeled and sold by their intended use rather than by place of origin as an aid to consumers—a change resisted by the industry.

Potato culture, like all modern agriculture, is heavily mechanized, mountains of spuds scooped out of the earth by huge machines and sent by conveyor belt on the first leg of their commercial journey. It is interesting to visit Long Island and see vast fields devoted to tubers, and New York not a major producer. Many of the large tracts are under death sentence— sold, idle, and gone to goldenrod while awaiting final execution into more housing developments and shopping malls.

Friends we stayed with said local people recognize an expanse of goldenrod as a sign of a potato field's imminent demise. Even the mighty tuber gives way to progress, with goldenrod the fatal symptom.

Today's potato is on the fast track as a commercial commodity, both for industrial use and as a basic food for man and beast. More than 250 billion pounds are grown annually in the United States, which lags far behind Russia and Europe in production. Five billion pounds alone are consumed by fast-fry Americans. In Lima, Peru, near where it all began, there is an International Potato Center dedicated to glorifying and promoting spuds, and it helps fund a potato museum in Washington, D.C. (now seeking a new location and sought by six states). Idaho plans to build a "tiny Disney World of potatoes." The National Museum of Natural History at the Smithsonian Institution is mounting an exhibit featuring potatoes as one of five things that changed the American contintents (the others being maize, sugar, the horse, and disease). A recent survey found that eight of ten American diners taste potatoes before meat, suggesting how far the potato has really come.

Even this is not the end. The contemporary white Irish tuber we know may be in for greater changes as researchers manipulate the spud genes to control everything from flavor to climate adaptability, ever seeking that Holy Grail of commerce, an eternal shelf life.

If I have a single garden favorite it is potatoes. They are useful, decorative, easy, and fun to grow, as versatile, basic, and valuable as any crop. It is doubtful that any other food encourages as much gastronomical ingenuity and variety as potatoes; they can be boiled, baked, fried, mashed, creamed, and roasted, served in soups, salads, stews, casseroles, and hashes, used in knishes, pie crusts, toppings, and even cakes. We also have couch potatoes.

The skins alone are tasty as snacks or hors d'oeuvres, offering valuable dietary fiber. Whole baked potatoes can be a main meal; when left over they are delicious quartered lengthwise, covered with thin cheese slices, and broiled briefly. An average spud contains only about 100 calories, approximately the same as an apple, and substantial amounts of vitamin C and iron. A potato is about 80 percent water, 18 percent carbohydrates (primarily starch), and 2 percent protein.

The book calls for planting whole small spuds or cutting large tubers so each piece has at least one eye and a couple of ounces of flesh to feed the emerging plant. I prefer medium-sized spuds cut in half, providing extra eyes and food on the theory that everything can use the best possible start in this life.

Curing the cut sections overnight, leaving them exposed to air, before planting helps form a protective crust that seals out disease organisms. Some growers brush the exposed surface with sulfur powder but I do not bother with this. I try to keep things as simple as possible, a principle that I think Farmer Bagley would go along with.

Potatoes do not have unreasonable cultural requirements, asking only for a rich, loamy soil, temperate climate, and steady water supply. The traditional planting method is to dig a four- or five-inch trench and place the sections, cut side down, every twelve inches, the rows about four feet apart. I add a sprinkling of greensand for potash and cheer to keep the tubers from getting soggy, and cover with soil.

As the plants grow, dirt can be mounded around them, a process known as "hilling." Tubers are merely swollen stems that tend to grow near the surface, and the extra earth protects them from direct sunlight, which turns the flesh green and unfit for consumption. A heavy mulch gives added protection from sunlight, along with smothering weeds, preserving moisture and keeping the tubers cool.

Potatoes also can be planted directly in mulch, a kind of mulch sandwich, which makes it possible to harvest them with no dirt to remove. I tried this but found that the mulch tended to sink down and expose some spuds to sunlight. The largest and best potatoes always seem to be the ones that get damaged. Paranoia also has its place in the garden.

We plant three varieties of spuds: reds, earlies, and keepers. Reds are especially tasty in early spring, succulent, the skin so tender it is almost transparent. Peggy has become adept at slipping her fingers under the soil and "stealing" a few premature tubers without damage to the plant or potato siblings still in the nest.

The keepers mature in about 110 days, are dried out of sunlight and stored in open containers. We keep them in the root cellar and they see us through the winter with leftovers to plant the following spring.

My fellow gardener Rit has another approach that I've never encountered elsewhere. He digs three-foot-wide trenches, about nine inches deep, and plants the pieces one foot apart, filling the trenches in as the potatoes grow, much as I grow leeks. He leaves the tubers in the ground to overwinter, covering them with heavy mulch, digging as needed. He claims they retain more flavor and do not sprout so early in the spring as when stored inside. I listen to him respectfully as he is the only gardener I know who grows potatoes and never has a potato beetle. Perhaps potato beetles dislike innovation, preferring to go with tradition.

Potatoes are justly celebrated for their nutritional virtues, flavor, versatility, and helping feed millions in an increasingly crowded and hungry world, but there are a few drawbacks which, in fairness, should be mentioned: They require planning and foresight, qualities that do not come easily to me.

Their primary demand is for an acid soil, which means preparing the plot in the fall (if I get around to it) by disking in rotted pine needles, leaves, or sawdust to lower the pH, the measure of alkalinity/acidity. Second, they cannot be exposed to raw manure without developing scab, an unsightly skin disease; even rotted manure should be dug or disked in months before planting. A third perversity is that they cannot follow other members of the nightshade family, including tomatoes, eggplant, and green peppers, all subject to the same ailments. This can be a nuisance in a small garden with limited space to maneuver or rotate crops.

Also, I should point out that potatoes are vulnerable to about a dozen diseases and are attacked by numerous common garden pests, among them terrorist potato beetles, potato psyllids (I have never seen a psyllid), flea beetles, leafhoppers, and an assemblage of anonymous foliage chewers and juice suckers who can transmit diseases. I recognize only one as a major threat—the passionate potato beetles.

I consider the many faces potatoes have to go with their numerous eyes as I methodically drop the cut sections in trenches, just as tradition dictates. Some three months from now, presumably, their offspring will be harvested, shorn of their secrecy as the potato rake bites into the earth to expose tender, almost transparent skins to light. Those that survive the digging, without being speared inadvertently or exposed to fatal sunscald, will feed us through the winter.

In late spring the unused potatoes will start to sprout. Even in the semi-darkness of the basement root cellar, some mysterious voice within tells them that spring is once more at hand, just as it must have alerted their diminutive and distant ancestors in Peru, and new foliage growing out of the eyes will reach for the light to continue this particular benefaction of nature.

The following recipe for adventuresome bakers is copied verbatim from *A Taste of Ireland in Food and Pictures* by Theodora Fitzgibbon (Pan Books Ltd., London, 1970). I am indebted to our friend Pam Johnson, who illustrated this book, for bringing it to my attention.

CHOCOLATE SANDWICH CAKE

This cake is unusual in that it contains mashed potato. This makes it hold the moisture and so prevents it becoming dry.

6 oz. (1½ cups) self-rising flour
6 oz. (⅔ cup) caster* sugar
6 oz. plain chocolate, melted,
 2 or 4 level tablesp. cocoa
½ teasp. salt

3 oz. (⅓ cup) cooked mashed
 potato
4 oz. (½ cup) butter
4 tablesp. milk
2 eggs

Cream the butter and sugar with the mashed potato, then add the melted chocolate or cocoa. Add the beaten eggs alternately with the flour and the salt. Finally pour in the milk, mixing well, to make a soft dropping consistency.

Well grease two 8-in. sandwich tins and divide the mixture equally between them. Cook in a moderate oven (400° F. electric; gas regulo 6) for 25–30 minutes. The top will be firm and springy to the touch when it is cooked. Let the cakes cool for a few minutes, then turn out onto a wire rack. The two sides are sandwiched together with whipped cream or chocolate icing.

*More coarse than confectioner's sugar but finer than our granulated sugar.

Summer

I was determined to know beans.
—Henry David Thoreau

I can never believe another summer is here, another gardening season under way, until the bush beans are planted. They are the first warm-weather seed crop to go in, my harbinger of summer. The earth is soft and warm and feels good against my hands. It has been a long winter and cold spring. I missed the feel of warm soil. It rejuvenates me. It gives me a feeling of wholeness, of completion, a new appreciation and awareness of the cycle of the seasons, the certainty of rebirth, and the great revolving wheel of life.

I have turned the soil, adding compost to the ever-sandy, every-hungry earth, and stretched two pieces of twine the length of the new bed, about nine inches apart. A sweet aroma arises from the freshly exposed soil. I do not rush to my task of planting but savor each step in this annual ritual. There will be subsequent plantings of beans but none with the meaning of this first crop. They are special, as if some of my own exuberance has been transferred to the beans. By summer's end, ritual will have become routine.

I do not follow the conventional spacing but put the seeds somewhat closer together. Nor will I thin them when they germinate. I expect all to take root and grow, and almost invariably they measure up to my high expectations, as if reluctant to disappoint me. Beans have the endearing trait of being reasonably predictable and responsive to favorable conditions. They are, in my experience, the easiest of all crops to grow. They were my first gardening success, so I have a sentimental attachment to them.

Beans do not protest being crowded. They do not shove one another aside in competition for breathing space and nutrients, nor do they show passive resistance or ill temper by bearing stingily. There is a bit of divinity in beans. They seem to like proximity, like city people born to cheek-to-jowl living. They return full measure, and more, for the care lavished on them. Beans are like heirs, born to security, being legumes with the ability to produce their own vital nitrogen. They can afford to be above the fray, dispensing their nutrient largess like philanthropists.

Once planted they are largely on their own, other than for frequent waterings. The first step in germination is for the tiny wormlike radicle to anchor itself in the soil, the other end of this incipient root elongating into the stem. Everyone who has grown bush beans is familiar with the sight of the hook-shaped hypocotyl, linking radicle and cotyledons, poking through the earth. As the seed coat softens and splits, the cotyledons divide like little wings, doubling in size the first twenty-four hours after being exposed to moisture.

With a mighty thrust the hypocotyl frees itself at one end, hoisting aloft the cotyledons with force enough to lift a three-quarter-pound weight, according to studies at Cornell University.

Watching the tiny plant emerge from the confining earth,

the new leaves forming to sing the joyous song of new life, must be one of the most satisfying and reassuring sights in gardening.

Some gardeners believe that bush-bean seeds emerge better and more reliably if sown with the hilum, or eye, placed down, a practice recommended for lima beans. Other claim it makes no difference or too little to bother with. I have never experimented with so-called emergence based on seed orientation, but let the beans greet the earth as they will, and have had no problems with germination.

It is advisable to keep soil with germinating seeds moist, and even to cover it with a light mulch, just enough to blunt the heat of the summer sun. When the plants reach a respectable size, six inches or so high, more mulch can be added to keep the roots damp. Not too much mulch. Farmer Bagley pointed out that beans like the sun's warmth on their feet.

The first planting will be ready in approximately sixty days. Beans should be harvested when they are about four to six inches long, or they quickly get stringy and tough. The first picking is the most welcome and abundant; the basket fairly overflows with tender young shoots that pop and spurt juices when snapped.

Invariably I miss a few of the wily beans. This is a trick they play. They try to avoid detection so they can produce seeds to reproduce themselves. I try to pick as clean as possible to encourage new growth. Each bush must be tilted to find the elusive beans that try to outwit me. Often they lurk on the underside of the bush, sagging of its own weight, near the ground.

The bees share my enthusiasm for this morning, hovering around as I move from plant to plant. They are welcome visitors and pleasant garden companions in this task. I especially enjoy the soft hum of insects harmonizing with the song of birds and the gentle breezes of morning. Once I saw a young field hand picking beans while wearing a headset attached to a radio on his belt. I thought it one of the more astonishing sights I had ever seen, a man attuned to artificial sounds rather than the music of nature, and I knew then that the race was in trouble.

Usually I take only three pickings per planting. By then the beans have largely exhausted their largess and goodwill and are turning cranky, the pods starting to get tough and stringy. I replant every couple of weeks to assure a continuing supply, just as the book recommends.

After the third picking the plants are pulled and composted. For them it is the end of the line. Only a few late pods from the last planting, along with any I missed, are left on the plants to dry and be saved for next year's seed.

Beans are so prolific that there is no keeping up with the outpouring. Invariably I overestimate our consumption and underestimate their fecundity. When we have had our fill of fresh beans, we can some and process others as dilly beans, a small work of garden art. It is always a happy reminder of summer to enter the root cellar on a winter day and see the shelf lined with jars of dilly beans, so wonderfully green and erect imprisoned in glass. I can almost smell the fragrance of plants long gone and hear the bees.

Most of the beans, after the initial picking, are given away. I once had a long lecture on the folly of not selling extra produce, and my only defense was that I get pleasure out of giving away that which I grow, a kind of gift of the self, but I did not convince my more practical, economic-minded critic. It would be more virtuous on my part if I were hard pressed for the money.

If I miscalculate my plantings and the crops overlap so a late picking of one comes atop a first picking of another, the kitchen sink can hardly accommodate this mountain of beans until they can be used or distributed. They are rinsed and soaked in cold water briefly to recover from the trauma of picking, and then put in plastic bags and chilled to preserve freshness.

In midsummer the pole beans also begin to pour forth, a virtual cornucopia of beans. I plant six or eight seeds around each leg of the tripod, thinning to four plants per pole. The vines eagerly climb the supports, with a bit of encouragement (to be commented upon subsequently), maturing in about sixty-five days. Dangling a foot long, festooned from their green triangle-teepees, they could be ornaments on odd-shaped Christmas trees, a rather amusing and delightful sight.

Beans have not had the respect they deserve. They are victims of derogatory expressions like "not worth a hill of beans" and "full of beans" to denote negative qualities. They also have an unfortunate reputation for causing flatulence, particularly dried beans. I can do nothing about linguistic insult, but dried beans are easily enough defused from causing gas, according to experts, by soaking for several hours, frequently changing the water, and cooking them in a large volume of water which is discarded. Some nutrients are unfortunately lost with the water but the beans themselves remain a valuable food.

Beans are grown throughout the world as a basic crop for humans and domestic animals. There are said to be as many as 1,200 varieties, about half of them named. Bush beans, often called snap beans, green beans, or just beans, are the most widely grown, an excellent source of vitamins, calcium, and iron. One pound of raw green beans contains only 143 calories.

I am, admittedly, an unabashed and uncompromising champion of beans. All beans. I admire their simplicity, ease with which they are grown, exquisite design and aesthetic beauty, taste, nutritional benefits, and versatility. I am therefore pleased to give the following unsolicited testimonial to beans:

BEANS belong in every home garden. They are one of the most virtuous and easiest crops grown, relatively disease and pest free, yielding mightily for the space taken, not demanding in soil requirements or care needed. Beans, as nitrogen-fixing legumes, enrich soil fertility and improve tilth. They are a no-nonsense food, valued by the economy-minded and nutrition-conscious alike.

Cooked with corn and whole grains, beans are among the few sources of inexpensive protein, almost indispensable in a vegetarian diet. They are also a gourmet's delight. They have a noble heritage and history. They come in many colors and shapes and can be dried, frozen, or canned, and eaten raw or cooked. They are an altogether positive force in any garden, adding cheer, dignity, and a solid sense of achievement while doing wonders for the gardener's larder and morale.

PEGGY'S DILLY BEANS
(makes about seven pints)

Brine:

3 lbs. green beans (approx.)	4 cups water
7 dill heads or 7 tsp. dill seed	4 cups vinegar
7 garlic cloves	5 Tbsp. salt
21 peppercorns	

Into each pint jar put one dill head, one clove of garlic, and three peppercorns. Wash beans, trim ends, and pack lengthwise tightly into clean wide-mouth pint jars; make sure to pack beans in tightly.

Boil brine mixture in enameled or stainless-steel pan and fill jars, leaving one-half inch headroom.

Put on lids and rings which have been boiled five minutes and process jars in boiling-water bath for ten minutes. Start timing after water returns to boil.

Remove, tighten lids, cool, store.

There's husbandry in heaven . . .
—William Shakespeare

Pole beans are one of the wonders of the garden. They can easily climb an eight-foot pole or shimmy up twine. I have no idea how high they could go given their way and a sufficiently long pole or support. They may have inspired *Jack and the Beanstalk.* With their antics, they do invite hyperbole.

Pole beans pose an obvious question: Why do they climb when most plants remain, sensibly it would seem, on the ground? Why do only a few plants have this gymnastic ability? Did some clever forebear long ago get the idea, work out the mechanics, and pass it along to his heirs and perhaps a few friends? Or did some others like what they saw and borrowed or stole the idea?

Relatively few plants have mastered this trick. Among them, along with pole beans, are certain garden peas, morning glories, cucurbits, and honeysuckle. Charles Darwin was fascinated by climbing plants; he studied more than a hundred varieties and wrote a book about them in support of natural selection, observing that they existed in the wild surrounded by thick vegetation and climbing toward the light was their struggle for life.

Through experiments, Darwin found that the climbing equipment grew out of other organs. He held that so many widely different forms of climbing plants would not have been possible unless all plants possessed some slight power of movement. But why do only a few beleaguered plants climb and not others? What is their special secret? Once more science has figured out the how but not the why—the great mystery that bedevils all efforts to explain first causes.

The process that enables certain plants to climb is called thigmotropism—moving in response to contact with a solid or rigid surface. Giving it a name neither adds nor detracts from its wonder, the little trick passed along in a genetic packet which was unknown in Darwin's time. All climbing plants respond to the same touch stimulus but the climbing mechanism varies among plants. All are variations on the basic idea; there are no patents in nature.

Climbing peas, as they grow upward in response to sunlight, anchor themselves with tiny threadlike tendrils that are merely specialized leaves which suggest elongated stems. The tendrils spiral around a fence or other support in a coiling motion that has been likened to a monkey wrapping its tail around a branch.

Each spurt of growth is followed by new tendrils attaching the growing plant for the next upward thrust. Eventually the vines reach the top of the support or climb as high as their genes or external conditions permit. The powerful threadlike tendrils carry the full weight of the plant and its pods with the strength of wire. When the plant is dead the faithful tendrils still hold fast as if reluctant to relinquish their grip. Some are still clinging to the fence when it is rolled and stored.

Pole beans, revealing a mind of their own, do not form tendrils as such but the entire leaf-bearing vine spirals around a pole or support as the plant ascends. Pole beans invariably grow counterclockwise. I have tried to entice them to go the opposite way but they would have none of·it. Only later I learned what a presumption this was. I was attempting to defy not only nature but the heavens themselves.

Some climbing plants are so responsive to touch that they take off within minutes of making contact with any solid object. I suspect they may even sense nearby objects and reach out for them, almost like throwing little lassos. I have seen errant pea tendrils wrap themselves around a rake handle several inches distant when the tool was left leaning against the fence.

More remarkable, one wayward pole-bean vine shinnied halfway up its pole in the traditional manner and suddenly, for reasons unknown, managed to "leap" a couple of feet to a cucumber cage where it grew beans among the cucumbers all summer. The cucumbers took this in a good spirit. I seemed to be the only one puzzled and inconvenienced by the ensuing land-bridge garden obstacle, and speculated whether someone had been giving my pole beans steroids to extend their natural athletic prowess.

Pole beans show other eccentricities, perhaps as a result of being left-handed. New plants often take off on the ground seeking a support of their own choosing. They adore mounting nearby row markers and trying to choke neighboring peppers. It is one thing to climb for an edge in survival, but quite another to attempt to throttle an unsuspecting pepper neighbor like a common mugger. I cannot believe this is what evolution intended when it came up with thigmotropism. I disentangled bean and pepper and forced the bean into its proper airborne niche, on the path to righteousness and the heavens themselves.

We come now to the crucial question posed by pole beans and their like: What is it that gives them their strange power to climb and move? Science has cracked the mystery of how thigmotropism works, if not why. The cells of vines or tendrils away from the point of contact with an object grow rapidly larger and faster than those on the side where they touch, but no one knows why this is so. The uneven growth imposes a twisting or wrapping motion. Whatever underlying force makes this possible, it has proved an effective means of upward plant locomotion.

This leaves unanswered another question: Why do pole beans climb counterclockwise? A botany professor I consulted gave the problem an interesting twist. "They only grow that way in the Northern Hemisphere," he said. "In the Southern Hemisphere they go the opposite direction. It has something to do with the spin of the earth, but don't ask me to explain how . . ."

That at least clarified why I had not been able to induce my pole beans to reverse direction. I was challenging cosmic forces. Since talking to the professor I have not felt quite the same toward pole beans; I find myself watching them out of the corner of my eye. It is unnerving to learn that what appears to be a simple garden plant is taking orders directly from the great intelligence of the universe that governs all living things on

Earth, even beans reaching toward the heavens they answer to. There is something awesome about it. Even unearthly.

> Go make thy garden fair as thou canst
> Thou workest never alone;
> Perchance he whose plot is next to
>   thine
> Will see it and mend his own.
> —Elizabeth Rundle Charles

On a cloudy day in late June Peggy and I attend a gardening workshop devoted to raised beds. We enrolled by mail and it is our first such experience. We look forward to some kind of revelation. About two dozen of us gather at the county agricultural department's demonstration plot, a small but tidy fenced-in area. The county agent, a woman who wears blue jeans, has a jaunty, confident manner. She leads us from one raised bed to another, explaining the various crops being grown and the virtues of the method.

All of us listen attentively except for one middle-aged man, a gardener most likely. He is preoccupied with some ants and furtively tries to smash them with his shoe. I do not know his grievance against the ants. They cause no offense and are not even in the beds, but he seems determined to wipe them out. I suppose he has a phobia, compulsion, or is programmed to kill anything that crawls or walks on more than four legs. There are many of his kind.

The workshop is well handled but if there are new revelations about raised beds I miss them with my own preoccupation with the man who is after the ants. The county agent emphasizes how easily the beds are made and plants maintained. Simply assemble four boards, usually some form of rectangle, and scoop the earth from the adjacent paths into the frame. She bought her wood and materials out of her budget, she explains, adding that it is also possible to make them without sides (if you do not have a bureaucratic budget to draw upon) simply by mounding the earth.

The advantages are numerous, which is probably why raised beds have become so popular, almost a rage, among gardeners. There is no walking on the beds and compacting the soil; they are tidy, plants do better in the deep, loose soil and are less trouble to tend. It is easier to keep track of what is going on in a small enclosed rectangle than in an undefined area.

Once the soil is built up and friable it can be turned with a shovel or light tiller. Another advantage, rarely mentioned, is that raised beds are kinder to tender or aged backs. There is less bending and strain; many older people find them especially helpful.

My friend Stu converted to raised beds for purely technical reasons. Stu is big on technical advances. He made his frames twelve inches high, twelve feet long and four feet wide, a popular size. Raised beds can be longer or shorter but usually no wider than four feet (and often three) for ease in tending.

Before installing the boxes, Stu had the topsoil scraped off the entire garden by a bulldozer and pushed into a huge pile to draw from. He then took things a step further, installing a series of rigid, removable hoops across the beds. By stretching transparent plastic sheeting over the hoops the raised beds become cold frames for early spring crops or for use in the fall to prolong the season.

In the spring, as soon as the weather warms, Stu removes the hoops and plastic covers and the transplants have a good start, aided by a drip irrigation system that waters automatically. Stu is very enthusiastic about the beds (Stu is very enthusiastic about everything) and tells me to get with the times. "Raised beds are the only way to go!" he exclaims. "By the way, do you need some topsoil?"

For a long time I resisted raised beds. Somehow they did

not appeal to me despite their obvious advantages. The garden, I thought, would have an artificial, manicured appearance. It would not look like a garden. I probably also resisted because everybody else was adopting them. I could hear Farmer Bagley saying, "If the good Lord intended for beds to be raised, he would of raised them himself. It ain't natural." That was good enough for me.

Then I reconsidered. Was I not being close-minded? So what if they were another fad? Why not give them a chance? I experimented. To my chagrin I liked raised beds. They were everything claimed for them. Humble pie was mine.

At first we had only a few, then on a spring day we visited "Plimoth Plantation," the famed replica of the Pilgrims' first settlement in Plymouth, Massachusetts. I had never been there before and was startled to see that every house had a kitchen garden made of raised beds. The Pilgrims had brought the method with them from England. It was old hat even then. For the early settlers the raised beds were both supermarket and drugstore, supplying food and medications, herbs being virtually the only pharmacopoeia they had.

Most of the beds were enclosed with crude planks but some were held in place by stones or thick tree limbs. A costumed "settler," calling herself Mrs. Winslow, said women tended the beds and the soil was improved with "muck" (animal litter). She explained that she put fresh manure on her beds in the spring, thus turning them into hot beds so the seeds would germinate and give her an early start. That in 1627, the time frame we were supposed to be locked into.

There was no getting the "settlers" to stop playing their well-rehearsed roles. I asked a man in period dress, a fierce-looking fellow with period patches on his pants and period beard, about the raised beds. "They give order," he snapped. "It is the duty of every Christian to bring order to the world. Only a savage would plant any other way."

I had not considered that viewpoint. I was thinking gardening, not theology. Who was I to defy the Almighty and upset the divine plan? Gradually I have increased our number of raised beds until we now have several spread around, some just 4×4 boxes made of salvaged wood. I would have more long rectangular beds but new lumber is expensive and used stock for the sides is hard to come by since the town dump started calling itself a sanitary landfill and picking was prohibited; we prefer waste and tidiness to recycling or conservation of materials in the name of progress.

I am not about to use stones or tree limbs for side supports. Most of my raised beds are simply mounded earth without sides. I find them easier to care for than the traditional flat surface. The soil does not seem to dry out so quickly, they are easier on the old back, and I am doing my bit to bring order to the world.

> *We will now discuss in a little more detail the Struggle for Existence.*
> —Charles Darwin

We awaken this morning to find the garden blanketed by mist, as if a cloud lay on the earth and green vegetation rises out of it. By the time we have breakfast the night's vapors are beginning to lift. Later, when I go into the garden, the mist is gone and only beads of dew glisten on shiny leaves.

I spend this Sunday morning thinning and weeding the carrots. It is a tedious job but one I rather enjoy. The tedium is lessened by the sound of wind in the surrounding pines and by distant church bells. By now I know from experimentation that it is largely futile to transplant carrots; the thinnings seldom take and when they do the roots are almost invariably crooked.

Still, this knowledge does not deter me. I cannot resist the temptation to fill in the blank spaces in the rows with the thin-nings, giving them their chance to fulfill their mission. This must represent some deep and unsuspected optimism in me, attempting that which has so little chance of success. Again, perhaps, it is not optimism at all but simply a refusal to accept a reality of which I do not approve, which suggests an unfortunate Calvinist streak in my makeup, of which I also do not approve.

The weather is near perfect for slugs, damp with little sunshine to dry out the earth. The soaked mulch must be ideal from a slug's point of view. No longer must they bother to burrow and hide among the lettuce or cabbage leaves but lie boldly on top. Peggy says they luxuriate like people at the beach. I find them even on the bush beans where they never appeared before. I toss them over the fence so they and the birds can work it out from there.

Slugs do not have a favorable image. People cringe at the touch of their slimy bodies. It is hard to find a good word for them in my researches. This makes slugs unusual if not somewhat unique; almost every garden pest, studied long and diligently enough, can be found to have some redeeming feature. Even the profaned squash bug has its handsome shield design. A grasshopper was clocked laying a thousand eggs in fifteen minutes, which should qualify for some distinction. Prejudice must not blind us to achievement.

I pluck a slug from the beans and study it to see if I can find a hidden personality or some extraordinary feature that has been overlooked. I try to be objective and fair but nothing is apparent. I put the slug on a cabbage leaf and take it in the house to examine it under a magnifying glass. This does not improve the slug image and may even set it back a bit. Had it been attending to its Sabbath devotions instead of eating my beans it would not be in this unlikely situation.

My slug is approximately two inches long, about half the length the book calls for, grayish in tone with vague brown markings on its back and a lighter-colored belly. It is wormlike in shape, without legs, and has a soft body with no shell; lack of a shell is the major difference between a slug and a snail.

The slug, wriggling on the cabbage leaf, appears to have no proper head, the body suddenly terminating in two tiny tentacles tipped with eyes, so-called eye stalks that resemble twin periscopes. I touch it and it withdraws the periscopes into a small mantle, much like a monk's cowl, and plumps up its body. It seems to think it is hidden when it covers its eyes.

Slugs are notorious for their slow pace ("sluggish"). A slug is said to take eight days to travel one mile, compared to fifteen days for a snail ("snail's pace"). The rate of locomotion must be of greater interest to researchers on grants than to the creatures themselves. I doubt if either slugs or snails travel a mile in their entire life and they probably could not care less. Time and speed seem to be of concern only to man.

Nature must have been in a capricious mood when she made slimy repulsiveness a slug's primary defense. The sticky mucus clings to fingers tenaciously and, in the garden, can be removed only by rubbing it off with dirt; even then it seems to linger.

Slugs presumably find one another attractive enough, although accounts of their sex life are skimpy. Each individual possesses both sexes but they still need a partner to reproduce, one taking the male role, the other female. I assume they can change about if either gets bored but I profess no expertise in such matters. This sexual versatility and interchange should eliminate many problems that bedevil other species in their relationships.

Slugs are not celebrated for their intelligence. They leave behind a telltale silvery mucus trail that is easily followed and often leads to their early demise. Individual slugs are said to build their own mucus highways which harden into silvery trails they follow, a snail version of hardtopping. They also reportedly form mucus ropes to suspend themselves from various supports or when going from one level to another.

I try to goad my captive slug into building a mucus trail or rope before releasing it but the frantic creature is obsessed with escaping from the cabbage leaf and shows no inclination to reveal its slug secrets. It is a spunky little fellow and moves surprisingly fast for having no legs and a reputation for slowness. I refer to slugs as "my pets" and tell people who find them in produce I give away to return them to me or provide a good home. None have returned so I assume that all have good homes.

Gardening books recommend the use of shingles to trap slugs that sleep during the heat of day. The witless creatures theoretically crawl under the shingle during siesta for protection from the sun and can be disposed of. I have had little success with the method and like to think my slugs, like my squash bugs, are a more brainy lot, not so easily duped.

The most common method of discouraging slugs is to sprinkle their trails with sand, cinders, diatomaceous earth with its sharp silicon skeletal remains, or some other rough material to scratch their soft bodies. Dusting them with hydrated lime or wood ashes also has a disagreeable effect. Caustic substances are said to cause them to produce protective mucus in such quantities that they become desiccated and die, self-destructing, in effect, the ultimate in biological warfare. People with allergies may sympathize with their plight.

Once the garden is mulched, slugs love to take refuge under the cool, damp organic matter, building their mucus highways to commute on. This keeps some gardeners from mulching. I consider slugs only a nuisance, the convenience of mulch outweighing the disadvantages of slugs.

Slugs are held to be most active when the temperature in between 60 and 70 degrees and dampness prevails. They gladly forgo a shingle to frolic and feed in a juicy head of lettuce or cabbage that provides soothing darkness, humidity, air conditioning, and conviviality with friends and family. They may be more intelligent than we suspect.

The use of stale beer in a saucer to trap roistering slugs has received wide publicity. Some slugs do get loaded and drown but others appear to take a nip and scoot away to sleep it off. I have no quarrel with this method but do think beer could be better used before it gets stale. Drunken revelry may not be the worst way to go, even for a slug.

An enterprising entomologist experimented to find out if slugs have a preference in beers, a kind of taste test to develop a marketing strategy to kill slugs. Like most marketing strategies it was not designed for the consumer's ultimate advantage. The experiments determined that slugs seem to consider Brand X as good as Brand Y to drown in.

Further testing revealed that it was not even the alcohol that attracted the slugs. Rather, it was the fermented yeasts in the brews. Slugs are not the common souses they were believed to be, but may be victims of hidden hunger, a dietary deficiency, simply trying to improve their nutritional status.

I searched a long time before finding any kind words for slugs, finally uncovering them in the *Encyclopedia Americana*, which notes that although slugs and snails are considered slow and insignificant, there are "few animals that have mastered so successfully greater portions of the wet and dry areas of the earth's surface"—at least a limited testimonial.

The writer, a professor, then made a provocative statement: "While they [slugs and snails] lack some senses familiar to man, they possess sensitivities wholly unfamiliar to him." To our peril we often demean or ignore other life forms and their works because of our own limited sensitivities and lack of understanding. We have not learned to respect our ignorance, an achievement that may be the beginning of wisdom.

I have nothing against slugs. Their damage is often more superficial than substantive. Commercial agriculture is more concerned with cosmetic appearance than substance, a standard that has been sold to the public with its attendant problems. The price may be higher than we think.

I recognize that mine is not a popular point of view. Other aesthetic sensibilities are more easily offended than mine. Life, it seems, is always reduced to point of view, usually shaped by that which serves our own interests, values, and prejudices. But because other creatures do not serve us, are they, therefore, worthless? Even the hated mosquito protects vulnerable wetlands, as poison ivy defends fragile land areas.

Not all cultures share our disdain, hatred, and revulsion of so-called lower life forms. India is said to have hospitals that provide private rooms just to care for sick and dying insects, including lice, fleas, and cockroaches, a tidbit I picked up in an excerpt from *Significa*, a compilation of odd facts by Irving Wallace, his son, and his daughter. The Wallaces claim this has been going on since the third century B.C. when a Buddhist ruler taught that humans should harm no beings, a philosophy shared by the Hindus and Jains, the latter adherents of an Indian religion originating in the sixth century B.C. that espouses immortality and the transmigration of the soul.

The insect room in one animal hospital was described as being between floorboards and ground, with grain dropped to the patients through cracks between the boards. A visitor in 1689 reported that "in order to feed the fleas and other bugs that needed meat, a poor man was occasionally hired to sleep with them as a sort of live feast." The modern insect room allegedly is sealed after a year, and twelve or fifteen years later, "when all the bugs have presumably died a natural death, the room is cleared out and the decayed matter is sold as fertilizer."

I am not about to endow an insect hospital, nor do I consider myself an apologist or defender of slugs. But there may be more to them, as there is to most creatures, than meets the eye, or magnifying glass. Even the lowly and despised slug on the cabbage leaf beside me may have an unknown role in the great scheme that we, as the professor suggested, are not capable of comprehending. Our values may often be more dangerous to us than some of the creatures we try to eradicate.

I take my sermon of tolerance from a framed motto that hung outside the bathroom of my Uncle George's boardinghouse in Kansas when I was a boy: "Pay your rent promptly the first of the month. Don't throw your coffee grounds in the stool. Live and let live."

Uncle George was a man of modest aspirations and would not have presumed to cosmic truths, but is not Planet Earth itself a vast boardinghouse serving many different kinds of tenants, and do we not all have the obligation to respect the rights of our fellow boarders and not throw coffee grounds in the stool?

> O'er folded blooms
>   On swirls of musk,
> The beetle booms adown the glooms
>   And bumps along the dusk.
>   —James Whitcomb Riley

Once more the Colorados have beaten me to the punch. I had not expected them so soon and am forced into an impromptu counterattack. The first potato beetle patrol of the year nets more than 200 egg clusters and 119 adults, including laggards and fornicating couples and not counting the grubs that fall to my unwilling hand.

In the future I will carry a can of kerosene to avoid the unpleasantness of squishing between thumb and forefinger, although kerosene has its own disadvantages: The sight of thrashing bodies in the lethal brew is unsettling. There is also the danger of spilling it in the soil, violating sound principles of organic gardening.

The beetles fly and crawl over the plants and one another in their lust for food and mates. They have a beachhead and pay little attention to me. The word is out that I am an easy touch, offering quality sustenance without adverse side effects. I have no illusions about wiping out the wily beetles; the most I hope for is control.

Timing is the key, experts say, pointing out that insect damage is less weakening to plants early and late in the season than in mid-season. This is reassuring but we generally get a respectable potato harvest even when the plants are reduced to little more than nubs.

Not only are the tubers gestating in secret below but the plants themselves can be deceptive, producing beautiful vegetation and poor crops. I recall a year when we had luxuriant growth above and nothing but midgies and blanks below. Peggy compared it to waking up Christmas morning and finding your stocking empty.

I had marked the calendar to begin beetle patrol in mid-June but, as usual, forgot or did not get around to it. Often the "bugs" catch me by surprise. Each year they seem to arrive earlier and in greater strength. I noticed the current invasion quite by accident when dumping kitchen middens; they had infested a volunteer growing out of the compost. Immediate action was necessary. In short order they can leave plants little more than a few skeletal leaves dangling from dispirited stems covered by multitudes of foraging fornicating beetles, a kind of beetle statement.

I have done extensive research but it has not been very helpful in combating the beetles. It may even lend some sympathy for their cause. Most gardening literature dismisses potato beetles in a cavalier way, it seems to me, simply describing them as one of the more serious garden pests and listing poisons they succumb to, or used to succumb to; it is not easy to keep up with which pests have developed immunity to which poisons. Since I am interested in control rather than beetle genocide I concentrate on their life history and evolutionary follies, hoping for as bloodless a resolution as possible to our annual confrontation. The beetles seem to have higher aspirations.

Several species of beetles attack potatoes but here we are concerned with the notorious Colorado potato beetle. It is stubby, about three-eighths of an inch long, and orange-brown in tone with five vertical black stripes on each wing cover and polka dots over the rest of the body; the number of dots on a beetle determines its species. Beetles belong to the scientific order Coleoptera, which in Greek means "sheath wings;" if that advances matters any.

With sound backing I refer to their offspring as grubs. One of my references sternly notes, "Some people call all young insects 'larvae,' but this is a careless use of language. . . . In scientific language, a young animal which does not look like its parents is called a 'larva' (plural, 'larvae'). . . . A young insect which *does* look like its parents should be called a 'nymph.' . . . Some insect larvae have special names of their own. . . . The larva of a beetle is a grub," a scientific dictum I defer to.

This is a timely place for me to confess that referring to all insects and their like collectively as "bugs" is license on my part, if not "a careless use of language." True bugs belong to one of the original Linnaean orders known as Hemiptera, and while they have many differences, all have one feature in common: piercing / sucking mouthparts, like such prominent members as bedbugs and squash bugs, whose lineage goes back some 215 million years. Like their biting and chewing compatriots, they dine indiscriminately at my expense, and certainly they owe me the convenience of referring to the lot of them simply as "bugs."

Those ruthless biting and chewing foragers, the Colorados, whose plump, humpbacked young do not the least resemble the adults, are believed to have originated in central Mexico; they migrated to the Rocky Mountain area of Colorado, remaining just long enough to be identified with the state and prosper before moving along in the finest American tradition of opportunism.

While in Colorado they lived frugally on nightshade and wild members of the potato family. When tamed tubers were planted by early settlers the beetles took off, spreading throughout the United States and Europe. Early on they were almost wiped out by the insecticide Paris green but soon achieved immunity and threatened to wipe out potatoes as a crop.

After World War II more deadly pesticides were introduced, touching off an "arms race" between beetles and progressively toxic chemicals. Ever more powerful substances were developed. The Colorados learned to handle each in turn. Eventually the poisons became so lethal that they posed a greater threat to people eating the potatoes than to beetles eating the plants.

A 1988 *New York Times* editorial reported that it took the Colorados on Long Island two years or less to develop resistance to each of nine pesticides, adding that "some 447 insect species are now resistant to members of all major classes of insecticide. Despite increasing expenditures on pesticides, now at $6.5 billion a year, insects, diseases, and weeds destroy a third of America's crops. That's the same proportion as in the 1940's and indeed the same as in the Middle Ages." We do not seem to be making much progress.

The life-style of Colorados is not particularly innovative or inspiring as such things go. Beetle mothers lay clusters of orange-yellow eggs on the undersides of leaves where, like those of squash bugs, they are hard to spot. The eggs hatch in four to nine days, the grubs, reluctant to leave home, dining on the leaf where they were born. Usually they feed in a little half-circle, or arc, retreating without breaking ranks, like an army falling back; as the leaf gets steadily smaller, they move on to destroy other leaves and, finally, whole plants.

The grubs go through four growth stages, each time getting a little larger and hungrier. After the final molt they burrow into the earth and emerge as adults. The whole process takes about a month, three generations per season in these parts, more than enough for the Colorados to keep up their end of things.

Potato beetles that hatch in the fall overwinter in the soil to emerge the following summer. The female feeds for a few days, getting it all together, and then starts laying eggs, a cycle that has been going on for millions of years.

I never know when to expect the Colorados. Each year they seem to vary their arrival date. The book claims they respond to soil temperature but I suspect they answer to some beetle imperative known only to them and they do not want to be taken for granted.

By now the Colorados seem to think they have a good thing going; all problems have been worked out and no further improvements are necessary. That may be a rash assumption. One practice makes them vulnerable. The egg clusters laid on leaves, even on the underside, reveal the presence of adults nearby, making egg and adult accident prone. The brilliant color of the eggs adds to the risk. It may be presumptuous to second-guess nature or evolution but it does seem that this reproductive strategy could be improved.

The flaw apparently has been recognized and rectified by a relative of theirs, the blister beetle, also known as an old-fashioned potato beetle and capable of causing a blister upon contact. They lay eggs in the soil where they cannot readily be found, and the odds may favor them for long-term survival. I have not come up with a suggested solution for the more serious problem that potato beetles, squash bugs, and other garden marauders face along with the rest of us, eating and multiplying themselves into extinction.

Obviously it is difficult to alter habits ingrained over millions of years. Once living organisms embark on a path it is almost impossible to change direction. Evolution may represent less real progress among the species than a series of irreversible biological blunders and all of us are simply trying to make the best of what we have to work with. This theory appeals to me. It would tend to explain much that is now incomprehensible.

The biggest thing potato beetles and their beetle relatives have going for them is their numbers. Of some ten million different kinds of insect species alive today (fewer than one million named), two-fifths of all those known are beetles. They have done remarkably well considering the stiff competition.

There are said to be 350,000 species of beetles alone (compared to only 5,000 species of mammals), which would seem to give them a leg up in the insect world. Some are among the largest of any species of insect. One is so tiny that it is described as being smaller than a large protozoa. The family includes the lead-cable borer, a small beetle with such powerful jaws that it can pierce a quarter-inch bar of solid lead. Another is known as the "confused flour beetle." More than 100 different beetle species live north of the Rio Grande, sharing our lives and food.

This multitude inspired the observation that the Creator must have been inordinantly fond of beetles, but there is also the possibility that they got out of hand early on and not even the Creator could control them.

It is to the Colorados' credit that they have made a name for themselves among such competing superstars as the ravenous Japanese beetle, the cherished weed-eating Australian beetle, and dung beetles, which spend their days rolling around a turd which they ultimately will lay their eggs in if first it does not, as the French entomologist Fabre told us, roll backward to flatten them or get stolen by another dung beetle.

The Colorados, as I see it, have made their mark largely by having a game plan and sticking to it, reducing life to essentials with single-minded dedication to eating and reproducing. They are, above all, obsessed with sex, usually coupled even while eating, pushing togetherness to its outer limits.

Colorados are never distracted from the business at hand. Their concentration is so great that they are oblivious to danger. Threatened while copulating, they do not break apart and take wing to save their individual skins; instead they fall to earth, still locked together in love's embrace. Is this stupidity, self-confidence, blind obedience to the life force, or merely a fatalistic assurance that there are plenty more where they came from? The only thing that matters for them is to get the job done, an ideal that assures success in all endeavors.

Several methods are advanced to combat potato beetles short of using violent poisons. If they get completely out of hand, I dust them with rotenone powder, the same desperation measure employed against squash bugs, but it is effective only against the juicy, soft-bodied grubs and must strike directly to make any lasting impression.

I read about a gardener who claimed he let his beetles eat unlimited amounts of nightshade that grew nearby until they poisoned themselves. I do not have nightshade and do not intend to plant it. I also fail to understand why sensible beetles would commit suicide by eating "deadly nightshade" when there are unpoisoned spuds for the taking.

Some innovative gardeners dust damp potato plants with bran; the unsuspecting beetles eat the bran, consume water, swell,

100 · W I L L I A M   L O N G G O O D

and burst. Somehow this does not seem quite sporting. Others use the "bug-juice" method, a mix of garden insects and water which is blended, strained, and sprayed on plants; bacterial and fungal pathogens in the spray are supposed to wipe out unwanted bugs, a kind of germ warfare which may, in its way, be as indiscriminate as pesticides, taking the wanted along with the unwanted, allies and foes indistinguishable to the infecting pathogens.

A gardener I read about claimed that mulch deters Colorados, a claim that startled me. I use mulch and my beetles are not deterred; they even seem to like snuggling down in the mulch to hide from me. Others claim success interplanting potatoes with garden flax, horseradish, garlic, and green beans. I do not grow flax or horseradish, but have tried garlic, and green beans often grow next to the potatoes; my beetles did not appear to be annoyed or distracted, let alone repelled. I also doused my plants with dissolved epsom salts, another sure cure I read about. Small white spots appeared on the leaves but the Colorados were undaunted.

The most hopeful news is that a new form of BT *(Bacillus thuringiensis)* has been invented to do to potato beetles what a companion BT does to cabbage worms. This bacterium, if effective as claimed, could be a serious setback to the Colorados, disrupting their game plan and forcing them to revise their strategy.

Meanwhile I continue to handpick the beetles, mosquitoes feast on me, birds eat the mosquitoes, something else eats the birds, and so on up and down the biotic pyramid.

> So, naturalists observe, a flea
> Hatch smaller fleas that on him prey;
> And these have smaller still to bite
>   'em;
> And so proceed ad infinitum.
>   —Jonathan Swift

Amoebas at the start
Were not complex;
They tore themselves apart
And started Sex.
—Arthur Guterman

There are, it seems, fashions in insects, as in all things, and they go in and out of style with the times and changing conditions. To declare a prominent pest no longer a serious menace is the kiss of death to its status, suggesting that it is obsolete, another victim of progress or new thinking.

This small garden truth was revealed to me long ago with the appearance of the Colorado potato beetles. We had been gardening for several years before the Colorados showed up, but from the beginning we had beetles working over the potatoes. This puzzled me. The only potato beetle mentioned in my gardening books was the Colorado. Our beetles looked nothing like those pictured.

Instead of being short and squat with five black stripes on each wing cover, like the Colorados, our beetles were long and slender and had only three stripes, more elegant, really. Who were these terrorists ravaging our potatoes? Imposters? Some new streamlined variety that evolution was experimenting with at my expense? Cucumber beetles, which they somewhat resembled, confused or gone berserk for want of their regular fare?

Then the prolific Colorados showed up and immediately took over by force of numbers, leaving the originals to play second fiddle, at least second beetle. They seemed to exist harmoniously enough, sharing quarters and provender and laying eggs side by side, joined by nervous flea beetles that chewed shotgun holes in the foliage and leafhoppers making prodigious leaps when not sucking juices from leaves and causing wilt and disease. It all seemed a bit much but not the worst, considering the possibilities; in gardening you learn to take comfort in possibilities not realized.

The potato patch may represent natural balance at its finest. The high-flying Colorados and three-linears leave less food for those who hop, leap, suck, and chew, and the flea beetles and leafhoppers leave less leaf surface for the others to lay eggs on, which I present as positive thinking at its finest. My role is that of the uninvited guest who provides the feast and nursery, gets the leftovers, and clears up the mess after the others are gone. It is all very neat, another of nature's complete circles.

Eventually I took the problem of the mystery bugs to the county agent, describing them by phone. She promptly identified them as "three-liners." "They're old-fashioned potato beetles," she said. "They've been around a long time." She spoke almost with disdain, as if they were not worthy of serious consideration.

That was my first brush with the ephemeral nature of insect fame in the garden, its shaky foundation of success. For many years the three-liners, along with blister beetles (also, as noted, called old-fashioned potato beetles although they have a more varied and balanced diet), had the potato field to themselves. They were doing an adequate job, it would seem, but suddenly out of Colorado came those hordes of greedy interlopers soon to be acclaimed the superstars in the competitive insect world.

This raises many questions. Why was there a need for a new potato beetle? Did nature or evolution consider Colorados a new and improved model? Why did previously undistinguished bugs living anonymously on wild potatoes in Colorado suddenly explode in numbers to upset the potato cart? Why did those displaced submit so meekly? Whatever the reasons, the Colorados quickly confirmed their new celebrity status with their gargantuan appetites, startling fecundity, poise, and ability to colonize new territories, basic talents or abilities of all true overachievers.

I have studied the two beetle rivals at hand, old and new, trying to answer questions they raise about redundancy, tactics, and insect personality. The Colorados brought a new strategy to the field: power sex, a willingness to be slaughtered in wholesale numbers in order to produce torrents of offspring, even, as pointed out before, refusing to split when caught while copulating, perishing together still locked in love or whatever.

The old-fashioned three-liners have more traditional values of self-survival. They are wary and skittish, taking wing at the suggestion of threat. If disturbed while copulating, the partners take off individually, each for him- or herself, which is not unique to their kind. "Beget and be gone" could be their motto; "he or she who copulates and flies away lives to procreate another day." I do not see this as any lack of dedication or want of team spirit, merely a basic difference in beetle philosophy.

The essential difference between the two is the three-liner's wariness. The Colorados passed up this quality in favor of power sex. Three-liners appear to be more interested in individual long-term survival rather than in spectacular short-term gains through overwhelming numbers. Is it better to live long and modestly or briefly and well?

The only time the skittish three-liners can be handpicked is in early morning when it is still cool and they are sluggish, but the trouble is that I, too, am sluggish at that hour, no better able than they to arouse myself. As the day becomes warmer, they are progressively more active, almost impossible to catch. Any disturbance in the potato patch in midday causes pandemonium. Spray from the hose leads to frenzy, while the imperturbable Colorados never break their concentration, continuing to fornicate, forage, or both at once.

I do not know what to make of all this. My observations lack scientific validity. They will never appear in a learned journal. They seem to go nowhere in explaining what evolution was shooting for when it introduced a beetle with sexual overdrive into an already crowded field. Why does nature keep mucking around with the delicate balance? Why not leave well enough alone?

At dusk, on my final beetle patrol of the day, I catch a three-liner; maybe it is drowsy, off-guard, or preoccupied with finding a partner to snug down with for the night. I hold it up and study it closely, eyeball to eyeball, wondering if it is capable of fear or terror, and once more I am guilty of offending science with my anthropomorphism; or is its wariness merely a conditioned reflex or instinct like procreation itself? But is not fear, like hope, a common denominator of all life, part of a shared original heritage from the deep where it is all said to have begun in a single speck of vitalized matter?

The horny exoskeleton presses against my fingers, legs and wings struggling to get free. This one doomed little insect epitomizes all of the creatures sacrificed for our convenience or well-being or because they violate our prejudices. This is our ultimatum to nature: "Bother us and you must go?" I relentlessly plunge the three-liner into the kerosene and there is a final convulsive twitching of wings and legs. Hereafter I shall keep our dispute impersonal and faceless.

The Colorados dominate their garden rivals for the moment, but with what assurance that they will prevail? Do they possess real staying power or are they a mere flash in the potato patch? They could bring about their own downfall by not absorbing the lessons of long-term survival the three-liners have to teach. Not all of evolution's experimental deviations are successful.

Personally I am heartened that the old-fashioned three-liner is still hanging in there, although outdated, downgraded, and practically forgotten; reminding us that prudence is still a valuable commodity in survival. Times change rapidly, traditions are forgotten, the once-honored is no longer esteemed. I am encouraged to see something from the past endure and still making its mark, however modest, in today's high-speed, high-tech, fast-track, public-relations-skewed world where content is secondary to style and form. The patient, prudent, wary three-liner may yet regain its former prominence in the shifting limelight of garden fashions.

The ant finds kingdoms in a foot of ground.
—Stephen Vincent Benét

Unexpected allies rally to my aid this morning: Tiny black ants crawl all over the potato plants attacking the grubs of potato beetles that I missed during yesterday's massacre. It is a grisly sight, this balancing of nature, although favorable to me. Ants by the thousands virtually cover the juicy, reddish-black humpback beetle grubs that squirt so revoltingly when pinched. The ants devour their prey on the spot, not so much, as far as I can see, as taking a few tasty grub steaks back to their nest for the kids or saving some for a rainy day.

I would have expected ants to be more provident. Have they, too, gone the way of the shiftless grasshopper with its absorption in immediate gratification and no thought of tomorrow? Are they, too, victims of progress and its imperatives? But I may do them an injustice. They could be taking the food in their crops, or "social stomach," to regurgitate and feed their young or helpless ants no longer able to feed themselves. Ants are like that.

My concern of the moment is where have all of these hungry beetle grubs come from after I purged the plants less than twenty-four hours ago, cutting short so many beetle careers? Are they brought in during the night, under cover of darkness, from neighboring gardens, a kind of beetle Berlin airlift? They are everywhere. They chew methodically on a leaf, retreating in order without breaking their arc formation, to move on to another leaf and then another. The foliage where they have foraged is little more than tattered stems and bare stalks.

I concentrate on the defenseless grubs. They lack the protection of a tough outer covering like their parents who wear chitin skeletons as a coat of armor. The grubs are not shrewd enough to remain on the undersides of the leaves where they hatched, out of sight, but dine on top in full view. This seems a shortcoming in their programming. The grubs offer no resistance when squished, other than squirting juices and staining my hands. Handpicking is not for the squeemish.

The grubs are small but larger than the attacking ants, not the least prepossessing with their soft, slimy bodies. I have heard them described as "gross," "disgusting," and even "revolting," although that may be overdoing it, and could not help developing egos. The adult Colorado, unlike its offspring, makes a good first impression, well formed if undistinguished in manner because of its lack of verve or dash, but always imperturbable, possibly dignified, even under duress. The grubs have no personality and are lethargic except for eating with enthusiasm.

I welcome the assistance of the ants but am not sure I find them more desirable than the potato beetles and their numerous progeny. Where will the rampaging ants go after they finish off the juicy grubs? Will they return to wherever they came from or take up permanent residence in the garden, creating new problems for me?

It is not that these small black ants are really troublesome. They do no particular harm, have modest appetites at best, and get rid of pests like beetle grubs. They live quietly in the earth, minding their manners and young, help aerate the soil, and break down organic matter. They lead uneventful lives, the reason little has been written about them compared to their more glamorous kin.

Competition for recognition is fierce in the ant world, with more than 3,500 described species and a greater total of individuals than any other land animals. About the best I could learn about my tiny visitors, *Monomorium minimum*, is that they are "often discovered throwing up tiny piles of sand in the garden or on lawns or golf courses," and may live in the burrows of larger ants as slaves or parasites, taking refuge in smaller tunnels or holes if kicked out.

These small ants have not made the big time like the famous leaf-cutter or Atta ants with their fabulous underground gardens of fungus, which is their sole food; other ants keep slave aphids which they "milk," stroking their bellies for their honeydew; there are ferocious warrior ants with murderous jaws, stinging fire ants, ants with venomous fangs, ants that fire caustic ballistic chemicals, army ants on permanent bivouac, revolutionaries that kidnap their queen to start a new colony, and exotics that store honeydew in the bodies of their own kind, forcing them to eat until they balloon out and resemble small barrels, known as repletes, which are attached to the ceiling in underground nests for use during hard times.

Such achievements must be rather intimidating and discouraging to small black garden-dwelling ants of no distinction. Why did they settle for so little?

My own objection to these tiny bland creatures is personal and, I fear, trivial, if not frivolous, in the larger scheme. They crawl up pants legs exploring sensitive areas, tending to distract and even irritate during the performance of garden chores, but not so disconcerting as stepping on a nest of yellow jackets and having them attack the same tender spot, a misadventure I once suffered while cutting grass in New Jersey.

I admire *Monomorium minimum's* industry, their willingness to pitch in and lend a hand, but am not sure I want a lasting or intimate relationship. I am not even sure I care to be beholden to them. Such is the problem we often face with our allies:

how to get rid of them or discharge our obligation after they have served their purpose? Is every ally a potential nuisance or enemy, holding a due bill over our heads?

> *Love is indestructible . . .*
> —Robert Southy

Tristram and Isolde! Romeo and Juliet! Adam and Eve! Edward and Wally! Ron and Nancy! George and Barbara! (Poppy and Babs).

While planting beans today (in the rain), I found two dead Colorados from last year's invasion, their bodies still coupled in death.

> *Pleasures lie thickest where no pleasures seem:*
> *There's not a leaf that falls upon the ground*
> *But holds some joy of silence or of sound,*
> *Some spirits begotten of a summer dream.*
> —Laman Blanchard

How delightful to watch young bees in their "play flights," trying out their new wings, zipping recklessly through the air in front of the hives, barely missing one another and workers coming in laden with nectar and pollen. These are days of holiday for them. Soon they will take over their life work and adult responsibility, wearing out those fragile wings and dying in six weeks, victims of summer's urgencies.

Do my playful young bees have a message for us? Does the garden and its perimeter hold an unknown dimension? Is there more for the busy inhabitants than the endless search for food, grim procreation, relentless warfare, the shackles of natural law? Are we beholden to the depressing dictum that all life is at war?

Nature may have been more generous and even-handed than we suspect in dispensing her greatest of all gifts—joy in life. The great Charles Darwin, always pursuing the riddle of being, observed that "happiness is never better exhibited than by young animals, such as puppies, kittens, lambs, etc., when playing together like our own children. Even insects play together as has been described by that excellent observer P. Huber who saw ants chasing and pretending to bite one another, like so many puppies."

Darwin was demonstrating the likeness of species. I admit to never having seen ants frolicking at play, but how much do I know about their private lives away from work? Other creatures considered beneath our notice may have their own diversions and amusements, even sorrows, not recognized by our standards of what constitutes joy, happiness, or grief.

If all of us, all members of all species, all of life, did in truth arise from the same atom of living matter, addressed by Donald Culross Peattie as "the cold batrachian jelly by which we vertebrates are linked to the things that creep and writhe and are blind yet breed and have being," if such be true, as science holds, can we believe that pleasure in living, the sweet savoring of existence, is restricted only to a chosen few able to articulate their feelings?

My young bees at play, like P. Huber's ants, proclaim that joy is universal and those not sharing it are robbed of their birthright.

There is no gathering the rose without being
pricked by the thorns.

—Bidapi

It was just a year ago that the deer appeared, and now, upon awakening, I find myself looking out the window to see if they have returned. I can tell at once by the pole beans. That is first choice for the deer. It is an unsettling sight to greet your pole beans in the morning and find them missing half of their foliage.

The deer easily jumped the four-foot fence during the night. There were at least two, possibly more. I could not tell for sure because of the number of hoofprints and the damage. Those sharp hooves bite into the soft earth, churning it up unmercifully. Along with stripping the lower half of the bean vines the raiders had polished off a row of cabbage and a few broccoli appetizers.

I was warned that once deer find you they will come back. Why not? That seems only sensible. Do we not also return to good restaurants or handouts? But this "customer loyalty" can be deadly for deer. Some hunters put out salt licks, get the deer in the habit of visiting them regularly, and shoot the animals once the hunting season begins.

I called the county agricultural agent to ask if she could suggest anything for my deer problem.

"Oh dear," she said.

"Yes," I replied.

"That's a tough one," she said. After a long pause she gave the name of a fungicide which "some people say repels deer."

"That's not exactly what I had in mind. Any other ideas?"

She said I could buy deer fence but it was expensive. I had never heard of it before. What was it? She said deer fence is five or six feet high "and then shoots of at a forty-five-degree angle."

"No other suggestions?"

"Well, some people cut soap shavings and hang them on the fence. I don't recall what kind of soap they use."

I said that did not appeal to me. Besides, you would have to keep putting more out after rain washed them away.

"I suppose that's true."

I thanked her and went about my business, harvesting a row of bush beans the deer had overlooked.

My previous firsthand experience with deer had been limited to a single encounter when our son Bret was young and I took him to an animal farm where animals wandered among the visitors. Bret carried his lunch in a paper bag, peanut butter and jelly sandwiches and an apple. One of the social dear ate it, bag and all, in a single gulp.

Live deer on Cape Cod usually make themselves scarce, although a sizable herd is maintained for hunters. Most live in the wooded Cape Cod National Seashore, on the lower Cape, because of the explosive development that is destroying habitats for animals and humans alike. Occasionally during hunting season I have seen dead deer, bleeding from the nostrils, slung over a pickup hood going to or from a deer checkpoint. Bureaucracy is very conscientious about keeping score.

Several years ago I went to a local farm for eggs and saw a dead deer suspended by its hind legs from a tripod. Nearby three men were drinking beer and laughing, celebrating the kill before butchering the carcass. Another time there was a dead deer at the side of the road, still warm after being hit by a car. Someone had called the police; there was nothing to do but admire the regal animal in death.

Only a few times have I seen live deer on the Cape. Once was on a back road when a young male with small antlers stood a couple hundred yards away, statuesque and beautiful. We stopped to admire the creature but almost at once it bounded into the nearby woods. A more unusual sighting was seeing four deer frolicking in a yard adjoining Route 6 at dusk on a summer evening, running and playing like children, oblivious of the traffic. It was such an odd place to see deer, so unexpected, that at first I thought they were dogs. God knows what happened to them.

After the first garden deer raid last year I spent the day trying to repair the damage. Would they return? I kept asking myself. They did. A couple nights later they ate higher on the pole beans, apparently standing on hind legs. They also finished off several heads of lettuce. Fortunately, they confined themselves, thus far, to the back part of the garden, farthest from the house.

I took my problem to Bill. He is not a gardener or naturalist but can fix practically anything. Why not deer? He said the answer was obvious: "Leave a floodlight on all night." He promptly produced a long extension cord from his "wonderful garage" (as I always refer to it), which has an inventory like a Sears warehouse. He also brought a floodlight but it did not work. I assured him I had a light.

That night I focused the light on the far end of the garden. The deer used it to find a row of newly transplanted broccoli and a few more heads of lettuce. They were getting bolder, dining closer to the house. So much for obvious solutions.

Did Bill have a less obvious solution? He does not go down easily. So light did not work; then sound would. Hook up a radio tuned to an all-night station and "let it blast!"

"What about our sleep?"

"You want to get rid of the deer, don't you?" Bill is always practical. First things first.

I was not confident, but the noise at least might give them nervous indigestion. Give it a try! Waves of hard rock pounding out of the garden kept us awake much of the night. It did not deter the deer. Music to eat by! The remaining vegetables looked pale and shaken by their nocturnal exposure to hard rock. I tried to console myself. Deer, too, had to eat, did they not? But so much? So often? Always the same garden?

Everyone I consulted offered the same advice: "Get a dawg." No thanks! I called the local feed and grain, in desperation, to ask about the fungicide recommended by the county agent. They had never heard of it. No one had ever asked for it before. Other consultants offered other solutions: Drink beer and pee all along the fence (How? Have a pee party?). Sprinkle blood-meal all around the perimeter of the garden (At more than $1 a pound?). Fasten chunks of human hair to the fence (Whose?).

Squash bugs, potato beetles, now deer. It does keep a body on his toes.

I next tried the ultimate source, or resource—the library. Perhaps reference books would offer a clue. I read that deer have been around for some 35 million years and are native to America. They are prized as game by hunters, popular for their meat, their heads often used as trophies and some of their organs sold in Asia as aphrodisiacs. Deer have a four-chambered stomach, are related to cattle, have thirty-two to thirty-four teeth, and four toes on each foot. All but one species lack a gallbladder. They feed on leaves, buds, twigs from woody branches, and grass. Not a word about peanut butter and jelly sandwiches and garden delicacies.

It was hardly fascinating information but did give me an idea: I would test their intelligence. I would raise the rear fence they jumped over by adding above it the fencing the peas had grown on. That would make it eight feet high. If they could not jump it, were they smart enough to follow the extended fence in back around the corner where it was still only four feet high on the sides?

That was the end of the nocturnal raids—for then. I am not sure whether the deer flunked their intelligence test or simply did not come back for reasons of their own. I like to think it was the latter. It is understandable if they could not solve the problem. Deer have only been around a mere 35 million years, hardly time enough to figure things out like, say, insects or squirrels, which have a longer history. Deer are still evolutionary babes in the woods. Given a few million more years they may smarten up enough not to be taken in by the salt-lick scam or end up slung over the hood of a pickup, bleeding from the nostrils, on the way to a deer checkpoint.

Although the raids were over for that summer, the deer returned, perhaps on a sentimental journey, several weeks later. On a crisp fall morning I looked out the bedroom window and there, outside the fence in back, were a doe and her fawn. They were looking in wistfully, it seemed to me, as if the doe were telling her fawn about the good old days in Bill's garden and what fine dining it was, and how good things never last in this ever-changing world. . .

They made no effort to jump the fence or even seriously explore the possibilities. They just stood together for a long time, nuzzling and looking in. What a stately and magnificent sight! Peggy and I watched the pair from the house until, finally, they strolled leisurely away to disappear in the woods, probably oblivious that it was the start of the hunting season.

I have heard about hunters who kept deer in their sights too long without shooting and they never did pull the trigger. It was too much for them. One spoke of the deer's eyes, their softness. He said he was unable to fire. At least one gave up hunting after such an experience. Surely as the power and beauty of life, the respect for life, all life, bite deeper into that part of our being we call soul, it becomes increasingly less attractive to take life.

I was too optimistic about having gotten rid of the deer. They did return with more serious intent. The following spring I looked out the study window and saw the doe and her fawn, the fawn now quite large, in the garden devouring leftover winter kale. It was mid-morning. I shouted at them. They looked up, unconcerned, and continued dining. I had to go almost into the garden, flailing my arms, before they took off over the fence in a vanishing flash of white tails.

That did it. Early plantings were in and if the deer returned to snack nothing would be left. Gradually a strategy of deterrence had been gestating. I extended the fence posts with timbers and nailed horizontal sections of strapping between the elongated posts, about two feet higher than the fence, and stretched rope from the dump between posts where the wood strips were too short to reach.

On a sunny Sunday afternoon Kaolin, a young artist friend, helped us decorate the new barriers. She and Peggy festooned rope and strapping with strips of colorful fabric, dangling aluminum-foil plates, wind chimes improvised of clapper cans within cans, and cans containing shells, pebbles, and other rattling objects, along with suspended plastic yogurt and milk containers and other salvaged artifacts that would flutter, blow, and rattle in the wind. Pam suggested empty cat food cans brushing against their detached lids. Lily did her bit by supplying us with the empty cat food cans. Others added their own decorative touches. The only rule was that nothing could be bought.

The completed fence suggests the creative impulse gone berserk, a wild combination of what appears to be tattered laundry drying in the wind and leftovers from a bankrupt, low-level flea market. It is visually jarring, an abomination on nature, but apparently effective, at least for the moment while the deer regroup, no more easily defeated, I assume, than squirrels at the winter feeder.

The deer have not returned since the new "system" went into operation several weeks ago. I do not know if it scared / unnerved them, violated their aesthetic sense, or they simply preferred not to associate with people of such bizarre tastes. A deliveryman looked at it and shook his head. Peggy considers it "rather jaunty." I describe it as art by committee. Someone suggested turning it into a tourist attraction and selling advertising space. Because the deer invariably came after dark, it seemed fitting to call it "Not Tonight, Deer."

From the study window I look out at this artistic endeavor as such, dreary, drooping, and forlorn in today's overcast and rain, and speculate on where it fits into the struggle for existence as one species tries to get a leg up on another, or at least to keep another from getting a leg over the fence. I doubt if it has a proper role in evolution, and it might even throw natural selection out of kilter. I am amused but not yet reassured or confident, keeping an uneasy watch on the garden and surrounding woods where even now the deer may be plotting their own strategy of return, saying to one another, "What do you make of people like that?"

> *The insect . . . brings with him something that does not seem to belong to the customs, the morale, the psychology of our Globe. One would say that it comes from another planet, more monstrous, more dynamic, more insensate, more atrocious, more infernal than ours.*
> —Maurice Maeterlinck

A praying mantis is already on the job when I check out the morning garden, perched among the bush beans, camouflaged, in her customary worshipful posture while awaiting breakfast. An unwary white butterfly flits by. Mantis rears up menacingly, gossamer wings outspread, to strike with a lightning thrust. The butterfly is impaled on cruel pruning-hook forelegs, skewered with sawtooth hind legs and thighs that are serrated razor blades. Mantis leisurely tears the luckless creature to pieces with her powerful jaws, devours it, and resumes her devotions. *Mantis religiosa* is well described as a religious fraud.

Mantis is a hardened, ruthless, dedicated killer with a gluttonous and indiscriminating appetite. She consumes wasps, butterflies, moths, crickets, bees, grasshoppers, and just about anything that comes along, a bloodied philosopher who takes whatever provender fate sends her way. She is so unselective that she will eat other mantids, her spouse, and, in hard times, her own offspring. The female will devour her partner after or even during copulation. Males seem to accept this misfortune stoically. A male has been known to continue mating after his mate chewed off his head, literally losing his head in love.

Mantis must be one of nature's outstanding achievements, perfectly engineered for her life work, a virtual killing machine. Every part of the odd-shaped body is designed for a lethal end; even her position before striking, rearing back, wings out-stretched, forelegs at the ready, paralyzes the victim with fear so it meekly submits to execution. Mantis probably eats a few of my bees and other beneficials, along with the pests, but I like to think the balance is in her favor. I consider her a wel-come garden visitor.

Mantis is said to be the only insect with a flexible neck that permits the head to swing completely around so she can see directly behind her, another part of the deadly arsenal. But I have read that the dragonfly's head is on a ball-and-socket joint that can swivel almost completely around and up and down as well. A supple neck must give both of these rapacious killers an edge in their bloody work.

Almost every insect is engineered with some special talent for earning a living. Mantids hunt for their enemies while hid-den by protective coloration. Dragonflies, known to me in my youth as darning needles, are considered the most agile of all flying insects. I noted earlier that one authority claims they zoom along at 60 miles per hour, while another holds that 35 is the top flying speed for any insect. Most insects are said to poke along at a mere 5 to 8 miles per hour. Bees fly at about 15 miles an hour, carrying their own weight in nectar, wings beating 250 times a second, literally worn out by endless labor, bringing death after about six weeks in the summer.

A garden is a lively and popular place in the growing season, attracting regular seasonal residents and itinerants, the latter migratory workers, in effect, stopping off for refreshments on their way here or there, a pit stop at my fast-food emporium. Some work for me, others against me, and the rest are neutral or indifferent. Some partake of the garden, others of their fellows. Half of the world's insects are believed to prey on other insects. Only 10 percent of all garden insects are believed to do 90 percent of all damage. Most are neither helpful nor harmful, just sort of hanging around, doing their thing, bit players in the drama of existence.

All of these creatures, residents and visitors alike, contribute to the rich ferment of garden life, adding zest and variety. They pollinate plants, aerate and improve soil, decompose and bury dead animals and plants, become food themselves for beneficial predators, excrete their wastes as fertilizer, and, finally, they die, returning to the earth mother that which they took from it and whence they came, completing their role in the great cycle.

These are my guests, my wards, in a manner of speaking. I bear even the worst of them no ill will nor do I begrudge them shelter and sustenance so long as they do not get out of hand. I am, in truth, an admirer of these various callers who have found so many inspiring and wonderous ways to tap into the garden economy, even those I call pests.

They have their own economy, just as we do. A leaf is an energy source to be translated into more beetles, squash bugs, slugs, grasshoppers, earwigs, or whatever. Eating is itself a form of capital investment. I am their banker, their source of income.

The habits of these creatures have been worked out through the ages, an adjustment here, a correction there, not necessarily improvements, scientists emphasize, but each minute alteration helping to better cope with existing conditions. These mutations, or "sports" as they are known, represent natural selection or "survival of the fittest" in action. Each species is different. No two that are redundant can compete for the limited food in the same habitat; one must change or be wiped out.

The story began almost 400 million years ago, we are told, with that hardy precursor of all flying insects, the ubiquitous cockroach, who was then much larger than now, which is fortunate for urban dwellers. The pioneering flying roach was soon followed by lightning-fast silverfish, and giant dragonflies with a thirty-inch wingspan, terrorists of prehistoric skies.

Things moved swiftly after that and today I am host to the descendants of these and other innovators, vagabonds, and virtuosos. They live symbiotically, in mutuality, commensalism, parasitism, in harmony, indifference, and perpetual warfare, each individual trying to survive and reproduce; yes, above all to reproduce, to complete its link and assure the next in the ongoing chain of life. Here, in the garden, live and die the combatants, non-combatants, foes, friends, and hangers-on, sharing a bloody battlefield marked by a deceptive facade of serenity.

A garden, according to Webster, is "a piece of ground for the cultivation of herbs, fruits, flowers, or vegetables." But that is too limited. A garden is a microcosm of the world. Each plant and creature is seeking an edge, an advantage, in the struggle for survival, possibly even now honing or altering techniques to outdo the competition. That is the story of life itself, as true for plants and bugs as for us.

Little is known about the relationships of the multitudes of plants, insects, and other creatures that inhabit this world we share with them, even the few that coexist in a garden. We do not know how extensive or interrelated is the interlocking web of life or the penalty for disrupting it. We have only fragmented and incomplete information. We live by many dangerous assumptions.

The basic structure of insect life appears straightforward enough: Herbivores and omnivores eat plants. Carnivores and omnivores eat herbivores. Then omnivores and carnivores eat one another. It is all quite orderly, a laissez-faire economy, life and death dispensed in a free market. Talents and luck are not distributed equitably. The more clever, unscrupulous, and better adapted live, the others perish, survival often depending on the effectiveness of strategies and biological engineering in the struggle to live.

All insects have more or less the same basic equipment: bodies made up of three parts, six legs, and a hard, protective covering of chitin (wearing their skeleton); most have two pairs of wings, sensory antennae, compound eyes, and powerful, chewing, jawlike mandibles or piercing/sucking mouthparts. From here they take off with their ingenious and amazing variations, each filling its particular niche in the great scheme.

One of the garden diners I encounter is a tomato hornworm, a handsome specimen with elegant white stripes, taking its morning nourishment. It is well hidden with its green coloring among the tomato plant's green leaves. But the worm made a fatal mistake, chewing away the protective leaves that provided effective camouflage, and it is now visible among the bare stems. The creatures black droppings also give it away, circumstantial evidence its undoing.

The worm rears up menacingly as I approach, a posture that has given its parent the name of sphinx moth. But it is all bluff. The worm, with its little horn of a tail, has no defense other than protective coloration. I do not disturb it. Another foe has already struck. Numerous white cocoons, like little upright grains of white rice, are on its back.

A braconid wasp laid its eggs in the caterpillar. The larvae, after dining on their host, are pupating in the white cocoons, which will tip open on top to release tiny young wasps, leaving dead the parasitized tomato worm that gave them life. Each egg the wasp lays produces many offspring. In one study two thousand wasps of another variety emerged from a single egg. Parasitic wasps, practicing their multiple-birth polyem-bryony, are valuable garden allies, one of the most important and deadly predators of leaf-eating insects.

Bugs have done extensive experimenting and innovating with reproduction. Some have worked things out by parthenogen-esis so the female produces young without fertilization by a male. For others a single mating lasts a lifetime. I assume these techniques were designed by nature for the usual purpose—to convey some advantage in survival, although they may be no more than experimentation for its own sake, pure research, as it were, possibly nature demonstrating the versatility and art-istry of the life force; art itself is a kind of playing with life, trying to tease it into being more than it is. The various inno-vations in reproduction have made no great headway in replac-ing the traditional method, so far as I can see, but nature may recognize no standard method or technique, ends justifying means.

I leave the doomed hornworm to check out the bush beans. There, tiny leafhoppers, those agile acrobats, make prodigious leaps forward, backward, sideways. Almost invisible flea bee-tles hop about chewing holes in the leaves, joined by flies and gnats. It looks like a circus. A daddy longlegs dines on the leafhoppers and flea beetles, and a small spider with red eyes skulking in a filmy web among the leaves seems to have its sights on the daddy longlegs. Some nearby beet leaves are splotchy from the larvae of leaf miners working within, doing their mischief out of sight. The damage is slight. I leave the predators to take care of them.

Underfoot, scurrying about in the damp mulch, are sow-bugs or pillbugs, which curl into a little ball when disturbed; there are centipedes, millipedes, earwigs, crickets, beetles, ants, and others, each on its own business in its own way. Over-head, groups of white cabbage butterflies flit about, less one eaten by the mantis. Some of the butterfly worm offspring dine on cabbage plants but they should be controlled by the parasitic wasps. Maggots in the ground may be attacked by rove beetles that travel in gangs, like so many muggers, stalking game bigger than themselves.

Aphids by the thousands perform antics on the celery. They are notorious breeders, lacking any sense of proportion or restraint. Cabbage aphids in a New York study, practicing parthenogenesis, averaged forty-one young per female with sixteen generations in six months. The bearing females, to give them their due, are known as "stem mothers"; if all descendants of one species of female aphid lived, the total would be 524 billion progeny in one year. In the fall the aphids produce males that mate with the females, who produce fertile eggs that overwinter to get things under way again come spring.

Most aphids are wingless but when threatened have a neat trick of simply sprouting wings to fly elsewhere, like humans hoping to flee into space to escape a ravaged planet, a kind of "flight square" as they say in chess. Aphids also have an unusual defense, producing under duress a sticky glob they push into the faces of startled pursuers by backing into them.

Several ladybird beetles are on the celery, so I am not too concerned about the aphids. A ladybird beetle can eat forty aphids in an hour. Aphids are a nuisance to me but a vital food for many of the predators working in my behalf. Another consumer of aphids is the ferocious aphis lion, the larvae of the exquisite but foul-smelling lacewing, known as the "skunk of the insect world." Her young lions are so hungry that they eat their newborn siblings, unless the prudent if odorous mother lays her eggs singly on tops of grass and weeds, safely out of reach of the firstborn.

Each creature practices its own particular tricks to make a living and try to escape death. The bot fly is claimed to zip along at 50 miles an hour. Robber flies, ambush bugs, ladybird beetles, and monarch butterflies feign death when threatened.

Walking sticks look like parts of tree limbs they cling to. The bombardier beetle, practicing chemical warfare, can accurately fire a stream of offensive spray heated to 95°F, described as a kind of rocket fuel, from the tip of its abdomen.

Hover flies, with no stingers or other means of defense, mimic bees. A variety of beetle is said to have developed an appetite for poisons, cigarettes, mustard plasters, and red pepper, although we are not told how it fares on this diet. Other creatures have protective stinging hairs, spines, and scales, or emit poisonous fluids, gases, waxes, resins, and vile odors.

A grasshopper makes a mighty leap as I approach. It is a greedy diner but also an accomplished musician, able to play by scraping legs together, legs against wings, or wing against wing, a versatile troubadour singing love songs amidst a dirge of death, a member of the nocturnal orchestra I support.

Skullduggery is an ancient art among insects. Female fireflies, whose artistry I admire on summer nights, alter their flashing pattern to lure and devour amorous suitors of other species, some of the victims containing a disagreeable chemical which makes them unappetizing to birds, now conferring that protection on the femmes fatales who ate them. The splendid monarch butterfly, an occasional garden visitor, also has blood that is distasteful to birds, travels a thousand or more miles to mate, and must lay its eggs on milkweed for the young to survive. Other butterflies mimic the unsavory, colorful monarchs for protection.

Industrious ants keep slave aphids like herds of cattle, as noted before, "milking" them for their honeydew and clipping their wings to prevent escape. Aphid eggs are kept warm underground in the ants' nest to start a new "herd" in the spring.

Many animals have more than one means of defense, often several which they use in sequence, saving the "most costly," such as chemical warfare, until the last, according to Dr. Thomas Eisner, a Cornell University entomologist. Their primary defense is the hard armor-like external skeleton. Many insects, particularly the young, can regenerate a lost appendage or get along nicely with a missing one.

Theirs is a world without mercy or compassion. One insect has been observed eating a second while itself being devoured by a third. Many techniques have been devised and refined over the eons for survival. Many scientists who study insects consider them the most successful form of life known.

The most awesome and effective weapon insects have for survival is their ability to reproduce in astronomical numbers. My squash bugs and potato beetles, which I consider prolific, are modest performers in this respect, small potatoes, really, compared to those on the fast track. Our salvation, and theirs, is that so few survive.

Termites are probably the superstars of fecundity. An East African termite queen lays one egg every two seconds, 43,000 a day. The queen of an Australian species lays 8,640 a day, 3,153,000 per year, a pace maintained for up to fifty years, which seems to be carrying fecundity, or even overcompensation, a bit far.

Not quite so spectacular but still impressive is the nearer-to-home dragonfly, which may lay 11,000 eggs in a clump. A praying mantis deposits 1,000 or so eggs but only a couple become adults. A honeybee queen, known to beekeepers as an "egg-laying machine," lays 2,000 eggs a day, some 1,500,000 in her career.

Even slow breeders like the seventeen-year locusts, which are not locusts at all but cicadas, produce some 40,000 offspring under a single tree, but their song is brief, their mortality high before they breed, and the nymphs vanish into the earth to pupate for another seventeen years, a tactic of saturation breeding at infrequent intervals to confuse predators. Cicadas, also called "harvest flies," for their timing, like to think things over. They obviously take the long view; some varieties remain underground only thirteen years, others less, impatient to get things moving.

Legendary tales are recalled of great swarms of locusts and grasshoppers darkening skies and leaving the earth stripped bare, only holes remaining to show where plants had grown. A single locust swarm in Nebraska, in the 1870s, was ten miles wide, three hundred miles long, and a mile high; moving at 5 miles an hour it took six hours to pass a fixed point and was calculated to number more than 124 billion individuals. Often such enormous populations collapsed as suddenly as they appeared, some of the factors known, others only poorly understood.

An overriding reason for the collapse was that the vast numbers overextended the earth's carrying capacity, a lesson we could learn from them. Such multitudes are rare today, probably due to loss of open space for breeding, unfavorable conditions generally, and various natural and man-made controls. The insects themselves may have become discouraged by their failure to achieve lasting benefits from such rash population outbursts, another lesson worth noting; there is nothing like a population explosion to ruin things for everyone.

An average female insect is said to lay about 250 eggs, more or less, and while the figure is not sensational neither is it inconsequential. But fertility alone does not explain the success of insects. Equally important is their rapid breeding cycle. Humans average about three generations per century. Insects may run off as many or more in a season. Aphids are good for one generation a week when the temperature reaches 80 degrees. Such rapid succession permits experimentation by the species, adapting quickly to novel or adverse conditions, changing tactics, even altering physical characteristics.

Through adaptive mechanisms, based on mutations, insects have become immune to the most powerful poisons and learned to live in changed climates and environments. A classic example often cited is how a certain moth in London, following the Industrial Revolution, gradually took on the darker coloring of a few individuals to blend in with the city's polluted, smoky air, making them harder to detect. For the fast-breeding insects, evolution is the primary means, or process, or gaining an edge in the struggle for life.

Many statistics and monographs document the importance of insects in our lives. The measure I like best is that some thirty thousand articles a year are said to appear in one thousand journals devoted exclusively to entomology. Insects, in one way or another, impact almost every area of human endeavor, including our food, health, economics, and social activities. The fast-breeding fruit fly, which reproduces every ten days, was instrumental in bringing understanding of genetic transference through studies revealing that DNA is the same in all forms of life, differing only in the instructions carried. We may be closer to bugs than we like to think.

Biologists occasionally amuse themselves by speculating on the number of individual insects in the world. This is outside the parameters of a modest garden book but the figures tossed off startle and give an idea of the possibilities. The number of creatures in the soil alone is staggering. Soil counts are considered the most reliable method of determining insect populations. A Pennsylvania study found 425 million insects and other creatures living in the soil per acre. In my small plot, if those figures hold true, there would be some 57 million insects and other creatures, plus the microorganisms which are more numerous than the stars in the heavens.

I stare at this tiny piece of earth beneath me, apparently inert and silent, and yet teeming with life, a frenzy of creatures burrowing, hiding, stalking, deceiving, attacking, fleeing, lurking, and dying, an ongoing pageant of life and death played out in a subterranean stage, species and individuals existing in some kind of commerce and equilibrium unknown to those of us above.

The most cheering conclusion I draw from all of this is that so few of the insects we share our lives and gardens with are considered harmful. In the United States the number of so-called pests is held to be only around ten thousand, about 1 percent of the nearly 1 million insects studied and named. Scientists believe there may be 10 million or more species in all. One way and another they help make life possible, if at times difficult.

Insects are, above all, survivors. Darwin found them on deserted islands where not even lichen could grow, subsisting on parasites carried by visiting sea birds. A small brown moth fed on feathers. Insects have mastered and occupy the entire earth, flourishing in the frozen wastes of the Arctic and Antarctic, atop mountains, in deserts, volcanoes, in the sea itself.

These creatures are worthy of admiration and respect. They are likely to be around when our kind is gone, victims of our own ingenuity or stupidity, which often seem to come to the same thing. It is easy enough to mistake ignorance for wisdom, folly for progress. Insects, after all, have had millions of years' experience hanging in there. They have not made our mistake of trying to leapfrog time and overreach the earth's hospitality and tolerance. We humans, virtual newcomers on earth, are still trying to learn how to cope with a difficult situation we do not quite understand. Insects have much to teach us.

> *Too many creatures*
> *both insects and humans*
> *estimate their own value*
> *by the amount of minor irritation*
> *they are able to cause*
> *to greater personalities than themselves.*
> —Don Marquis

July 19
Bug Patrol Report:

On the evening of this glorious summer day I examine the squash and pumpkins for squash bugs. On fewer than a dozen plants I find 242 egg patches, averaging about three dozen per cluster; some individual leaves have a dozen clutches of eggs, representing extensive bug industry and aspirations.

I am surprised to find that the volunteer butternut growing out of the compost heap is the most heavily infested of all. It is almost solid eggs. This defies the conventional wisdom organic gardeners live by—that a healthy plant is more immune to insect attack than weaker, less well-nourished growth. Volunteers are usually the strongest plants in the garden. My squash bugs do not seem to respect articles of faith.

Along with the eggs are hundreds of tiny gray nymphs staggering about getting their sea (or garden) legs before going to work on the leaves in earnest. Despite all of the eggs and nymphs, I find only four adults, all four hiding under a zucchini leaf like couples on a picnic. While I prey on the squash bugs, the mosquitoes and flies chew unmercifully on me, keeping nature more or less in balance, at least momentarily, with me on the short end.

July 21

Another splendid outpouring of squash-bug eggs: 132 new patches destroyed despite the massacre of only two days ago.

This time I find only one adult, which I like to think is progress of sorts, but I am left pondering where all the new eggs came from.

I also find, unexpectedly, a half-dozen potato beetles on the squash plants. I assume they are paying a social call on the squash bugs. Or are they guest artists displaying their own egg-laying technique, a kind of workshop? They also could be young mothers discussing their new role.

My search-and-destroy mission uncovers several dozen nymphs, obviously from eggs missed the last time around. Most of the new egg clusters are larger than those uncovered previously. They are, generally, deposited in a workmanlike, professional manner, but occasionally there is a small irregular clutch suggesting a botched-up job by an amateur. First-rate egg patches are, as I have observed, in a tight alignment somewhat resembling racked pool balls.

I notice an oddity on a squash plant: several clusters of distinctive yellowish eggs, apparently left by an itinerant potato beetle en route to or from the potato patch, possibly practicing on the squash before getting down to serious business on the potatoes.

Things which you do not hope happen more
frequently than things which you do hope.
—Plautus

Dill must be the most pervasive, determined, contrary growth in the garden. I plant row after row and usually it refuses to germinate in the herb bed. But as a volunteer it grows everywhere, particularly where it is not wanted, proliferating like a weed. Dill weed is well named.

It grows profusely between the rows of peas, in beds of lettuce and onions, among beans and leeks. Each year it reseeds itself to come up like a mat of new grass—but only in spots of its own choosing. We no longer plant dill, letting the volunteers go to seed, and they never fail to reestablish themselves on their own terms.

Peggy is especially fond of dill, for both practical and aesthetic reasons. She uses it in cooking and puts small bouquets of the aromatic foliage on the windowsill over the kitchen sink. On windy days outdoors the exquisite ferns dance in poetic unison like so many ballerinas. When I weed, I am forever being admonished to "be careful of the dill."

I have spent hours surreptitiously pulling dill up from unwanted places where it was choking out the resident crop. Dill is so willful and sure of itself that the soil can be rototilled, churned up, or turned under and the seeds still manage to resurface and grow. There is no suppressing dill once it makes up its mind. Respected and treated well, volunteer dill tolerates some transplanting, if it approves of the new location.

I particularly like the word *volunteer*. It suggests something noble, a giving of self, rising above petty self-interest or the minimal demands of law and society. The dictionary, less romantic but more precise, defines a volunteer as "one who enters into, or offers himself for, any service of his own free will." "Free will" is the key. In the garden a volunteer is simply any plant that grows from a seed not planted intentionally, usually of unknown origin, dropped by a bird, blown in by the wind, spread in compost or manure, or fallen from a plant that went to seed.

This definition, while accurate enough, is narrow. A volunteer grows primarily in a spot of its own choosing under conditions it finds suitable. The essence of a volunteer is that it is not dictated to; it is a free agent exercising "free will."

Volunteers give a lilt to gardens by adding an element of serendipity to a fairly ordered enterprise. I delight in those little surprises when a green shoot pokes its head up unexpectedly from a mystery seed and I must wait to see what develops. I admire volunteers not only for their practical food contribution but also their spirit and joie de vivre. They are true democrats as well as survivors.

It is almost impossible to trace their lineage. They do not expect to be cosseted or pampered. They know they must make it on their own and not through special treatment or family connections. They usually have already survived a winter outdoors and are confident of their survival skills. They are, in a sense, self-made plants, worthy of respect.

Because volunteers are not distracted or disciplined by human intervention or management, they tend to grow in the most unlikely, unexpected, and often outrageous and unwanted places. In my garden they delight in growing between the regular fence and adjoining "rabbit-guard" fence where it is almost impossible to get to them.

Volunteers usually must struggle against great odds to survive. Those that make it are a fine expression of the life force, like an errant dandelion, a volunteer itself of sorts, growing through an almost invisible crack in concrete or asphalt.

Volunteers are hardy and invariably lend an element of mystery and surprise. Occasionally I let a few plants go to seed, counting on the seeds sending up new plants the following year, planned volunteers, as it were.

Volunteers are the antithesis of common commercial packaged hybrid seeds, those unnatural genetic unions that live passively and leave no heirs. Hybrids possess no real tolerance for adversity, other than possible resistance bred into them to specific misfortunes. They have no prospect of immortality; they are beginning and end of their line.

It must be discouraging to be a hybrid, "born" in a greenhouse or under rigidly controlled field conditions, hand-pollinated or gene-spliced in a genetic assembly line, germinated and raised under artificial lights or plastic in a sterile medium, laced with a chemical broadside of automated growth promoters and conditioners, fungicides, hormones, fertilizers, weed killers, pesticides, and who knows what else, totally dependent upon mechanical life-support systems down to ersatz sunshine, timed waterings, and forced heat, factory packaged, promoted, marketed, and sent into the world of gardens without individual personality or character, every seed in every package a clone, so rigorously controlled that it will produce a plant almost the mirror image of every other, designed for appearance rather than taste, a triumph of cosmetic scientific ingenuity, technology, and public relations, serving the purse before the palate.

Volunteers, unlike hybrids, develop a character and personality of their own. Their consciousness has been raised, often to such astronomical levels that there is no denying them. Like dill. Volunteers understand that the first law of life is to survive and reproduce, not just to look pretty for camera or table. They are an inspiring example of "keeping a stiff upper lip and looking out for number one," if one admires that sort of thing.

Some of the finest volunteers are distributed from compost. Often seeds take root and grow in the heap itself. I recall an epic zucchini that grew out of our compost in New Jersey, a Paul (or Paula) Bunyon among zucchinis. When its domestic kin petered out or succumbed, the compost volunteer remained robust, pouring out fruit relentlessly until cold weather finally cut it down. I have always regretted not having kept seed from that overachiever zucchini.

Some gardeners, instead of taking their chances with volunteers, plant directly into their compost piles. Janet, the most beautiful gardener I know, keeps horses and always has a pile of rotted manure handy. She slips seeds directly into the composted manure and grows glorious pumpkins and squash, both notorious gluttons for food. Before season's end she invariably has a box in front of her house filled with surplus squash, and a sign, "Help yourself."

Every year we have a crop of volunteer potatoes, some of

them, oddly enough, growing far from the previous year's patch, probably spread from compost or tossed aside during harvesting and forgotten. Often these volunteers grow larger than the certified seed potatoes I planted. Sometimes the out-of-the-patch spuds outwit the wily potato beetles and go untouched; sometimes they are the most heavily attacked of all. There is no figuring such things.

Our annual crop of volunteers invariably includes tomatoes, most from compost or forebears left to rot on the ground; often they germinate and grow in great self-defeating smothering clumps. Cherry tomatoes are the most abundant because they are the most likely to have been left on the ground to rot the previous season. Several years ago I planted a few cherries and now they reseed themselves annually, providing handy and tasty garden snacking.

The problem with tomato volunteers is that there is no telling the variety until the fruit forms. The seedlings all look much alike, at least to me. I have tried transplanting volunteer tomatoes, taking my chances, but generally they do not do well, as if sulking because I took over.

Volunteer tomatoes occasionally grow directly out of the compost heap, producing excellent foliage but small amounts of fruit because of the excess fertility. I generally leave such plants so their canopy of leaves will protect the pile from drying out. At season's end these plants are composted, returning the borrowed nutrients, closing the loop.

One year volunteer tomatoes were our salvation. That was the summer of the great garden wipeout. The tomatoes we planted grew no more than a foot high and produced sickly, deformed fruit. Zucchini, pumpkins, butternut squash, and eggplant bore no fruit. Broccoli flowered without heading. Successive plantings of parsley refused to germinate. The celery was stunted and tasted like wet rope. Even the ever-faithful bush beans faltered. Other gardeners told similar morbid tales, while some professed to have had a fair to good year.

One woman claimed it was her best garden ever. How to explain such things?

The fall plantings failed, like their spring predecessors. I was about to write the year off as a full-blown disaster but the tomato volunteers made a dramatic rally, enabling us to have tomatoes late into fall with extras to give away. Since then volunteer tomatoes have been part of my gardening strategy, a kind of fail-safe backup.

An odd thing about volunteer tomatoes: They do not germinate in the garden until after plants grown inside under lights are transplanted outdoors. And yet, by season's end, the volunteers have largely caught up and are producing almost as well as their domesticated and pampered relatives. Maybe it is their hardiness and self-confidence from having survived the winter outdoors. I have saved the seeds of such volunteers and planted them in flats the following year but after my interference they show no inclination to outperform or even match the seeds I buy or save from the regular plantings.

Our most unforgettable experience with volunteers was the year we moved here. I brought several pickup loads of topsoil from our former Cape Cod garden, just like a French peasant, and piled it about eight feet high, awaiting completion of the house and a new garden. The following spring a volunteer cucumber grew out of that huge mound of earth. It grew and kept growing. Never was there such an outpouring of cucumbers, tender, succulent, almost a foot long. The vines ran some twenty feet, the roots burrowed long and deep in the friable soil. I saved seed from the cukes and kept that remarkable strain going for several years until it got tired.

The pile of transplanted topsoil, including some brought from New Jersey to the previous garden, also produced potatoes from red spuds thrown into the compost the year before. The vines were lush, the potatoes huge. I used to tell visitors that was what garden books meant when they called for hilling potatoes. The joke was lost on most non-gardeners. One nodded and said, "It must be a lot of trouble to grow potatoes." Another visitor, a gardener himself, wryly said, "You seem to take hilling potatoes a bit too seriously."

The most unusual volunteers we ever had were sunflowers, probably from seed dropped by bird visitors to the house feeder in the winter. After the first plant went to seed, we had sunflowers for many succeeding years. It was delightful to watch blue jays hanging upside down, their weight bending the stately ten-foot stalks almost double, struggling to get out the seeds. Jays are born comedians.

The volunteer sunflowers eventually gave out and I left it at that, which I believe is the right way to handle all volunteers: Leave the decision to them when to quit, as well as when to start, although I have been tempted, at times, to slip out under cover of night and plant a few volunteers myself just to make sure they do not forget or overlook me.

> *In nature's infinite book of secrecy*
> *A little I can read.*
> —William Shakespeare

Nature speaks with many voices in a garden. The plants themselves ask to be heard, but we must listen carefully to what they have to say. Their message is about the ongoing strife we call balance or equilibrium when neither attacker nor attacked has an advantage. If one does not look or listen too intently the stalemate may be mistaken for peace or tranquility. But this is an illusion.

Plants do not play a passive role in their ongoing war with insects. They have their own means of defense and may even take the initiative, although they do not go so far in aggression as the notorious Venus flytrap, pitcher, and sundew, plants which "eat" insects as a way of getting nitrogen missing in the

soil where they grow. Ordinary garden plants are not carnivores. They are simply looking for peaceful coexistence, going
about the business of self-defense with less violence, histrion-
ics, or celebrity.

The silent, complex relationships between bugs and plants,
and between the plants themselves, are among the more interesting tales a garden has to tell. The gardener also plays his
role; wittingly or unwittingly he may be mediator, catalyst, or
even antagonist in the mysterious forces that rule his realm.
Unfortunately, this convergence of energies, combatants, and
allies composes a garden drama rarely if ever seen in action.
We observe only the end result and are left to puzzle out what
happened and why.

Plants have many means of defense: active, passive, mechanical, chemical, biological. Most defy simple categories or
understanding. Some have hairs, thorns, or bristles to discourage chewing insects. Others grow a "beard," stiff bristles that
deter assailants such as the Mexican bean beetle and leafhoppers; a careless leafhopper may be fatally impaled if it does not
look before it leaps.

Certain plants produce substances or noxious odors toxic to
both insects and other animals. Mustard plants excrete a compound that keeps wormlike potato nematodes in the soil from
hatching. Adult nematodes are put off by the exudates of some
asparagus varieties. Poisonous rhubarb leaves seem to confer
protection for the entire plant against insects; rhubarb can be
grown outside the garden with little danger of attack.

Some vegetables produce hormones that cause insects to
become deformed or fail to develop as adults. Oats and flax
have compounds that repel certain soil fungi. Various members of the nightshade family are toxic to certain creatures.
Some plants are believed to contain tiny sacs of poison that are
released when bitten into. The pyrethrum flower is so deadly
that it is used as an insecticide, and rotenone is made from the

roots of several tropical plants; both are popular among organic gardeners because they are natural products that break down quickly, leaving no harmful residue.

The wily bugs are not so easily put off or defeated by plant ruses and defenses but counterattack with ingenious schemes and mechanisms of their own. Some can detect and avoid harmful plant secretions or hormones. Some insects are even attracted by former repellents, having learned to excrete or store poisons safely in their bodies. Chemical warfare plays a large role in this ongoing conflict.

Treachery and trickery also play their part. Monarch butterflies store in their cells a poison found in milkweed, their favorite food, but a predator eating a monarch may die. The shrewd viceroy butterfly, sensing opportunity here, mimics the monarch to avoid being eaten, a deceptive "piggyback" protective mechanism adopted by many creatures to outwit their tormentors.

Plants, like insects, alter tactics to meet changing conditions and challenges, using different strategies for different enemies, keeping up with the times. Nothing remains still, which is the only constant in the tableau of intrigue, violence, subterfuge, and biological dexterity that composes garden life—and death.

Plants have displayed remarkable initiative and inventiveness in coming up with defenses based on their insect enemies' likes, dislikes, character, and life-styles. It is difficult to deny them credit for a certain kind of intelligence vital to their survival, which may be the ultimate test of intelligence in any species.

Researchers have broken the various plant defenses into three major categories. *Organic Plant Protection*, a Rodale Press publication, classifies them as nonpreference, antibiosis, and tolerance.

Plants opting for nonpreference seem to depend more on psychology than harsh measures or confrontation. They repel by offering discomforts or a lack of insect amenities, much as an unfriendly landlord evicts or discourages undesirable tenants by withholding hot water or providing uncomfortable beds. Plants utilize such irritants as color, smell, texture, hairs, or fuzz that may not feel good or may affect the way light is reflected, or even produce oils or chemicals that cling unpleasantly to wings or feet. This is not the stuff of the Welcome Wagon.

These various shortcomings offend a discerning bug's aesthetics and standards of comfort, prompting it to seek more suitable lodging and meals elsewhere, as well as a more congenial place to lay her eggs; no one wants to raise a family in uncomfortable or unwelcoming surroundings.

Antibiosis is a more aggressive and even violent defense, giving certain plants the ability to "prevent, injure, or destroy insect life." The word itself means an association between organisms that is harmful to one. Here our figurative landlord turns nasty, even maniacal. The hostile plant can cause its victims to fall into a stupor, vomit, fail to grow, become sterile, or suffer other indignities.

The knockout punch comes from so-called phytoalexins, volatile oils produced by certain plants. Some plants are believed to manufacture the compounds only when under attack; others, like garlic and marigolds, contain a built-in supply and merely await an oppressor to pull the trigger.

One researcher credits this vigorous defense with wiping out the plaguelike swarms of locusts that periodically devastated the Great Plains in the last century. Charles H. Brett, an entomologist, holds that the locusts' diet was changed when alfalfa was planted in the region in place of natural growths, and this change of diet "played tricks" with the locusts' bodies, an effect comparable to that of people drinking whisky instead of milk.

The locusts, it is said, did not actually vanish but changed into a smaller, less virulent form, malformed and disease prone.

Fed their former natural diet, the locusts allegedly reverted to the original shape of species gathered during the 1800s, another dramatic example, if true, of the subtle but profound effects of disrupting natural forces.

Tolerance, the third defense category, is a kind of turn-the-other-cheek response, suggesting a godly and forgiving nature, one rarely found in landlords or tenants. Here the landlord passively suffers blows and insults in hopes of reforming or coexisting with an errant tenant oppressor.

Tolerant plants do not try to repel, disable, or destroy their assailants but to regenerate damaged tissue fast enough to produce a crop. Dr. Frederick R. Lawson, entomologist, points out that some plants can lose up to almost a third of their leaves without much loss of yield, a kind of testimonial to the virtue of passive resistance in an angry, vengeful world.

Timing is said to be everything in repairing damage, with injury less weakening to plants early and late in the season than in midsummer, as observed earlier. One study showed that potatoes can recover from 67 percent damage early or late in the season with only slight reduction in yield. In midsummer, as little as 30 percent leaf damage can cut production. This is not unique or even unusual among crops; mature bean plants can produce when completely stripped of their foliage.

The type of injury is as important as the timing. A single bite by a virus bearer can do in a plant, but most vegetables can withstand extensive damage from ordinary chewing insects. The magic figure beyond which damage cuts yields generally is held to be about 30 percent. Why 30 percent? Nature apparently settled on that as a threshold for reasons of her own.

The story becomes progressively complex. As new resistant plant varieties are developed, insects overcome each new defense and the vulnerable plants must keep coming up with something new. Three-quarters of all crops planted today are said to be resistant to some insects or disease. More than 100 varieties are resistant to at least 25 insects. Over 150 have protection against an array of plant diseases.

Because plants and insects alike produce so many generations in rapid succession, change and adaptation move along swiftly. In the ongoing struggle different plant strategies are developed for different insect attackers. But what works against one enemy may not work against another and plants and insects often fail to act or interact the same way in different locations, further confusing things. As plants evolve new ways to resist or repel insect assault, the bugs come up with tricks of their own to avoid tripping alarms that activate various defenses.

Plants, unwittingly, bring on many of their own problems. Insects are known to be attracted to them by sight, scent, and taste, and now it is suspected that there may be still another, until recently unknown, attractant: sound. Scientists have discovered that when plants are deprived of water they give off a high-frequency signal as their cells break down. Studies are now underway to find out whether this is an auditory signal, a kind of dinner bell, summoning pests to move in for the final feast.

As plants gradually revealed their innermost secrets, growers tried to assist them by matching them with other plants of similar needs or able to help one another in some way. This ancient method, now known as companion planting, is popular among organic gardeners. It depends primarily on pairing plants to promote growth, protect their neighbors, and increase productivity either directly or indirectly.

Companion planting has many facets, some understood, others rooted in theory or what seems to be wishful thinking. A primary tenet is the use of diversified crops rather than a monoculture which sends off an intensified signal inviting concentrated insect attack; others are growing repellent plants, trap or decoy plants to lure pests away from a more valuable crop, and production-enhancing combinations.

A tall sun-loving plant is well matched with a shorter one that likes some shade. Plants whose roots are at different levels or have dissimilar soil requirements may be grown closer together than competing plants. Selective interplanting, along with conferring protection, can provide an interchange or giving of nutrients.

The Indians practiced companion planting intuitively when they grew corn and pumpkins in conjunction with beans, known to the Iroquois as the "three sisters." While supplying the Indians with valuable protein (corn and beans), the "three sisters" took care of one another's needs. The corn and pumpkins, both heavy feeders, utilized nitrogen provided by the beans. Beans climbed on the corn. The pumpkins, with their sharp protective bristles, or spines, kept away harmful insects; together they formed an ideal community of mutual assistance.

Almost every gardener today, organic or otherwise, practices some form of companion planting. Most of us probably grow radishes with carrots to mark the row until the tiny carrot seeds sprout, and to seduce root maggots away from tender young carrot roots. Crop diversification provides the grower with a varied diet, while assuring dispersal of pests and a complex of predators to prey on them. It is only sensible to plant nitrogen-hungry crops where legumes grew.

The dedicated companion planter believes certain herbs attract beneficial insects while others repel pests. Dill, mint, basil, pennyroyal, and sage are variously held to promote helpful insects; tansy is considered a repellent. Certain flowers are touted as discouraging bugs, among them marigolds, asters, nasturtiums, and even innocent petunias.

I have tried most of these with only limited or indifferent success. The number of variables makes it difficult to determine the effectiveness. Some seem to work at times, others rarely or never. Protective onions and leeks have been chewed to the ground, nasturtiums devoured with gusto, and tansy, which spreads like a weed, attracted flies. Some repellents have been devoured before the crop they were supposed to protect.

I do not mean to disparage companion planting. It offers many advantages and often makes sense. I especially admire the theory. The problem is that the various elements, particularly bugs and plants, so often refuse to follow the rules laid down for them, a not uncommon failing in many theories, especially those that pit dogma against experience.

The delicate balance never seems to last long in the garden, or at least it keeps changing character. New insect- and disease-resistant plants are periodically introduced but immunity wears out after a few years, often about five, and yet another new resistant variety must be developed to keep the delicate balance in line.

Relationships are further destabilized by the gardener's own intervention. Each new application of fertilizer, pesticides, minerals, or change of soil composition and structure alters the equilibrium. Imported biological controls—ladybird beetles, parasitic wasps, praying mantises, and other purchased predators—create new conditions and alignments.

Revolutionary techniques and technologies now on the drawing board will have further unsettling effects and unknown consequences. Gene manipulation in plants is sure to have a profound impact. Science is studying ways of using bugs to attack their own in odd new ways.

Killer nematodes are already available, dried out, refrigerated, shipped, reconstituted by adding water, and sprayed on plants. Presto! Instant nematodes. Those regenerated microscopic worms, puffed up and factory aggressive, are said to be lethal to a variety of pests while harmless to humans, pets, plants, and birds. We do not know what long-term effect they may have on soil or plant biotas. DDT was once hailed as our savior. Deadly chlordane, now banned from use in food, was recommended for crops and available for the taking. Too often technology is a mechanized or biological noose we slip around our necks, and once in place is not easily removed.

While high-tech biological warfare unfolds in factories and advertising agencies, the traditional plant-insect strife continues unabated year after year, in front of me, mostly unseen. The wounds of battle appear on plants but I rarely observe the actual assault or hear the call to arms.

Each day we square off anew. The assailants throw themselves at one another, wave after wave, perishing, falling back, regrouping to try again, experimenting with new tactics and strategies, a kind of hoax they live and die with, unaware that they are locked into a higher strategy we celebrate as the delicate balance of nature.

I can almost believe that plants discuss their common problem of bug harassment, comparing techniques and suggesting new defenses. *The Secret Life of Plants* reported that plants emote, feel, and respond to kind words from their keepers; and if so, why not carry on conversations or counsels among themselves for their mutual benefit?

But a recent panel of scientists at a session of the American Association for the Advancement of Science, the nation's foremost scientific body, rejected the notion that a household philodendron can be happy or sad, and five of the six panelists held that plants have no emotional reaction to events around them. The one dissenting expert, Cleve Backster, a lie-detector expert whose experiments led to *The Secret Life*, insisted he had registered by polygraph distress among boiling brine shrimp.

Mr. Backster not only refused to back down, but said a more recent study revealed that yogurt has emotions too, and some yogurt was pleased or jealous when other yogurt was fed milk. I have no opinion on whether boiling brine shrimp display emotional distress or yogurt exhibits feelings, but I like to think the plants are able to discuss common problems and how to keep the bugs at bay. I also like to think I may be supported in this by Yale biology students who, in an informal poll reported by the *New York Times*, indicated that they believe plants do indeed have a secret life.

I confess to being puzzled by the business of built-in plant protection. What good to have complete security against some pests and none against others at hand? What good to build up immunity to one disease if another silent subversive killer lurks in the wings waiting to strike?

I ponder these questions as I consider the day's body count: Half the cabbage seedlings have gone under, several new onions are missing, the kale, replanted three times, has suffered new losses; even rhubarb leaves are riddled—and just after I declared them virtually pestproof. This mortality is high even for an organic garden. I am further dismayed by the day's wind damage; what the bugs do not eat, the unrelenting wind batters or weakens for tomorrow's feast; such is gardening in this ocean outpost.

Just who are these superbugs of such skill and shameless guile demolishing my efforts? Have the plants given up all thought of self-defense and now look to me for the protection I fail to give them? Is St. Jude the final recourse for both of us?

The onions are especially baffling. The book lists only one insect that eats young onions—the ubiquitous but wily garden springtail (which also has a varied diet of beans, beets, chard, and squash). I admit to never having seen a springtail in action but read that they are tiny wingless insects with dark yellow spots and a "taillike appendage to hurtle themselves into the air," not too easily missed, if visible, or forgotten if seen, I would think.

Oddly enough, the defense for these performers is said to be spraying the onion foliage with garlic and water. Only one creature seems to eat garlic: my fellow man (without me). It is listed as both insecticide and repellent. But if I use garlic to drive the springtails, or whatever, away from the onions, why will they not simply eat other crops in their varied diet? Have I resolved one problem only to create another? That is the fate of many environmental "solutions."

I have a similar dilemma with the kale. I find none of the several insects listed as its enemies, no web among the foliage with celery-leaf tiers, whatever they are, frolicking within. There is not just chewing damage. Entire plants are missing. Vanished overnight! And what mysterious assassin is attacking the rhubarb? I uncover no snout-nosed beetle, the intrepid rhubarb curculio, which I would not recognize. Does this anonymous assailant not know the leaves are poisonous? Has it developed immunity, or even a taste for toxic delicacies?

This suggests a new and unexplored area of plant-insect research: Bugs may not only develop immunity to plant defenses but acquire new tastes as well. I have long noted that if pests cannot find their food of choice, most will, sensibly, try something else and possibly develop a liking for it. Squash bugs go after cucumbers when squash is not available. Last year I found an early Colorado potato beetle, who had arrived before the potatoes sprouted, dining on the spinach. Does spinach now have to find a defense against the Colorados? Is there no end to it?

If of a more visionary turn of mind, I might consider that in this unusual seashore garden ecosystem, bugs come from all over the country for the "season," like the tourists, to enjoy the cooling ocean breezes and excellent dining, bringing with them exotic tastes and behavior learned elsewhere, and my unworldly plants have neither the means nor experience to cope with them. Some days I feel less like a gardener than a restauranteur preparing quality cuisine al fresco for unbidden guests, telling myself that anything I get is a bonus and gardening its own reward.

I read in garden publications testimonials from others who grow without the use of chemicals or pesticides and they invariably conclude triumphantly: ". . . and not a bug in sight, not a blemished plant in the whole garden!" My friend Rit looks at me with perplexity when I recount my bug woes. He has never seen a potato beetle! What do they like? Nothing eats his plants! Why not?—and him only a few miles away, undermining any comforting theory I have of washashore invading vacationing bugs. Does he suspect me of having organic paranoia?

All of this depresses me. I am filled with envy. It makes me feel that I am not only doing a lousy job of gardening but letting the organic team down as well, like the suffering and vanquished plants in my care, not keeping up my end of things.

"Don't be ridiculous," I said. "They would not dare." "Oh, yes, they would," chorused half an acre of Brussels sprouts . . .
—Prince Charles

This is the season of the cabbage butterfly. Dozens, possibly hundreds, flutter daintily in the early July garden, awaiting the chance to lay their tiny white eggs at the base of an unwary cabbage plant. It is said that every white cabbage butterfly killed prevents a hundred cabbage worms. The green caterpillars that attack the plants are not really a serious problem, certainly nothing to get emotional or paranoid about like, say, potato beetles or squash bugs.

Cabbage worms show little intelligence or initiative in avoiding detection and destruction; like the eggs, they can be removed by hand, or controlled by dusting plants with a mixture of wood ashes, flour, and fine table salt, or sprayed with the insecticide BT, which has a solid track record going back to 1901.

Cabbage maggots are more troublesome. They are the larvae of a small black fly that lays its eggs in the soil near the stem, and the emerging maggots burrow into the earth to humble the plant's roots. They are more clever and insidious than the visible, forthright caterpillars working overhead.

More bold and daring gardeners control cabbage maggots with diazinon, a powerful insecticide. The more timid and resourceful use companion planting, such as circling cabbage with garlic or onions, or put small squares of tarpaper snugly around plant stems to foil the egg-laying fly. They also may dust the surrounding area with wood ashes, or cover the entire plant with cheesecloth or a floating row cover, although the latter verges on overprotectiveness and may undermine the developing plant's character.

Several enemies of cabbage are specialists, taking their victim's name as part of theirs, a kind of proprietary arrogance, and prefer cabbage as their main dish. Among them are the striped cabbage worm and that whimsical traveler, the cabbage looper, with its odd, looping, end-to-end gait. BT is effective against most caterpillars or worms. I have not found them much of a problem.

Cole crops are, generally, grown wherever the climate is cool and moist. Cabbage, particularly, is found all over the world in many colors and shapes; more than five hundred varieties are grown in the United States alone. I have personally had good luck with cabbage and hold it in high esteem. It is an asset to any garden whether grown for food or merely as decoration. I find it demeaning to cabbage to refer to people considered low in intelligence as "cabbageheads," just as the term "couch potatoes," for those who spend too much time watching television, does little to enhance the image of potatoes or dedicated viewers.

While intellect is not relevant to the role of cabbage in the garden, I suspect that cabbages are collectively more intelligent than many of their more flamboyant companions and, possibly, a cut above those who defame them. I knew one gardener who claimed he had many fascinating conversations with cabbages. He said they act sensibly, listen attentively, never interrupt, keep their opinions to themselves, and keep a civil tongue in their cabbage heads. They make excellent garden companions in every way, he added, and confessed that he sometimes feels troubled when eating them.

Talking to vegetables may not be as odd or unusual as it seems. Many people report that vegetables respond favorably when spoken to soothingly, part of their secret life. Prince Charles is very big on talking to plants and hearing their side of things, as befits the heir to the British throne.

An extensive conversation he had with garden vegetables was reported in the *New York Times*, although I thought him a bit off base in describing a row of leeks as "cocky little things." He did explain that they were prize leeks, which may account for it; common leeks are known for their modesty and decorum. I regret that Prince Charles did not report on his dialogues with cabbages, although he did speak favorably of their kin, brussels sprouts.

While I have never carried on a conversation with a cabbage, or even a brussels sprout, I appreciate their excellent qualities and lineage. Wild cabbage is said to have originated in the Near East and was brought to Europe, where it was tamed some four thousand years ago. It is hailed as one of the first vegetables to be domesticated.

Cabbage and kale were brought to America in 1540 by the French explorer Jacques Cartier, according to *Green Immigrants*, by Clare Shaver Haughton, and planted along the St. Lawrence to provide food for his men through the winter, a patrician background that cabbage carries with becoming modesty.

Close relatives of cabbage, along with brussels sprouts, are broccoli and cauliflower, and more distant kin include kohl-rabi, rape, mustard, Chinese cabbage, collards, and rutabagas, all known for their strong family orientation. Cauliflower, brussels sprouts, and kale bear the distinguished name *Brassica oleracea acephala*, which means cabbage without a head. Kale and collards, recruited from Asia Minor, were around for centuries before head cabbage was developed in the Middle Ages, according to my sources. The record does not reveal when cabbage started to talk.

The various cole crops are rich in vitamins and minerals and provide valuable fiber, now considered so essential to good health. Cabbage juice was once considered an effective treatment for ulcers, although I never knew anyone who tried it and have not heard the remedy mentioned for years. More conventionally, cabbage is eaten raw, as coleslaw, or in soup, cooked, stuffed, or preserved as sauerkraut; it has many expressions and champions.

Few garden plants are more striking than cabbage with its huge, shiny leaves and noble head, a splendid sight glistening with morning dew. Cabbage is relatively easy to grow, making few demands beyond requiring plenty of moisture and a rich soil providing reasonable amounts of nitrogen and potash. Cabbage often fares well in seasons when less well-adjusted plants falter or fail altogether. I have had rows of vibrant cabbage in years when the rest of the garden was poor and even the hardy broccoli mysteriously went to seed without forming heads.

Cabbage is celebrated for having fewer diseases than many vegetables and shows a stiff upper lip in adversity, often recovering from near-fatal maladies and a poor start that cuts down plants of lesser spirit.

Biologists now theorize that plants are territorial, much like animals, including people, taking care of their own turf, and many, possibly all, produce chemicals that either aid or repel other plants. I can believe this about cabbage; it seems to get along with its neighbors but tolerates no familiarity or aggressive togetherness. Some consider cabbage haughty and overbearing, even elitist. I like to think it is quiet pride in its distinguished background and accomplishments.

Along with its other virtues, cabbage will last well into the winter if refrigerated or otherwise kept cool. We have had it keep until spring in the basement root cellar, tightly wrapped in plastic. Some gardeners preserve cabbage by pulling the entire plant and hanging it intact from a joist in a cool garage, or burying the root in a bucket of damp sand. I have never tried these methods, lacking the prescribed cool garage, and burying a plant in a bucket of damp sand is more trouble than I care to go to. I also dislike the idea of an artificial support system to sustain life, and am reluctant to risk giving cabbage an inflated idea of its importance.

I am personally not overly fond of the taste of cabbage. Almost invariably we grow more than we can use and end up throwing it away. But every year I grow it again for its many admirable qualities of personality, character, background, decorative charm, leadership, and the possibility of engaging it in conversation.

Who loves a garden still his Eden keeps,
Perennial pleasures plants, and wholesome harvest
reaps.
—Amos Bronson Alcott

*S*ummer is moving along. The sun beats down relentlessly and all of the plants are dutifully setting fruit: tomatoes, eggplants, pumpkins, zucchinis, butternut squash, cucumbers, and peppers. I give each a shot of manure tea from a fifty-five-gallon steel drum from which the top was removed with a steel chisel. The manure is in a burlap bag, brewing in the barrel of water. A board on top of the barrel reduces evaporation and keeps the bees from drowning. A shot of the rich manure tea and the plants seem to shudder and take off as the fermented juice hits their roots.

Pole beans seem especially responsive. They are producing heroically. Maybe they are nervous, seeing how the nearby bush beans that gave out early went to the compost heap. The climbing vines have reached the top of their eight-foot poles and the thick foliage has turned the tripods into green wigwams.

No longer must I stand on a milk carton to pick beans at the top of the tripod. Now they come down to me, dangling in clusters, and picking them reminds me of milking a cow. The beans remain surprisingly tender even when quite large and have more flavor and body than snap beans; they also have more staying power. A single planting of pole beans lasts the season, compared to replanting snap or bush beans every couple of weeks.

Pole beans have an oddment that I have never read about but have come to expect: In late August they slow down, as if bushed, you might say, or taking a breather, and then come on strong again in September, continuing to produce until the weather turns chilly. This may be due to some kind of unusual local condition or an eccentricity of the beans themselves. I usually stop picking one of the wigwams just before this final outburst and let the pods go to seed for the following year. Sometimes I do not get around to picking the seed beans and vines and pods look shriveled and forlorn on the naked poles as winter plays its hand.

We have planted Kentucky Wonder pole beans for many years. Carol, a former newspaper colleague, got me started with that variety, lamenting that she had not eaten them since she left home in the Midwest. "There's nothing like Kentucky Wonders," she said, sighing. Could I have planted anything else? The seed catalogues recommend new varieties but out of loyalty to Carol and past performance of the beans we stay with Kentucky Wonders. Carol, now a confirmed city person, never writes without asking how the Kentucky Wonders are doing, even out of season.

The beans are now at their peak, delicious, cooked with lots of boiling water, about five minutes, so they stay crisp and green. Served with a touch of butter and seasoning, they are one of summer's culinary delights. Pole beans are also delicious served cold, with dressing, as bean salad. Because of their body, they make superb dilly beans.

A favorite of Peggy's is a salad plate made by French-slicing the beans and cooking them by the blanch method, just until tender. Serve on a platter, elegantly arranged in a bed of fresh garden lettuce, with new potatoes boiled in their jackets and sliced, along with sliced onions, black olives (tuna, if desired), and a drizzle of vinaigrette dressing. Potatoes and beans can be served hot or cold.

I come in with the day's harvest of pole beans and Peggy looks at the overflowing basket with dismay. "More beans!" she exclaims and her eyes seem to glaze over. "Where will we put them? The refrigerator is already full." She says we are like the Sorcerer's Apprentice. We turned on this onslaught of beans and now cannot turn it off. "Master! Master! . . ."

I am no longer intimidated from picking the pole beans when the plants are wet for fear of spreading disease—a threat the experts warn against. Nothing could stop them. Not even disease. I might welcome a little blight to slow production. I have already supplied all of our friends but still the relentless beans pour in.

They remind me of a green squash we grew in New Jersey. A friend brought the seeds from England. Never was there such an outpouring of squash. We brought in armloads every day. Finally we could not look green squash in the stem. We could not give it away fast enough. The plant went berserk. It ran clear around the garden and started a second circuit as if gone crazy with the life force. In desperation I ripped it out of the ground. That rich black New Jersey soil was unbelievable. I used to bring in tomatoes until every kitchen surface was covered. There was almost no place to eat dinner. And more tomatoes to come! The life force can overdo it. You cannot let it get the upper hand.

Now it is pole beans. We sit at the kitchen table after dinner, canning dilly beans. The brine cooks on the stove. The house has the acrid smell of boiling vinegar and spices. When the beans are packed in widemouth jars, the uneven ends trimmed off, Peggy adds the hot mixture and I screw on the lids for final processing. But more beans await us in the refrigerator. The vines on the poles outside palpitate with the expectation of tomorrow's production.

Peggy observes that if ever we were up against it, we could practically get along with what we grow and put up. We would need relatively few staples, she says, primarily powdered milk, a few bags of soybeans, brown rice, and wheat; if necessary we could grow our own soybeans . . .

This is idle talk. We both know it but go over it occasionally in fanciful speculation. In more practical moments we recognize that it would be almost impossible to live off a kitchen garden in these times. But the garden could, and does, go far toward sustaining us.

Garden economics interest me. Writers often try to place a dollar value on the savings from growing your own vegetables. I have seen figures ranging up to several hundred dollars annually. I do not know how such sums are arrived at but suspect they may be overly optimistic.

A garden is economic simplicity itself. Production and consumption must be in some kind of balance. There can be no creative financing. This is real economics. No credits or deficits. No "buy now pay later" with its attendant bondage. Strictly cash and carry! You cannot consume more than you produce. For extra produce there is always a market. If one does not sell or runs out of friends to give the surplus to, there is the ever-hungry compost heap.

A garden is marvelously versatile. It offers options and alternatives. If one crop fails, another can take its place, a kind of fail-safe. Our menu on any given day, especially in summer, is dictated largely by what is available in the garden. For the discerning cook, there is the joy and beauty of produce at its peak of freshness and flavor, uncontaminated by chemicals. You do not say, "What shall we have for dinner?" More likely it is, "There's lots of broccoli and zucchini (or whatever) coming in. How can it be prepared in an interesting way?"

You eat and think differently when you have a garden. You have different expectations. One way and another, a garden is in your thoughts every day, what you are going to do in it or take from it. There is no ignoring it. A garden demands its share of time and attention; it helps shape the economy of our lives.

A garden imposes its own discipline and guidelines but at the same time is flexible and tolerant. If you cannot grow one crop, you can grow another. A gardener may fumble and falter but, unlike adversity and inadequacy in most other endeavors, he need not go hungry. Something is always out there. At least enough to make a meal. That, as they say, must be the bottom line.

If one gardens only for economy, I offer the advice of Tom. We knew him back in New Jersey when we lived in a garden apartment early in our marriage. Tom came around every evening in a van selling vegetables and fruits. He was a neighborhood fixture and favorite, part of a now-vanished way of suburban life that was then a reasonable compromise between urban and country living. That was before suburbia became a social stigma or label; it was a pleasant and affordable way of life.

Tom brought not only fresh produce but local gossip as well, dispensed with his own homilies and philosophy. He advised mothers how to feed and raise their young, he gave fathers social and economic advice. He kept the kids in line with candy bribes or an admonishing stern finger. He was a sort of Italian Jewish mother. I recall an afternoon when Tom showed up on his daily rounds while I was washing the car. He looked at me disapprovingly and said, "Pay somebody else to do it and earn money at what you do and you will come out ahead."

Economically, it was sound advice. I would probably have done better in monetary terms to have paid for the service and spent the time writing an article for magazines I was then selling regularly to. The same advice, I suspect, also applies to a garden. But there is a flaw in the argument: I enjoyed washing the car, just as I now enjoy working in the garden. What was my pleasure and sense of being somewhat self-sufficient worth? How is a value figure placed on pleasure? Do intangibles have a tangible price? Is pleasure cost-efficient? Does it have a bottom line? Do I better serve the economy of life by writing an article, washing a car, or planting a seed or tree?

If I wanted to place a monetary figure on garden-grown produce, I would not know how to go about it. What is the true price of a single home-grown cucumber, pepper, radish, or bean? There is the cost of seeds, electricity to grow seedlings in the house, running the pump for water from the well, and the wire fence and posts to keep out marauders.

I would have to factor in the cost of building up the soil, buying tools and their depreciation, rototilling, buying and replacing hoses and watering equipment, plastic and row covers for cold frames and cloches, the prorated cost of running and maintaining my old Jeep pickup, plus its insurance, to bring in manure and mulch, the cost of baskets, various soil amendments, and other paraphernalia.

If strict accounting methods were applied, would not there have to be a charge for use of the land? Certainly that is not just thrown in with produce bought from the supermarket. And what of my labor? How to put a price on that? Would it be my hourly wage if I worked at other employment—and what other employment? And what about overtime and weekends, taxes, and wear and tear on my clothes?

Since I am the sole keeper of the garden and a nonrenewable resource, like an oil well or gravel pit, am I not entitled to amortize my life-sustaining juices, diminishing energies, and labor? Is there compensating credit for goodwill from produce I give away? What role, if any, do capital gains play here?

If a gardener kept a proper profit-and-loss statement and put a price on his time, I doubt if a garden would be economically justified in strict monetary terms. Fortunately for me, time means nothing. In that respect I am fabulously wealthy. I can waste time as recklessly as any millionaire throwing away his money.

Time does not exist for me, despite the toll it takes on my diminishing energies and well-being. I refuse to recognize time as an economic force. I work at a pace and schedule dictated by body and spirit, not clock or computer, a benevolence that transcends marketplace economics. I have paid my dues to clock, calendar, and commerce. Instead of increasing my income I reduce my needs. I want nothing I do not have. I am satisfied.

The real economics of life lie beyond the paper transactions of speculators and middlemen. The only real depression a garden knows is a soil that will not produce food. That is the true meaning of bankruptcy. Too often the objects of commerce become the commerce of our lives. A garden is real wealth.

It would be presumptuous and foolish to recommend gardens for all. But there are said to be some 35 million—50 million by one count—of us who garden in the United States, so it figures in many lives, a sizable proportion of the population. There are probably as many reasons for gardening as there are gardeners. Even writing about gardens and gardening is an industry in itself, along with supplying the huge market that gardening represents. It is a powerful economic force in our national life, a spiritual force in our personal lives.

Everywhere water is a thing of beauty gleaming in the dewdrop, singing in the summer rain . . .
—John Ballantine Gough

The cucumbers are wilting in the mid-afternoon heat of this scorching July day. I soak them with the hose, trying to cheer them, but they wilt even more. There is a sound scientific reason for this but at the moment I attribute it to the natural perversity of cucumbers. The cucumber personality is erratic, wants everything its own way, and is easily distracted.

Other gardeners I know insist that cucumbers are easy to get on with and simple to grow. Steve, a neighbor, raises profuse numbers in soil piled in old tires, explaining that the sunbaked rubber warms the earth and promotes growth. He chuckles and adds that cucumbers could grow through asphalt. I accept his theory but do not care for tires in the garden. I also think we have overdone it coddling cucumbers.

I turn the hose on the tomatoes. They release a tantalizing aroma, as if expressing gratitude for this impromptu drink. Tomatoes take their responsibility as prima donnas and role models in the garden graciously. I spray other plants and they also perk up and seem pleased by such unexpected refreshment on a hot summer day. Indeed it should occur to the lot of them that they would shrivel and die if left to nature. They are wholly dependent on the moisture I provide; I stand between them and disaster.

We have not had a decent rain for weeks. The garden looks dispirited. Even the water I provide does not help much. This sandy soil refuses to hold moisture, and after a few days without rain or a deep hose soaking the plants begin to look forlorn, growth is slowed, and production declines. Depriving plants of water at any stage of growth has repercussions. Nature has a long memory; she may forgive but does not forget.

A steady water supply makes possible more intensive plantings, hastens maturity, and increases yields and quality. It is especially important not to let new seed beds dry out, and young plants with shallow roots, largely dependent on surface moisture, need to be watered frequently.

Every garden book properly emphasizes the need for water in growing plants and all living things. Most writers manage to work in the phrase that "plants drink their food." Writers are enamored by the phrase. I rather like it myself. They point out that water makes it possible for soil microbes to break down organic matter and minerals so they are available to plants.

Soil molecules are surrounded by water, and air bubbles form in the water among the particles. Loam soil, ideally, is composed of 40 percent clay, 40 percent humus, and the rest sand. About half the space between soil components is given to air and water. Tiny hair roots probe among the particles, taking carbon from the air bubbles and minerals in solution. These nutrients are available only in solution. "Plants drink their food." Nutrients are sucked up by the tiny root hairs in the form of sap and transported up the stem to the leaves.

A plant is often likened to a pump. The nutrient-rich water taken up by the roots is released through the leaves, a process originally called "perspiration" by its clergyman discoverer, but now bearing the more dignified name "transpiration." Plants are estimated to absorb from the soil up to a thousand times as much water as their cells require.

Trees are even bigger pumps. A full-grown willow can transpire up to five thousand gallons of water into the air in a single summer day. A tree pump is so powerful that it is said to exert a force of up to three thousand pounds per square inch, enough, theoretically, to lift a column of water more than a mile high, if trees grew that tall.

Trees are often compared to vast fountains spewing moisture into the air. The loss of trees on a large scale can change weather patterns and affect temperatures. The destruction of tropical rain forests in Latin America and the United States is believed to be changing climate and weather throughout the world.

Water is vital to almost every function of plant life. The protoplasm in leaf cells is 80 percent water. Photosynthesis depends on water. The life-giving glucose formed by photosynthesis is delivered in water. Soil nutrients can come only in water. If the pump supplying most of this water stops, the plant suffers and dies. Plant roots are constantly seeking nutrient-rich water.

Most vegetables are 90 percent water, and in ancient times cucumbers were used to assuage thirst on long desert journeys, the original thermos and possibly accounting for the haughtiness of cucumbers.

To produce one pound of tissue, a plant must take in two hundred to a thousand pounds of water, usually averaging in the upper range. Only about 1 percent of the water absorbed is retained as moisture or food. A single tomato plant gives off eleven or more quarts per day. The water required to grow one acre of corn in a normal season, if allowed to remain on the ground instead of being released into the air, would form a lake five feet deep. I read it, so it must be true, but I am not sure I believe it.

Water evaporation from plants is part of the great cycle of life. It lowers surrounding temperatures and refreshes the atmosphere. Describing a garden as a "cool oasis" is scientifically sound. The water trapped in the ground is continually released and the fixed amount of water covering three-quarters of the globe is recirculated by mighty weather systems that regulate rainfall over the earth's surface.

Nature has another and more compelling reason for making plants expel water into the atmosphere so lavishly. It is not just for our comfort and pleasure or merely to redistribute the earth's water. Rather, it is related to the endless search by plant roots for those nutrients vital to the cells' growth and health.

It has long been recognized that the primary chemicals plants require are oxygen, carbon, hydrogen, and nitrogen, the stuff of life itself. The first three are products of photosynthesis. Nitrogen is usually in good supply in the soil. But in addition plants need about a dozen hard-to-get mineral salts, among them sulfur, calcium, iron, potassium, phosphorus, and magnesium. These come from dissolved rock and bits of soil; many are extremely scarce although essential. Huge amounts of water must be sucked up by the roots for the plant to extract the necessary nutrients. The excess is released in transpiration.

Less than 2 percent of a plant's tissue is made up of minerals absorbed through the roots but that tiny amount is vital. The rest is taken from the air, primarily carbon dioxide breathed in through invisible pores in the leaves and water pulled in by the roots for use in photosynthesis.

The critical role of roots in seeking out mineral salts in groundwater was demonstrated in a well-known experiment cited in *Leaves*, by James Poling. A common winter rye plant was grown in a container holding two cubic feet of soil for four months. That one plant grew 13,800,000 roots that would have stretched 387 miles if laid end to end.

The leaves provided the roots with enough food to grow an average of 3 miles per day, amounting to 66 feet an hour or over 13 inches every minute. The main roots, in addition, we are told, grew 6,000 miles of water-absorbant root hairs, an

average of 50 miles of hair per day, another of nature's staggering extravagances.

The root of a plant or tree is one of life's great inventions.
Roots take many shapes and forms but all have one basic function: to anchor or support the vegetation above. The root system is commensurate with the growth on top and binds the
soil together, helps prevent erosion, aerates soil, and provides
a channel for water to follow.

Efficient nature decided that the supporting root should also
supply the plant with liquid minerals extracted from the earth.
The root, a "naked organ" incapable of growing leaves, has
four parts. At the apex is the "rootcap," a blunt driving force
that thrusts forcefully among soil and rock particles in search
of food. Behind it is the so-called zone of elongation, the only
part of the root that grows, and next are the delicate root hairs
which suck up nutrients, dying off quickly and being replaced
by new growth as the segment ahead forms new cells to expand.

The final section, the oldest part of the root, is made up of
woody growth, now acting as little more than a conduit or
pipeline transporting nutrients to the plant stem for delivery
aboveground, just as the root is fed sugar formed by photosynthesis in the leaves, everything working together, another of
nature's great harmonies.

Every gardener soon learns that crops vary in the amount of
water they require to reach maturity. This ranges from about
six to thirty inches. A lettuce plant needs about nine inches,
celery thirty inches; to produce a single stalk of corn demands
one pound of water.

For those who like statistics, and it is surprising how many
do, a heavy rain of one and a half inches is equal to only about
one gallon of water per square foot. Most vegetables need one
to two inches per week for a "thorough soaking." About two-
thirds of a gallon is necessary for one inch of water per square
foot of soil. A sprinkler would have to spew water steadily for
eight hours to wet dry earth to a depth of one foot.

A disconcerting fact to new gardeners is the amount of water it takes to penetrate soil to a depth of six or nine inches, where most plants have their roots. We have all been warned often enough that a light sprinkling is meaningless, doing more harm than good by causing shallow root development and weak plants.

There are various tests for soil dampness. The simplest is, after watering, to scuff the earth with your shoe, hardly high tech but effective enough. Usually the ground will turn up powder-dry under the surface. A more sophisticated method is to pull a weed. Rarely is one found with wet feet, even after prolonged watering. Weeds get along nicely without much water but vegetables cannot tolerate prolonged drought. Most vegetables are little more than domesticated and pampered weed offspring, their wild hardiness bred out of them, as dependent on us as we are on them.

Water does not reveal all of its secrets readily. For a long time I was puzzled why some plants, like the cucumber mentioned earlier, wilted when given a shot of cooling water on a hot summer afternoon. It is common enough knowledge that plants may give off more water from their leaves than they can absorb from the soil and the result is wilting. Everyone is also familiar with the sight of a plant drawing into itself in the afternoon heat, curling its leaves to expose less surface to the sun to cut moisture loss. But why should water actually cause more wilting?

I tardily learned the answer from T. Bedford Franklin, author of *Climates in Miniature*. He explains that on a hot day soil temperatures may be 80 or 90 degrees, with water temperature only 55 or 60. A plant's absorption of water slows down as soil temperature falls. Cold water applied to hot soil makes it impossible for the roots to supply the plant with as much water as before. The result is more wilting. I maligned the haughty, temperamental cucumber.

The prudent gardener leaves water in a barrel or pails to be warmed by the sun before dousing plants on a hot day, or waters after the sun has lost its intensity. The truly fortunate among us do not have to think about this but get a steady supply of rain. Rain is preferable to groundwater, as it contains nitrogen from the air, another of nature's little economies.

Nothing better illustrates the principle of too much or too little than a garden. There is too much or too little sun, too much or too little produce, too much or too little rain. Nothing in moderation. An excess or lack of water is a problem for most of us, either occasionally or chronically. Both extremes stress plants, inviting insect attack and disease.

Rarely is soil moisture in balance. Too much air from lack of moisture causes nitrogen to be released beyond the plants' capacity to utilize it and much is lost. Too much water drives out vital air spaces, depriving plants of oxygen and minerals. Saturated soil contains no oxygen, slowing the release of nitrogen and hindering growth.

Most plants fare better with too little water than too much. Excess moisture can "drown" roots, causing rot or mold and washing away nutrients. This is a difficulty primarily of clay or heavy soils with poor drainage. Sandy soils have the opposite problem, refusing to hold moisture and requiring frequent waterings that leach out nutrients, causing plant starvation or disease due to malnutrition.

The ideal is a "thorough soaking" once a week, as the book calls for, rather than repeated light waterings. But who has ideal conditions? With my porous sandy soil I am forced to take my chances with frequent waterings and trying to replace the lost nutrients.

Applying enough moisture is important. Keeping it from evaporating from the soil is equally important. Here the gardener tries, again, to disrupt a natural process for his own advantage, and in the process confronts a perversity of water. We expect water to obey gravity and sink into the soil, or seek its own level as it is supposed to, whatever that may be, but instead it tends not to migrate down but to rise to the top where the sun burns it off through evaporation. Science offers a neat explanation of how this happens:

As sun and heat evaporate the surface water, moisture in the earth rises through small cylinder-like passages in the soil. Water is lifted by capillary action, much as in a test tube, and through water molecules clinging together by cohesion. As water is lost at the top it is replaced by water rising from below, an upward migration that continues until the soil is completely dry and the gardener out of sorts.

One authority says this drying action can be prevented by breaking up the surface soil through cultivation, increasing the size of the soil passages so capillary action cannot take place. This is primarily a scientific explanation of what was once called "dust mulching." Gardeners and dirt farmers, with little knowledge of scientific principles, would break up soil particles to provide a larger surface area exposed to sun and heat, the ensuing dust cover conserving the moisture below.

But most gardeners today keep soil from drying out by using mulch, the method devised by nature herself.

How much water should be applied for ideal soil conditions? The answer, of course, depends on the type of soil. Experts recommend one or two inches per week but that assumes the soil has enough clay or humus to hold moisture for an extended period. All expert advice must make assumptions.

Water retention is, as we know, dependent on soil porosity. Sand is so granular that water pours through it. Clay particles are microscopic and tend to compact so tightly that they are almost impervious to water.

There are many ways to water a garden, from an old-fashioned watering can to modern drip irrigation automatically controlled. The latter system was developed in parched Israel, along with the use of rocks as mulch to conserve precious moisture in desert farming.

The method used is generally determined largely by the type of soil, climate or weather, personal inclination, and time available. I prefer to water by hand, with a hose, a luxury I can afford because I have time at my disposal. I primarily use a watering wand, a thirty-inch aluminum tube with attached dispenser that delivers a large volume of water in a gentle spray, much like a shower head, to the base of the plant without disturbing the soil.

Often I leave a shallow basin-like depression around plants so I can quickly flood it, enabling the water to sink in slowly and deeply without substantial evaporation. A similar technique I have used is to bury a large, perforated can (size #10) into the ground and fill the can with water, which seeps slowly into the earth at root depth; this works especially well with thirsty cucumbers.

I have a sprinkler but rarely use it. About half the water sprayed is lost through evaporation. Occasionally, on summer evenings, we turn on the sprinkler, "the dancing waters," more for our own pleasure than any good it does the plants.

The water arcs high over the garden, catching the late sun in dazzling rainbow colors and releasing the fragrance of grateful plants. It is aesthetically pleasing, a cheering sight when we sit on the deck with a cool drink before dinner. We are not alone in this pleasure. The garden orchestra is tuning up for the night's concert, refreshed by the water. Mosquitoes are girding for their nocturnal assault. Lily has a wary eye out for Michelob, who waits in ambush outside the garden.

I generally prefer to water by hand because it gives me another chance to see what is going on in the garden. Occasionally, after dinner, I sit in the metal chair and spray plants with the hose. This is not a good idea, according to the rules. It is said to leave plants damp for the night and subject to fungal disease, although I have never figured out why night dew and rain do not cause the same problems. I sometimes suspect that the plants do not know all the rules, or ignore them as I often do. A garden must provide pleasure as well as food, nourishment for the spirit as well as the body. If the rules get in the way of pleasure they occasionally must be dispensed with.

If the afternoon is particularly hot, I may lightly spray plants with the hose. Usually they perk up, other than the contrary cucurbits, which prefer scientific truth to a cool drink. It seems to do no particular harm. If it does set the plants back a bit, I am not distraught. I am out to win no prizes. I would rather hear Farmer Bagley say, "Your peas look pretty good," than win a blue ribbon at the county fair.

For many years gardeners were warned not to water during the heat of the day. Drops of water were said to create a lens, much like a magnifying glass, causing the concentrated rays of the sun to burn the leaves. That theory now seems to be largely discredited or abandoned. I have not heard it for a long time. Often, if you wait long enough, unsettling theories seem to be replaced by new theories of less concern.

If the plants seem particularly stressed or depressed by the intense heat of midday, I often give them an impromptu afternoon serving of manure tea. The brew is strong and aromatic from the beating sun. I can almost see the wilted cucumbers gulping the rich, warm tea, their roots "drinking their food," and hear them gratefully exclaim, "God! was I thirsty!"

But optics sharp it needs, I ween
To see what is not to be seen.
                    —John Trumbull

Mike, it turned out, was also a gardener and, like most of us, was delighted to give a tour of his garden. We had met in an adult education class and he revealed that he was a fisherman. Did he ever sell fish? Sure, drop by next Sunday.

I was impressed, startled really, by the garden's lushness. But I noticed that beetles were hard at his potatoes. I commented on the damage. Mike had an unexpected response. "Yes," he said, continuing our tour as if he and the beetles had nothing to do with one another.

"What will you do about them?" I asked.

"Nothing," he replied, leading the way out of the garden and starting to weigh out the fish.

"Why not?" I persisted. I was fascinated by his indifference. Did he spray, dust, handpick—anything?

"What are they to me?" he said, almost irritably. "I didn't bring them here."

"They're eating your plants."

"So?"

"You won't have any potatoes."

"Then I'll buy some from the market."

I had trouble hearing him because of a Beethoven symphony booming from a stereo on the nearby deck. I knew nothing of Mike's domestic arrangements but a young woman wearing a swimming suit was sunning on the deck while listening to the Ninth. The music blasted across the garden below, rolling over the vegetables in majestic waves.

"You don't spray?" I asked.

"No."

"Do you handpick?"

"No."

"What do you do?"

"Put a fish under every plant."

"Nothing else?"

"No."

"You don't mind losing your potatoes?"

"I'd rather not."

I could not think of a successful reply to this and let it drop. The symphony continued. I had heard that music can stimulate plants. Perhaps that was what Mike had in mind: The plants would be so charged, between the fish and music, that the beetles could not prevail.

I concentrated on the peppers while Mike wrapped up the cod for Peggy. The *Ode to Joy* thundered out. The peppers looked thoughtful but then seemed to fairly quiver in ecstasy. I asked Mike if the music was responsible for the garden's exuberance, but he took a more utilitarian view.

"It's the fish fertilizer," he said.

Mike, like the rest of us who do not use chemicals, could have employed several tried if not always true nontoxic defenses against the beetles. But he was having none of it. Why? I later pondered our conversation at length and came up with what could be a new approach to pest control, or non-control.

The fish and music had nothing to do with it. Mike, a former teacher who gave up the clamor and frustrations of the classroom for the solitude and perils of the sea, was blocking out, as the psychologists say. It was a clear case of denial. He did not want to believe those potato beetles were there devouring his plants, so for him they did not exist. I had intruded on his manufactured reality and that was why he was vexed.

Once the beetles' presence was acknowledged, he would be virtually compelled to do something about them. As long as he refused to see them, nothing was required of him. This suggests a kind of Freudian approach to pest control, a new twist to gardening without poisons.

It also suggests, on another level, that the way we manage

our gardens may indicate how we run our lives—the phantoms perceived that do not exist, monsters that exist but are not perceived, the fears and terrors we flee and those that find us, difficult and painful decisions to be made in trying to maintain the fragile realities we create, how we resolve the big questions of life and death, what it means to be a human being in a troubled world. But these are profound and unsettling matters that I do not feel like thinking about today. I am like Mike. Some other time, maybe.

Meanwhile, as Voltaire advised, let us tend our gardens, such as they are.

> *The awful shadow of some unseen Power*
> *Floats tho' unseen amongst us.*
> —Percy Bysshe Shelley

Beets, probably more than any garden crop, are entitled to an inferiority complex. Nutritionists often say the tops, which most people discard, have more nutritional punch than the roots which are eaten, and that pretty well exhausts their virtue. This is something of a libel. The tops do have vitamins A and C, along with some iron and calcium, but the roots have a respectable amount of vitamins B_1 and C. The only shortcoming of the roots, in my opinion, is the heavy sugar content, which is their great commercial appeal.

I like beet roots pickled, served hot with butter, or as borscht. Peggy hates beets in any form so we rarely have them, and then only to please me. Occasionally I give some to Ray, who prepares them for us as borscht (his Peggy also hates beets), but his enthusiasm seems forced and he never mentions beets unless I almost push them on him. Friendship has its limits. Beets may be its litmus test.

Even seed catalogues do not carry on ecstatically about beets as they do for most crops. Copywriters obviously do not like beets and show little compassion for nature's limitations. Beets are probably eaten more in the South, usually as "greens and grits," then in the North but that is not much of a testimonial. I have eaten yellow beets but they do not seem natural and have an unbeetlike taste. I cannot give them my support.

Nutrition and taste aside, beets are handsome plants and fun to grow. Each seed is really a fruit consisting of two to six individual seeds, each capable of producing a plant, so thinning is necessary. Beets are almost foolproof to grow, at least in my experience.

The leaves, if they do not get mottled and discouraged by bad-mouthing, blight, and other misadventures that pursue them, are an exquisite green-purple tone, a credit to any garden, worth growing for their decorative value alone. They are ceremonial in coloration and regal in bearing, and I intend to continue growing them to prove that I am willing to stand up and be counted on their behalf.

Beets have few pest enemies. I like to think this is due to their valor, disposition, and possible chemical exudates, but the uninformed and prejudiced claim that even common garden pests cannot tolerate them. They are worthy of our compassion, like any oppressed minority, despised and disparaged for reasons beyond their control.

I feel sorry for beets and am pleased to point out that I have had excellent luck growing old-fashioned Detroit dark reds, although tops and bottoms alike usually wind up in the compost.

RAY'S NO-NONSENSE BORSCHT

6 beets—peel, grate, and boil in 6 cups of water, simmer for 30 minutes.
Add 3/4 tsp. salt, 1/4 cup sugar (to taste), strain and chill.
To 1/2 pint of sour cream, add, slowly, the chilled borscht, mixing as

you go. Mix cream into borscht Russian style, not an American
dab floating pitifully on the top.
Original recipe calls for serving in "chilled clear bowls." Ray doesn't.

Some things that you grow you do not really like and take
them on simply because they are interesting, fun, or present a
challenge. Then you are faced with what to do with them, as
I am with beets. I read about a gardener who detested parsnips
but grew them anyway because he liked the way they looked.
When the parsnips were grown and harvested, he said they
had outlived their usefulness and threw them away.

I suppose we all grow certain things we have no intention of
eating or actually dislike for one reason or another. I have always
looked upon eating foods that your mate likes and you dislike,
and vice versa, as one of the obligations of marriage. Peggy
adores eggplant. I find it abominable, just as I like beets and
she despises them. I eat eggplant occasionally but you can eat
only so much eggplant parmesan, even in the name of marital
harmony, without imposing a terminal strain on the relationship.

Each year I plant a few eggplants because Peggy is so fond
of them but I have trouble growing eggplant, possibly because
they know how much I dislike them. They are one of the most
demanding and finicky of all plants and do not appreciate all
the trouble you must go to for them. Only now and then do
we have a good year with eggplant. Except for the few that
Peggy can use, most end up as compost, like the beets. No one
wants them. I cannot give them away. I never realized until
recently how many people hate eggplant. I find that encour-
aging.

People often ask me why I do not grow asparagus, and it
takes some explaining. Asparagus is one of the more troublesome plants to get started but once established the shoots are
available every spring with no further effort. It is another of

Peggy's favorites. For many years we grew asparagus. At first it was excellent, and I wondered why it was not grown in every garden. Then I learned about its insidious nature.

I first grew asparagus in New Jersey. Martha Washington plants were then popular but have been largely succeeded by other varieties as rust* has overcome plant resistance. Plant breeders are having a time trying to keep ahead of asparagus rust and keep developing new varieties. But all require much the same culture.

Asparagus is generally planted by digging a deep trench, preferably in an out-of-the-way place because the stalks come up year after year. The finger-like roots are spread out on the bottom of the trench, fanlike, lightly covered, and the trench is gradually filled in as the plants grow. It is necessary to have a good supply of compost or manure down where the roots are, just as it is for rhubarb; this is their food source for years to come.

The problem with asparagus arises if the stalks are allowed to go to seed; they are extremely determined. Oh, they are attractive all right, even beautiful, the tall, fernlike foliage producing charming red berries. I was then new to gardening and the asparagus seduced and took advantage of me.

Those charming berries fell to earth, took root, and soon volunteers were all over. This might have been all right but the roots were near the surface and produced only spindly stalks not fit for eating. Then they, too, went to seed and spread more volunteers. Soon we had an impossible tangle. It takes mulch, weeding, vigilance, and a firm hand to keep asparagus in line.

Several years ago Stu decided to try his luck with asparagus. He especially loved the fresh succulent stalks cooked almost as soon as they poked their heads up in the spring. For once, he

*A fungal disease that causes reddish or brownish spots on plants.

announced, he was going to have his fill of asparagus. Stu never does things by halves, so he dug a twenty-foot-square hole, some three feet deep, and filled it with asparagus plants and organic matter.

The first couple of years he had only a modest return as the new plants took root and gathered momentum. By the third year the stalks were thick, tender, and plentiful. Stu ate asparagus that Kay prepared until he turned a rather odd greenish color, and he gave away asparagus by the bushel. He would call on some pretext and say, "Oh, by the way, can you use some asparagus?" Stu is very big on "Oh, by the way . . ."

The fourth year the plants were so robust and belligerent from all that organic matter that they could hardly be cut with a machete. Stu and Kay could not keep up with the output. Even "Oh, by the way . . ." failed him. By then he had turned almost completely green. Then an unexpected thing happened. Other volunteer seeds from the rest of the garden were attracted to that banquet of concentrated organic matter. They moved in and began competing with the asparagus volunteers. Darwin would have been proud.

Finally it was a jungle. Asparagus and the other volunteers threatened to take over the entire garden. Stu could not get in to weed. There was a nightmarish quality about it, the making of a Kafka horror story or science fiction organic Armageddon featuring unstoppable asparagus on the march . . . Stu had no choice but to dig up the whole bed. He no longer speaks of asparagus and turns slightly green at the mention of it.

That is why I no longer grow asparagus.

One crop I have never grown is corn. It is popular with most gardeners. Some have only small plots but still manage a few rows and report success. Bill and Helen have less than one-fourth the area I cultivate but every year they plant several hills. They are generous friends and insist on sharing their meager return with us, which I feel is carrying friendship to its outer limits.

I am not exactly sure why I never grow corn. Certainly I have read the directions often enough and it does not seem too difficult. Bill claims he does not even use pesticides. Just a drop or two of mineral oil on the tassel of each forming ear and that keeps away the worms. Bill hates gardening and it is a measure of his devotion to Helen and corn that he suppresses the worms with oil.

I have room to grow corn. We both like it. I have thought about it often enough. I feel that never having had a go at corn suggests a lack of adventuresome spirit in me and even a deficiency in my gardening résumé. The only reason I can offer is a rather strange one and it goes back many years.

Early in our marriage we were looking to buy a house and visited a real estate agent in then-rural New Jersey. The agent and his wife, "Flo," had a fierce argument over his car telephone, and he showed us a partially converted chicken coop which he cheerfully said "needs some work." Passing the open fields, he began talking about corn.

The trick, he said, is to get it fresh. Right out of the field. The minute it is picked. "My wife and I back our car up close as we can get. Then we pick the corn and immediately put it in a gunny sack filled with ice. Then we run to the car. We drive home fast as we can. The water is in the pot boiling. On the way home my wife shucks the corn. We run into the house and pop the ears into the boiling water and eat them at once."

"But aren't they terribly hot?" I asked.

"Yes," he said, "but you can't wait or you lose the flavor. Flavor is everything in corn."

Every time I get the urge to grow corn, I think about the real estate agent and his wife Flo and somehow I never get around to planting corn.

Consider the little mouse, how sagacious an animal it is which never entrusts its life to one hole only.

—Plautus

The mouse who lives in the toolshed and I have an accommodation of sorts. At least I have accommodated to her. I had little choice in the matter. The mice long ago staked the toolshed out as their home, declaring squatter's sovereignty. Without taking extreme measures, which I am reluctant to do, there is little I can do about it.

The mouse, or mice, set up housekeeping shortly after we moved here in the outbuilding brought from our previous home. I had built it myself and it was sturdy enough to make the move undamaged on a trailer used to transport a bulldozer. The doors were nailed shut for the move. We rolled the stout little structure to and from the trailer on logs, and it was as simple as that. The toolshed was resettled on concrete blocks, facing where I planned to put the garden. The tools, removed for the move, were put back inside and we were more or less ready to start a new garden our first summer here, even before the house was completely finished.

The following winter the mice claimed it, or they may have come with the shed, migrants just like us. One way or another, they have occupied the toolshed so long now that they must consider it a mouse condominium. God alone knows how many generations of mouslings have called it home, mice being what they are.

The original nest was on the shelf, in a tin can holding assorted hose parts. The first time I put my hand in the can to get a washer and touched a furry little body, it gave me a start. It must have been traumatic for mouse. She, a gender assumption based on later evidence, ran frantically and hid under a sack of lime on the floor.

It was then fall and I was unwilling to evict the mice because it was late to find new winter quarters. I had no objection to them as tenants, other than the gamey smell they gave the place. On clear days I left the swinging doors open to air it. That excited Lily. She bounded inside to stand vigil under the upended wheelbarrow, hoping to disrupt the mouse tenancy and redress the local balance of nature. The mice, then and now, seem to prefer this precarious arrangement to finding new mice quarters. Lily does not share my sentiment about mice.

In the spring babies were in the nest. Inadvertently I picked up the can and mother mouse leaped out, leaving a half-dozen tiny pink bodies huddled together. I returned the can to the shelf and the mouse family and I went about our respective affairs.

The babies grew up, I assume, and made their own way in the mouse world. I have no idea how they worked it out but their numbers were never excessive, which seems rather remarkable and even astonishing. I never saw more than one or two of any size when I opened the door; they ran wildly as light violated their dark sanctuary.

How they get in and out of the toolshed is a mystery. There are no visible holes, cracks, or openings. They must squeeze under the doors, although this seems unlikely because of the tight fit. Assuming that Plautus is right, my sagacious mouse has not one "hole" but at least two.

Periodically, over the years, the mice change the location of their nest, each succeeding mouse mother perhaps having her own idea about proper circumstances for birthing. They developed a particular fondness for wooden pint strawberry boxes in which I kept twine, tags, and such. The nests always seemed to be lined with the same soft fluffy substance that looks wonderfully comfortable for "laying in," as it was once called.

The only damage the mice ever did was to chew a hole in a plastic tarp I had stored over the winter and to convert an old pair of cotton work gloves into nesting material for maternity use. I considered it a breach of etiquette but not contract and overlooked it in the name of harmony between the species.

One spring I soaked creosote into the plywood exterior of the toolshed and several days later found four dead baby mice on the floor. I had not considered the effect of the fumes on my mouse tenants. I felt bad about that.

This spring the mice apparently decided to upgrade their living quarters. I had stored four wooden bushel baskets, upside down, near the coiled hoses in a corner for the winter. When I removed the hoses I noticed a small hole in the top basket. That puzzled me but I gave it little thought at the time.

A week or so later I needed the baskets. Then I discovered that each one in the stack had a matching hole directly beneath the one on top. Between the bottom and second baskets the mouse mother had built an elaborate nest of the same soft, downy material, the remains of my work gloves. In the nest were four baby mice, not pink as they are at birth but not yet ready to abandon the nursery. I replaced the baskets, holes in alignment, until this latest mouse family was old enough to make its way in the world.

Later, after the young were gone, I removed the baskets. One full-grown mouse remained in the nest, the mother, prob-ably, ready to start a new family, or one of the last brood who refused to leave home; Cape Cod's young are notoriously reluctant to leave home. I needed the baskets, so I dumped nest and mouse in front of the toolshed and the mouse darted under a nearby cold frame. I composted the nest, still rather indignant about the holes in my baskets.

I have not seen the mice since then but trust that the mother is still around. The mouse smell is strong as ever, despite fre-quent airings. I have no idea if she is the original tenant, which is doubtful, or represents a later generation, a daughter or granddaughter many times removed, maybe a descendant of the original homesteader. Is there a line of succession among mice, a kind of mouse primogeniture?

I know little about mice, really, and reference books at hand are not terribly enlightening. My encyclopedia reveals that they are "the largest mammalian family in number of species, several hundred, at least, being recognized." It also notes that mice have learned to get on well with people, as if I needed to be told that. I could probably learn more details but the situation and relationship between us would not be drastically changed or improved if I knew their genealogy, statistics, or intimate secrets. Walt Whitman held that a mouse "is miracle enough to stagger sextillions of infidels," a rather imposing testimonial.

I am an admirer of mouse ingenuity. Last winter a tiny mouse took up housekeeping in the pantry (where was Lily?). It chewed a hole in the plastic base of the electric ice cream maker on the floor, where the wire entered the housing, to make its nest in the motor itself. The fluffy nest was discovered after the gears ground to a gasping halt. The culprit was caught in a Havahart trap, seduced by peanut butter, and released outdoors to pursue its career al fresco.

I do not know if mice are native to this country or are wash-ashores, as the Cape Cod natives call those of us not born here, like myself (they claim it takes three generations to make a native). I do know they, mice, have small but frequent families and reproduce in awesome numbers if ill fortune does not intervene.

I have read that some rodent populations mimic human populations in certain respects, as if they have spent too much time around us. This is especially true of rats. If they overpopulate in close quarters their social structure collapses into cannibalism and chaos, akin to the violence and discord in some of our large cities.

So far I have not had to deal with such urban difficulties in the toolshed, and I am not even sure they apply to mice as they do to their cousins, the rats. It makes no difference. I try to be a considerate landlord and they have been more or less tolerable if not exemplary tenants. I am not sure what nature, or whoever is in charge of the great scheme, has in mind, but mouse (or the mice) and I seem to have evolved a mode of life that suits both of us. At least we coexist on agreeable enough terms of live and let live in our private little universe, the toolshed.

Mouse update:

Much later, on a hot summer day, I go into the toolshed to get a stored floating row cover to protect some new broccoli plantings for fall. To my dismay the cover has been chewed unmercifully; "permeable" now means more holes than cover. I pick up a new tarp nearby; it has a hole chewed in it.

Under the hole in the tarp lies mouse. The light is poor and my eyes being what they are, I cannot see clearly. Mouse lies strangely still in her nest, my row cover reduced to the fluffy stuff mouse nests are made of. She tries to move but is unable to. Only then do I understand. Clinging to her are a half-dozen tiny pink mouslings. I have interrupted the little mouse mother nursing her newborns. I quickly replace the tarp and shut the door, leaving behind the quiet darkness for the new generation that presumably will inherit the toolshed.

> *O bed! O bed! delicious bed!*
> *That heaven upon earth to the weary head!*
> —Thomas Hood

I sit in the garden, on the green metal chair, reading a letter from a former newspaper colleague. The sun is so brilliant that it makes a glare on the paper and I must squint in order to read. The letter is typed, hurriedly, with many typos, words scratched out, or mistakes corrected with the flick of a ballpoint in a rushed proofreading job. No word processor for my correspondent. He, too, is a dinosaur, still writing on an outmoded mechanical machine, just as I do.

The letter is only of personal interest, the communication of those with little to bind them except a shared past—the problems of aging, ill health, recollections of days gone, the new dead. My former comrade in arms, as it were, is still writing but now only for tawdry detective pulps and the sensational supermarket press. Never mind, he enjoys it and the income is welcome, although he looks upon the result as something of a joke. "Imagine actually being paid to grind out such drivel and nonsense."

The only startling revelation is that he begins work every day when his "brainy cat, my alarm clock," touches her nose to his cheek promptly at 4:50 A.M. He is in front of his old portable, banging out the drivel and nonsense at 5:30.

Incredible! Imagine awakening voluntarily at 4:50 and actually being in front of a typewriter at 5:30! It verges upon the obscene. That was what I most disliked about newspaper work—the hours, the other side of the publicized glamour. When first hired, I spent several months on the "lobster shift," from 2 A.M. until 9 A.M. It almost did me in.

There can be nothing more melancholy than a newspaper office at 2 A.M., at least as it was in my day: the smell of stale coffee, stale cigarette smoke, and fermenting quiet desperation, a curious blend of old men on their way out and young men on their way in, the ghosts of disasters past, dim lights, being handed a fistful of obituaries to rewrite. The tyranny of "night rewrite" at its worst. I recall an editor on the lobster shift, a cheerful drunk, who always referred to breakfast as "the cocktail hour."

Even after being graduated from the lobster shift, I often worked nights. News knows no hours. People murder one another without respect for the clock or others' sleep. There are explosions, robberies, muggings, swindles, politicians caught in the wrong bed or with a hand in the municipal till; the blind get evicted, old people are taken advantage of, there are child abusers, rapists, corporate shenanigans, mass firings, strikes, demonstrations, fires, plane and train crashes, drug outrages, terrorists, hijackings, spouses taking off on one another, an ongoing and bloody saga of the expected and unexpected, the stuff the media live by, that strange compost called news.

There is no end to it. Excitements go on around the clock. I once interviewed a convicted burglar, a self-described "second-story man," who complained that he did not like the business (his word) he was in because he had to work at night when he would have preferred being home in bed. A man worthy of rehabilitation.

That is what I like most about gardening: the hours. I report only when and if I am ready, stay as long as I like, and work only as intensely as suits my mood. I am not drugged with fatigue. I need not force myself to perform. The option of whether or not to work and taking impromptu naps are among the great luxuries of life. An unsung attraction of gardening is that it allows the unburdened mind leisure to roam. One usually need not concentrate on the job to be done; hands and brain can be largely independent of one another.

One can dwell on the past, speculate on the future, or whatever. Time itself is an open vista. The most astonishing and irrelevant thoughts come when the mind is relaxed and receptive. The rare moments without mental stress are, I believe, essential to our well-being. Time and its imperatives and events roll over us and fall into their proper place. In these unplanned and unfettered moments we shape our inner world and position ourselves in it. How fitting that the Bible places creation in a garden!

In a garden nothing of great consequence usually happens before the sun is well up, other than a nocturnal raid by deer, woodchucks or other marauders, and the tardy sleeper is comforted by the thought that he should not work the plants while they are still damp with night dew. He has a chance to fortify himself with proper rest for the day's assaults and surprises.

Lack of sleep and the irritability and instability it brings may play a bigger role than suspected in shaping the world we live in. A decent night's sleep may be the beginning of a kinder and gentler world. Much of my life is spent trying to make up sleep I lost to the lobster shift. As my former colleague sits in front of his old portable inventing outrages to stimulate the jaded and weary shopper, and news is in the making, I am trying to even the score with the past, asleep and gearing up for any small shocks the garden holds for me this day.

Most insects, sensibly, do not stir before the sun is fairly warm. They depend on the gathering heat to get them underway, much as I do these days. They do not take unfair advantage of my lassitude, enabling both of us to get down to business about the same time. This may be nature at her finest.

There are exceptions, of course. There are exceptions to almost everything in this world (that is primarily what news is). Creatures such as slugs and cutworms do their work at night and sleep during the day, just as I did on the lobster shift, when and if I could fall asleep during the day, but they are low types and show little imagination or intelligence, easily taken in by a few shingles they use for motels or guilelessly drowning in a pan of stale beer. They get no sympathy from me. Not because of the damage they do but because of the hours they keep.

The extremes of zucchini are like goldfish nibbling
you to death; sooner or later they'll get you with
too little or too much.
　　　　　　　　　　　　　　　　—Ex-gardener's lament

I had intended to write a paean to zucchini but at the moment my vision is clouded. I went out to collect a few zukes to take with us to New Hampshire, for our son and his family, and there, on the leaves, were little gray crawling bodies. There is nothing like little gray crawling bodies to cloud your vision and even dampen your ardor for zucchini.

Zucchini, gray crawling bodies notwithstanding, is one of my favorite vegetables. To grow, that is. As food, I can take it or leave it, although I respect its multiple functional uses and lesser nutritional merit; it is probably the most versatile of all garden crops.

Zucchini can be boiled, fried, pickled, stuffed, eaten raw, or cooked, used in lasagna, pancakes, scrambled eggs, omelets, soups, salads, relishes, pasta, quiches, appetizers, baked goods, and pies; even the blossoms can be sautéed or eaten raw with vinaigrette. There is no end to its uses. Whole recipes books are devoted to zucchini alone. Keene, New Hampshire, holds an annual summer International Zucchini Festival, a kind of mecca for those with a passion for zucchini.

Zucchini is better known in other parts of the world than in the United States, variously called vegetable marrow, Italian squash, green squash, and cocozelle. Here it is generally referred to only as zucchini; it is a relative of the common pie pumpkin, if that gives it added status.

Zucchini's nutritional virtues are sound if modest. It is low in calories and fats and contains carbohydrates, some protein, vitamins, and minerals. Like tofu, it tends to take on the flavor of whatever it is paired with, much like an affable person lacking personality or flavor and adopting that of a stronger companion.

Zucchini is fairly easy to grow, usually planted in hills, four seeds or so per mound, and bears in about fifty-five days. It requires a rich soil and lots of water and is notorious for its fecundity. There are probably as many jokes about trying to give away surplus zucchini as there are zucchini to give away. Often such giveaways are so overgrown they can barely be lifted, let alone used; charity has its limits.

Zucchini is one of our garden regulars. We use it fresh throughout the season in many ways. Peggy also cans some as part of a vegetable mix with tomatoes, onions, and celery, and as pickled spears. Shredded and sautéd zucchini is frozen for frittatas. We tried to freeze shredded raw zucchini for use in cakes over the winter but that was too much even for the amiable zucchini.

I earlier recounted my adventures forcing zucchini in the spring by starting it inside under lights and transplanting the seedlings to a cold frame that must be protected with a cover at night. This was, as noted, started as an experiment, just to see if I could pull it off. By now it may be more of a small vanity of mine, trying to outwit the weather and nature, than any uncontrollable urge for early zucchini. My old garden calendars bear circles around various harvesting dates in June, with the triumphant notation "1st zuke" followed by up to four exclamation marks, depending on the date and degree of my cxultation.

I am not sure why I continue this bothersome spring ritual. Surely it means little or nothing to eat fresh zucchini before others have it. The ego returns are not that great. The nutritional dividends are marginal. It must be habit, compulsion, or maybe I just enjoy watching the little plants struggle to survive. Whatever my reasons (or problems), I do not recommend it for those with proper respect for the uses of time.

Whether given a jump start inside or allowed to germinate and grow outside at its own pace, zucchini may be the most clever plant in the garden. Certainly it is the most brainy in the squash family, which is not generally known for its intelligence. The leaves are so large, the stalks so thick and convoluted, that it is often impossible to find the green, camouflaged fruit lurking in the tangle below. Suddenly it appears, big as a baseball bat, fit only for composting.

This goes beyond wasted squash. The problem is compounded because the plant then believes it has achieved its life mission of reproducing itself and slows down or stops bearing altogether, a problem with most plants. Zucchini requires constant vigilance. It is a kind of garden censor, rewarding the conscientious and penalizing the lax and errant. It punishes foibles, exposes pretentions, and deflates illusions. It is a moral force in the garden.

One shortcoming of a work like this is that some creatures fail to get the attention or respect they deserve. I have acknowledged the menace of squash bugs but neglected borers. Squash bugs and borers are the primary assassins of zucchini. I never saw or heard of squash bugs until we came to Massachusetts but have always had to contend with borers. Like tomato hornworms and potato beetles, borers are garden celebrities.

The borer parent is a moth, another terrorist, but even critics agree that she is striking in appearance, with transparent wings and blackish-iridescent body. The moth lays her eggs conscientiously at the base of a zucchini plant and the ensuing larvae burrow under the soil until ready to take up residence in the stem of the plant.

The moth offspring is pearly white, an inch or so long, and eats lustily inside the stem, out of sight. Soon the starved leaves wilt. The entire plant collapses; once-proud stalks sprawl on the ground, often revealing a final outsized zuke, a last effort to perpetuate itself. The problem of what to do with excess zucchini is resolved.

Garden writers are very upbeat about getting rid of borers. They advise poking a pin into the stalk to impale the wormlike creature within, or taking a knife and delicately slitting the stem to stab and remove the feasting grub. Then pile soil around the wound. The injury heals, the plant recovers. Presto! Once more you have surplus zukes to unload.

The method has one flaw. It rarely works. At least for me. By the time the borer's presence is noted by wilting leaves, damage is already extensive. There may not be just one borer within but two or several. And where in the stem are they? Extensive probing and slitting may be necessary. If the borer or borers do not kill the plant, the surgery is almost sure to. Then there is the likelihood of introducing disease into the wound. I would never have made it as a surgeon.

A better method may be to inject BT into the stem with a hypodermic needle, obtainable from hardware supply houses for use in applying glue. I read about this only recently but have never tried it.

Vigilant gardeners are advised to examine the base of their plants for telltale evidence of the borer, its eggs, or excrement, the latter euphemistically known as "frass." It requires sharp eyes and a bit of doing, even for the dedicated, to spot tiny eggs or insect turds on the ground under a tangle of outsize plants, a preventive technique I have never mastered.

More courageous gardeners saturate soil around the plants with poisons to wipe out the larvae. Organic gardeners often try to outmaneuver them with guile, spreading their plantings around and making successive plantings. Eventually the moth disappears, her time over, and later plantings are usually borer free. One gardener I know spreads rotenone around the base of plants. I generally practice saturation plantings, hoping to grow enough for them and me. The theory seems simple enough:

If you plant enough, the borers are bound to miss some. Occasionally it works.

Several years ago I hit on a new method. The young plants in the cold frame were protected from the moth but when the plants grew larger and the cover was removed not one plant was hit. Others growing nearby were wiped out. Why?

I finally decided it was the close spacing. The plants inside the cold frame were so crowded that the moth could not get to the stems to lay eggs. The following year the same result. Was I on to something good? A breakthrough in borer control?

The third year we had the biggest zucchini outpouring ever. We could not give them away fast enough. I facetiously said to Peggy, "Where are the borers when we need them?" An unfortunate remark. Two days later they struck. Every plant in the garden was cut down. The borers were never worse. So much for innovation.

Subsequently Helen told me her method. She wraps old pantyhose around the base of her zucchinis to thwart the moth, a kind of birth control. She says it works perfectly. Now I am not especially eager to dress the plants in old pantyhose but it does sound worth a try. One thing bothers me: How will the proud zucchini feel about this indignity? How will it affect them as a moral force in the garden?

No paean to zucchini, even though aborted by bugs and borers, is complete without a favorite recipe. I personally think zucchini is at its best as frittata, also known as Italian omelet. Peggy serves it as a complete meal with a garden-fresh salad and homemade whole-wheat sourdough bread. Leftover frittata is excellent served cold or as a sandwich.

PEGGY'S FRITTATA

6 eggs
1 lb. zucchini (about one medium squash)
1 onion (medium size)

¼ cup grated Parmesan or Romano cheese
1 cup shredded cheddar cheese
1 Tbsp. olive oil
¼ tsp. oregano
   salt and pepper to taste

Trim off ends and coarsely grate zucchini, wrap in tea towel, and squeeze out excess juice. Set aside.

Dice onion and sauté in olive oil in large frying pan (with heat-proof handle) until translucent. Add zucchini and sauté until wilted. Sprinkle with salt, pepper, and oregano.

Beat eggs briskly with 2 tablespoons of water and pour over zucchini mix. Cook until slightly firm.

Sprinkle cheese on top of eggs and pop under preheated broiler. Cook until brown and bubbly. Remove from heat, cool for five minutes, cut and serve.

Serves four.

>   *This world is very odd we see,*
>   *We do not comprehend it;*
>   *But in one fact we all agree,*
>   *God won't, and we can't mend it.*
>   —Arthur Hugh Clough

W e are prepared to leave for New Hampshire. I have gathered a basket full of zucchinis when I find the squash nymphs and it is about to rain any minute. Peggy calls from the house. It is time to leave. We are already late. Will I be much longer? Gardening books never deal with crises like this.

It is not a good time to go away. We have had an extended dry spell. Everything desperately needs water. I look at the sky hopefully. Each time rain threatens it passes over. Even this early in the day the zucchinis have wilted slightly, practicing their trick of curling their leaves to conserve such moisture as there is. And what to do about the squash bugs?

I hurriedly handpick as many of the nymphs and egg clusters as I can find and sprinkle the leaves with rotenone powder. Almost at once the rain starts, washing off the insecticide before it can do any good. Peggy calls again. I retreat to the house. We take off with the basket of twenty-two zucchinis and my misgivings.

Back from New Hampshire after a three-day absence. I go to the garden almost at once. An army of marauding squash bugs, nymphs, and eggs await me. Where did so many come from in so short a time? Are all mine? Are there imports? I handpick as many as I can and dust the explosive numbers with rotenone. Many leaves are so devastated that they must be cut off and thrown away. Now all I need is a few borers working below while the squash bugs take the high road above.

A more serious problem for the entire garden is the lack of water. The rain came to nothing. Everything is wilted. Some plants are desperate, sagging almost to the ground. An emergency watering perks them up considerably. The hose says to them, "Don't give up. Help is on the way. Better days are ahead. Just hang in there for now. Chin up!"

While we were away a friend, a young woman, stayed with Lily but apparently she is not a great hand at gardening, although she announced, triumphantly, that she took some "great pictures" of the garden. She did not notice, or ignored, the plants' plight. She is in love and gardening does not hold high priority when one is in love. Gardening and love do not mix. I have seen more than one garden go under because its keeper fell in love.

I take stock of the damage that occurred during our absence. Weeds grew. Lettuce bolted. Heads of cabbage cracked. The broccoli started to flower. Bush beans got too big to use. The pole beans are so long and plentiful dangling from their tripods that they have a surrealistic effect. A new seed bed of fall spinach dried out. Fall cabbage seedling are "leggy." Everything needs a booster of fertilizer. The entire garden looks ragged and neglected. It always gets out of hand when we go away, even for a few days, as if to punish me.

Most of the problems could have been prevented with a little foresight and effort, a thought that fails to comfort me. I could have conserved moisture and kept down weeds by adding more mulch. Tilting the cabbage plants would have broken part of the root systems to interfere with water intake and keep the heads from cracking. I should have harvested the broccoli and beans before we left and covered the new spinach bed with wet burlap or a light mulch. The cabbage seedlings should have been transplanted.

The majority of these ailments can be more or less rectified with no great loss to the garden or dislocation of the great scheme. But some things are gone. A garden can be unreasonably demanding. Certain jobs must be performed at a given time or there is no second chance. Weather constantly changes. The season moves inexorably forward. The given allotment of growing days runs on relentlessly, like a clock ticking away the designated number of hours or days in a lifetime. There is just so much time for each living thing; each of us is on an invisible time schedule.

I sympathize with those who work at jobs with fixed hours and try to garden in their spare time, as I once did. This probably includes the majority of gardeners. It is difficult, often impossible, to fulfill domestic and job obligations and still meet a garden's needs. For the hurried and conscientious, a garden can impose unrelenting pressures. Often the gardener must make an unpleasant choice: What do I neglect?

A garden requires a certain amount of time devoted to it every week, but when that time is given may be more important than the number of hours worked. Gardens are flexible to a degree but may adjust their needs reluctantly, often to the detriment of crops that refuse to negotiate or compromise gracefully.

Everything in a garden has its moment of greatest need. If

that need is not met it may never be made up. If mature beans are not picked they cannot remain on the vine without loss of quality or being ruined altogether. The same is true of most plants. Each has its moment of perfection, then quality declines: Sugars turn to starch, the tender becomes stringy or tough, there is less flavor. Differences may be slight or subtle but they are there. The more discerning the palate, the greater the difference, the greater the loss.

For many plants the moment comes and goes swiftly. It is much like the development of children or young animals. Certain needs of the moment must be met or they can never be made up. Each living thing is beholden to its internal timetable. Each in its own time. If the moment of need or fulfillment slips by, it may be forever lost. We, the zucchini, beans, cabbage, and all the rest have more in common than we suspect. The clock ticks on . . .

Those "great pictures" of the garden did not turn out. There was no film in the camera. Love!

> *There is no ancient gentlemen but gardeners. . . .*
> *They hold up Adam's profession.*
> —William Shakespeare

Bret and his family are here for a visit and he talks with enthusiasm about his garden. It is doing fine but the bugs are terrible. Gardening is not easy where he lives, in southern New Hampshire. As soon as the ground thaws in the spring there is an unending procession of no-see-ums, midgies, black flies, greenheads, deer flies, assorted others, and always the fierce mosquitoes that can draw blood.

To work in the garden he has to wear a net. "But they can still get to you," he says. I feel for him. I have seen gardeners there wearing bee suits and veils to work outside at all. Once I saw a crew of road workers with blood-soaked towels around their necks.

Otherwise it is great, he says. The cabbages are huge. The squash has already run over the fence. The tomatoes recovered after a slow start due to an unusually cold spring. The clay soil is improving from all the manure he has tilled in. He is gaining on the weeds. "If only I had more room," he adds, his voice trailing off in that universal lament of gardeners.

Somehow I keep from smiling. I am remembering when he was finishing high school back in New Jersey during the high-flying 1960s. He and his friend Brian asked if they could take over the garden that summer. It took me a minute to recover. "What's up?" I asked.

"We want to learn how," he said.

Again it took some doing to absorb that. He had never looked at the garden, let alone worked in it. Why this sudden urge to garden? "Well," he said, pulling at his long hair, "people should be self-sufficient. A person should grow the food they eat. You know. . . ."

I resisted the temptation to say, "Like changing your life-style, right, man?" Instead, I said, "Sure, go ahead."

"What do we do first?"

"You start by turning the soil."

He and Brian went to his room and I overheard enough of their conversation to gather that this was the first step in a self-sufficiency program. Next they would start keeping chickens. Then they would open a vegetable stand, use the proceeds to buy a pickup truck, and expand the garden. As soon as the program was under way they would take a trip to Hawaii . . .

The program got started that afternoon. I watched from the study upstairs overlooking the garden. I was fascinated, stunned really, by this change in our son. He and Brian each had a shovel. But they seemed to have trouble getting up momentum. One would slowly turn a scoop of earth, then the other. The two shovels never worked together. The two entrepreneurs never stopped talking. They were in the garden for two hours. When they took off, the soil was almost intact, the shovels abandoned on the ground, the toolhouse door left open.

The following day they returned and did about the same amount of "work." This continued for a week. At the rate they were going summer would be over before the soil was prepared. Meanwhile quack grass threatened to take over the entire garden with its tangle of spreading spaghetti-like roots. Quack grass, also known as quick, twitch, and witchgrass, is almost impossible to get rid of. It advances by both dropping seeds on the earth and spreading rhizomes below. Quack grass may be the most pernicious of all garden weeds, exceeded outside the garden only by parasitic witchweed.

From my observation post I watched the program proceed, or fail to proceed. Bret and Brian were now stretched out on the ground to discuss their itinerary for Hawaii, the shovels already on vacation. After the pair knocked off for the afternoon I surreptitiously tore out some of the charging quack grass. Each day the gardeners reported excellent progress.

"What do we do next?" asked Bret.

"Keep forging ahead."

By June, the gardeners had vanished. The program was abandoned, the pilgrimage to Hawaii on hold. The garden was almost solid quack grass. I took over, cleaned the rust off the abandoned shovels, and salvaged what was left of the season by planting a few late crops.

Time passes. Bret went to college for two years and quit to go into construction so he could be "self-sufficient." ("If you quit school now, you are on your own," I admonished sternly.) He stayed in construction for about three years. Meanwhile we moved to Cape Cod and bought a large tract of forested land in New Hampshire, where I built a 12 × 12-foot cabin overlooking a beaver pond. Bret moved into the cabin, went back to school, and entered a new phase of self-sufficiency.

The cabin was uninsulated. No water, electricity, or outhouse. Only a small wood-burning stove, raised plywood board for a cot, makeshift table, a few old dishes and utensils, some cast-off pots and pans, and portable propane stove. Somehow he survived two frigid subzero New Hampshire winters in that tiny cabin.

He drew water from the nearby stream, studied by kerosene lamp, kept more or less warm burning wood from trees he cut down, sectioned, and split. He hiked a mile to and from the highway every day, using snowshoes when the snow was impossibly deep, and hitchhiked twenty miles to school. He usually did not get home until after dark, built a fire, drew water from the stream, cooked his dinner with propane gas, and studied by kerosene light. It was inspiring. Even awesome. All on his own. I went from skeptic to admirer. Self-sufficiency is not to be taken lightly.

Often he threatened to grow a garden but clearing out the huge trees and underbrush would have been an enormous undertaking and bringing in electricity to operate a well fantastically expensive. Bret was no more deterred by these obstacles than he had been by the rampaging quack grass back in New Jersey. The garden was part of what he called his "five-year plan." He made it sound like the hanging gardens of Babylon. Bret always thought big. He actually did cut down some trees for a clearing and planted four fruit trees.

One tree, a peach, saw early on that the game was up and promptly expired. The others—apple, plum, and cherry—after a valiant struggle were choked to death by new forest growth. Bret still was not discouraged and remained keenly interested in my garden. He often asked me how to grow this or that. He never failed to ask how the garden was doing, as one would inquire after a family member, even in mid-winter when nothing was growing. He had high standards for my gardens.

When he came to visit he invariably offered a hand with anything that needed doing. He was especially pleased to be of use in the garden, despite his lack of experience. I never saw anybody without a garden so involved in gardening. He was dedicated to the idea of gardening, if not the practice itself, a not uncommon phenomenon, I have learned.

It is to the dedicated gardener that we now turn, whether he or she actually gardens or not. There is more to gardening than dirt under the fingernails. I know a writer of how-to garden books who never goes near a garden. Gardening may be more state of mind than state of the art. Most dedicated gardeners I have known are, of necessity, fairly resolute. They have a sense of responsibility. Most are fairly stable in their personal habits. They are, for the most part, serious gardeners.

What is a serious gardener? Kipling's observation that half of a proper gardener's work is done upon his knees is a compelling statement of dedication but rules out too many of us with physical ailments or lack of inclination to work that way. I have an invalid friend who goes into the garden in a wheelchair.

I like to think that dedication has more to do with commitment than posture, a kind of unwritten contract between garden and tender. Regardless of vicissitudes or setbacks the serious gardener will stay the course. The dilettante or casual gardener tends to fold with the first winds or weeds of adversity.

There are exceptions. There may be more exceptions than model or "book" gardeners. But here we are concerned with dedication in its pure form. Based on personal observation, I offer the following case studies.

Bill was a bachelor, an alcoholic, a dedicated gardener. Every day he got drunk and every day he tended his garden. Dedication has many expressions. For him, gardening required more than ordinary commitment. His plot was near a wetland and the mosquitoes were savage. He always seemed to be rototilling. I often wondered what demons pursued him as he lurched behind his rototiller, followed by a cloud of mosquitoes.

Alcohol seemed to have preserved rather than to have killed him off. He was old, pitifully thin, toothless, and always wore a torn undershirt desperately in need of laundering. A little felt hat, several sizes too small, was perched on his head at a rakish angle. He was not your ordinary run-of-the-garden drunk; he had spirit and independence.

Once I made him a loaf of homemade bread. "What the hell is that?" he demanded. "You think I'm down here starving?" A few days later he stopped me and thrust out a brown paper bag. "I've got some old pig potatoes going to waste," he said gruffly. "You want 'em?" He gave what he had to give. I was touched. I have no idea how he lived. He had no known means of support other than the garden and occasionally rototilling for others. Still, he managed to buy his bottle every day. Resourcefulness is an asset in any gardener.

By nightfall he could not tell an onion from a potato. But there he was, back in the garden. The rototiller kept him from falling on his face as he fled his furies. What if he did run over a newly planted row of lettuce or mistake beets for weeds? In a world of uncertainties and irresolution, dedication is where you find it.

Herman was a German immigrant I knew back in Jersey, an excellent grower who practiced many tricks. He was the first gardener I knew to use silverfoil plates hung from strings to scare away crows. His entire backyard was garden. "You can't eat the grass," was his favorite expression, uttered in a heavy accent.

His plot was relatively small, intensely worked, and fabulously productive. It supplied most of the family's food throughout the year, including huge reserves of sauerkraut. A row of compost bins was lined up neatly behind the garage in Teutonic order. Nothing out of place. Not a weed to be seen.

Herman had secret sources of broken-down leaves, rotted chicken manure, and other organic treasures. He had a pleasant-like suspicion, almost paranoia, about guarding where they came from, as if he did not want to encourage competition or chance losing his edge.

Herman had a degenerated hip, could hardly walk, and was in constant pain. He could barely make it out to the garden. Once there, he clung to the fence, supported himself with a shovel or rake, or even crawled on hands and knees to do what needed doing. Pain was never allowed to get in the way of the garden's needs.

He was the first person I knew to have a hip replacement, a procedure then in its infancy and considered somewhat risky. He was willing to take his chances. "What is life without gardening?" he said. The operation was a success. When last I saw him he was starting to convert the front yard into a second garden. "You can't eat the grass," he announced solemnly.

Hoss is a clinical psychologist, passionately dedicated to his garden. I think of him as an aggressive gardener. He is forever exhorting his plants to perform better, whipping them on with this or that. They are prodded with the likes of strong manure tea, seaweed extract, fish fertilizer, and God knows what mysterious potions and admonitions secretely administered.

I picture Hoss in the garden at midnight, a chubby wraith who can lift a refrigerator without taking a deep breath, urging the plants to be all they can be and more, perhaps doing group therapy with the onions. Hoss claims to be an organic gardener and swears that he has no problem with insects. Not even root maggots on the broccoli and cabbage? I asked. No, he said. But under intense interrogation he admitted to using diazinon. I have urged him, in vain, to come out of the organic closet and declare himself the chemical assassin he is.

Several years ago Hoss and his wife, Susanne, lived in a rented house with a tiny garden ringed by tall trees. It was amazing how much he got out of that small sunless plot. Now, knowing how he browbeats and exhorts his plants, it is not so surprising. I once accused him of practicing psychotherapy on the tomatoes. He denied it, grinned happily, and declared, "They do it all on their own."

Susanne confided to me that Hoss's secret ambition was to grow bigger onions than I did. Until then I did not suspect that he was also a competitive gardener. He used to ask me casually how my garden was doing. "Terrible," I would reply. It seemed to cheer him no end.

"How are your onions?" he asked. His eyes narrowed to slits. He sucked in his breath. "Worst I've ever had," I said, curling thumb and forefinger in a huge circle. It was a lie but had the desired effect. Hoss made a hissing sound like a punctured balloon.

Eventually he and Susanne bought a house on a half-acre lot. They were hardly in before he cut down every tree and bought the biggest, most powerful rototiller made. He brought in seaweed, manure, and peat moss to build up the soil.

Hoss loved to demonstrate that brute rototiller, guiding it with one hand, just like the ads show. At the corners he hung on with both hands, struggling to keep the monster from tipping over or taking down his neighbor's fence. He kept explaining how, in the long run, expensive as the tiller was, it would be a great economy. "You know how much food costs nowadays at the supermarket," he exclaimed.

Soon the entire backyard was garden, except for a 6 × 6-foot plot grudgingly allocated to Susanne to grow herbs for potpourri. Long rows of tomatoes, shoulder to shoulder, were supported on old telephone wires stretched between two stout posts. There were tomatoes enough to supply a farmer's market. "You can't have too many tomatoes!" cried Hoss.

Peppers and melons grew out of slits in black plastic. The cabbage thrust through salvaged green carpeting. "If anything lays eggs on it, I can just throw them away," explained Hoss. He described himself as the only gardener on Cape Cod with a wall-to-wall cabbage patch.

To bring in the quantities of seaweed, mulch, manure, and peat to serve that huge garden, Hoss bought a big trailer. Then he bought a used pickup to haul the trailer. "It's worth the outlay," he said. "You know how much food costs at the super-market nowadays."

Next he bought an expensive kit for the rototiller. It would supply spare parts in an emergency. "You never know what can go wrong," explained Hoss. "Supposing something broke and I had to wait a week for parts. In the long run it's an economy. You know how much food costs at the supermarket nowadays. By the way, how is your garden doing? How are your onions?"

By then his garden was so lush and overgrown that you could barely see the house. Susanne's 6 × 6 herb bed had shrunk to 4 × 4. Hoss had so much garden to tend that he was out in the morning before going to work, back at noon to give it a boost, and again promptly after work whipping the plants on.

The garden was so full that there was no longer room for the rototiller between rows. There were no rows. Just solid plants. The monster tiller sat in the corner toolshed, brooding and unused. Hoss would fire it up for visitors to demonstrate how it performed.

Next he bought the biggest garden cart made, a splendid contraption that gleamed in the sunlight. It would make him more efficient, another economy in the long run. Like the monster tiller, it was better suited to a farm than garden; the cart was too big to get between the nonexistent rows.

Hoss would load the cart and push it gingerly around the perimeter of the garden on his neighbor's property or leave it on the side to glisten grandly in the sun. It was a rebuke to the ratty old wheelbarrow I inherited from Bret when he was a mason's helper in New Jersey; I never dared ask where it came from.

Hoss next invested in a costly automated drip-irrigation sys-tem, an economy that would, in the long run, save time and water. He planned to build a greenhouse to start plants in to get a jump on the season. Still another economy. I noted by my reckoning that every pepper he grew cost about $12 and lettuce a conservative $5. Hoss chuckled, cleared his throat, scraped his feet, and turned slightly pink.

"It's a lot of money," he said. "I'll admit that. But think how much it costs to buy food at the supermarket nowadays. By the way, how's your garden?"

"Terrible!"

"Hmmmm," he mused, looking happy. Then he tensed. "How are your onions?"

That was a while back. Hoss and Susanne now have a new house, this one on a heavily wooded hill where gardening seemed unlikely. But Hoss was up to the challenge. He whacked down some trees and put in raised beds, bolted and braced to last the ages. The best. They cost a fortune but were an economy in the long run because "they will last forever."

High-grade loam was bought for the beds. The new garden was under way. Now tomatoes and other produce pour forth. Pole beans climb the side of the house and must be picked from the upper deck. But it is not like the old place. The raised beds never overreach themselves. The monster tiller and splendid garden cart brood together, unused, in a metal shed. That is the way it is sometimes with economies.

I catch Hoss in a reflective mood. What does he get out of gardening other than fresh vegetables? He thinks a long time, as if he never considered it before. Finally he replies that it "is creative, making things grow, starting with a seed and helping it become a plant that feeds you. It's no economy, I'll admit that. At best we break even, not even counting the work that goes into it."

He thinks again and continues: "It's hard work. It's demanding. Sometimes I don't want to go out there. I'd rather read or watch TV. But I have to. The plants need me. That gives me a feeling of being useful. I get satisfaction out of it. When you work with your head all day, it helps you relax, putting your fingers in the earth. It gives a sense of reality. It does for me what I do for my clients."

Donna had the magic touch. She could violate every rule and the plants would smile and perform for her. They outdid themselves. They grew to extraordinary size and still retained flavor. Her peppers were big as buckets, unlike any others I ever tasted. I wish I could explain this. I cannot. I do not even have any theories about it. But I saw it; I swear it.

Donna was in her late twenties, single, lived in a room of a house owned by a married couple, and cared for their garden in exchange for rent. She was slender but had enormous energy and surprising strength. She was also attractive. She had a degree as an art teacher but was too restless and energetic for a classroom and did landscaping for a living. She had a hive of bees (the way I met her), an old pickup truck, and two dalmation dogs. One of the dogs was deaf; she taught it to obey sign language.

Donna knew intuitively about gardening what most of us have to learn from print, observation, and experience. She could grow anything. She merely dropped a seed into the earth and a plant fairly leaped forth bearing succulent fruit. She never seemed to have problems with plant diseases or pests. It was almost creepy.

I showed her an ailing cabbage in my garden. It looked pitiful. It had rejected everything I tried, like a patient turning its face to the wall, ready for the last rites. Donna bent down and examined the sick plant. She put a ring of dried manure around it, gave it water, and touched it gently here and there. The following day my sick cabbage was vibrant and healthy, its joie de vivre restored. How did she do it? Some mystic rite? A laying on of hands? An inborn talent? Supernatural intervention? What?

Donna was saving money to go to Texas to buy land. She had never been there but had "a feeling" she would like it. I thought it so much talk. I am used to dreamers. But after a couple of years she announced that she had saved money and was leaving for Texas.

She built a coffin-like box on top of the pickup to sleep in, loaded her few possessions, including the hive of bees and the dogs, and took off. Later she sent a letter and picture. She had bought a piece of land and built a small cabin. She had an extensive garden and was doing landscape work. She loved Texas.

Later we heard through a mutual friend that a flash flood had wiped her out. That did not stop Donna. She rebuilt her cabin on a higher part of the land, got another truck, and put in a new and larger garden. The friend reported that Donna's garden was a sensation in that parched land with its poor soil. No one could understand how she did it.

Donna came back to visit a couple of years later. She was vibrant as ever and seemed happy. She said her garden was doing "just fine." She was absolutely radiant. Dreams can come true. The Donnas of the world are the proof. Dreams and dedication are a powerful combination. Especially if you have the touch. The last we heard of Donna, she had married and had a child. She was still gardening.

Joe is usually described as a hardheaded businessman." Talk business with him and his eyes narrow. Talk politics and he grinds his teeth. Talk gardening and he mellows. His garden is his hobby, his love. Nothing is too good for hardheaded, tight-fisted Joe's garden.

He owns the biggest and most expensive rototiller made, and a second lighter one for cultivating. He had a hydraulic pump lift installed on the bed of his pickup. One spring he enlarged his garden and tilled in seventy bales of peat that cost a small fortune. He not only changes clothes when he goes into the garden, he changes personality. Business Hyde becomes Garden Jekyll.

Joe comes by his love for gardening honestly. He said his

father earned his living with a truck farm, taking produce into town and selling it, and young Joe helped. "My father didn't know anything about all these modern methods of gardening and farming. He just believed in putting enough manure into the soil. He never once had a soil test. All he did was work in manure, and he could grow anything."

Joe's eyes light up as he talks. He smiles. He laughs. There is no resemblance to Joe the hardheaded businessman. He is generous about giving away plants, produce, or advice. He is mellow except when discussing "those goddamned root maggots that ruined my broccoli." The eyes narrow. He grinds his teeth as he does when talking about Communists and bloodsuckers who won't work. He takes a hard line in the garden as well as out. Against garden pests he wages all-out chemical warfare. He has the same standards for his vegetables and his employees. By God, they better shape up or else!

"How are your peppers?" he asks. Joe is very big on peppers. I have noticed that many gardeners are partial to certain crops, like parents who have favorite children to whom they give special treatment.

"Terrible," I confess. "They haven't grown since I transplanted them."

He nods sympathetically, about the extent of his compassion for my kind of gardening. I am touched by his solicitude. Usually he chuckles when I recite my organic misfortunes, and he responds by proclaiming his chemical triumphs.

"Have you tried matches?" he asks.

"Matches?"

"Sure."

"What do you do—build a fire under the peppers? Give them a hot foot? Torch them?"

I think he is pulling my leg, but no, he is serious. He says I should get a book of matches, tear off the cover, and bury the matches lightly under the soil around the peppers. That feeds sulfur to the roots, he explains.

"You do it?" I ask.

"Sure."

"And it works?"

"I have great peppers."

I tell him I will try it.

"When the peppers start to flower, you should give them Epsom salts," he says.

It is too much. First a hot foot and now an enema!

"A teaspoon of Epsom salts to a quart of water," he adds. "Spray the entire plant until it is soaked. I think it's the magnesium."

"And you have already given them the match treatment?"

He nods.

As if I have not been humbled enough, he invites me to drop by his garden for some kale seedlings. "I've got more than I can use," he cries grandly. "I have to thin them. I've already given away a lot."

I suffer another organic indignity by going for some of his beautiful chemically ravaged kale seedlings to replace my pristine insect-ravaged plants. Joe advises me to place shingles around my tomato plants to shield them from the wind. He is surprisingly tolerant of the wind. He does not grind his teeth or narrow his eyes while discussing its perversities and treacheries. But he has no mercy for the pests attacking his beloved plants. He goes into a grand teeth-grinding slit-eyes fury. He is particularly enraged at the white cabbage butterflies. "Those sons of bitches!" he exclaims. "There's nothing you can do about them. . ."

Bret says he loves to garden but having to wear a net does detract a bit from the pleasure. He says it more with regret than resentment or anger. He also feels guilty about spending so much time in the garden when there is still so much to be done on their new home.

The cabin I built, where he lived when he went back to

school, is now his toolshed. It needs some work, he says. Porcupines gnawed on the plywood exterior to get at the glue. "I expect to get to it this year," he adds, looking somewhat harried as he considers all he has to do and so little time to do it. A garden does take time, I reply lamely.

Is there anything he can do to give me a hand while they are here visiting? he asks. I tell him that tomorrow maybe he will help me bring mulch in the garden. I piled it outside to let rain was out the salt. . . . "Why not now?" he cries. I am delighted although a bit startled. It is almost time for bed.

We go outdoors. The night air is cool. The moon is bright. We do not even need the floodlight on the house to see. The garden is still except for the insect chorus. There is only the moonlight, bright stars in a clear sky, shadows from the bean tripods against silvered soil, in the distance the soft murmur of the ocean, the poetry of a summer night.

I am especially pleased that we have these few minutes alone together, as well as welcoming the help. It seldom happens now. He is engrossed with his own life, his family, their new home, his career, his own friends, all of the demands on him. We have grown apart as we live apart and see little of one another. When we do infrequently get together it is as if we must start all over. Our conversation is largely perfunctory and superficial.

For any continuing relationship, whether of companions, friends, lovers, spouses, siblings, or parents and children, there must be continuity. We quickly lose track of the small swirls and eddies in the current of daily life that shape the texture and content of being. Letters take time and most people dislike writing. The phone better reveals mind than heart.

I live too much to myself. Bret, perhaps, because he is younger, is too much with others. Each of us is isolated in his own way at our respective stages of life. Now here we are, my son and I, alone together in the garden, between us so much shared past and yet almost strangers. There is just the moonlight and shadows, the stillness and pulsations of the ocean, and insect music on the night air.

At first neither of us talks much as we bring load after load of the wet thatch from the pile outside the gate. Then we begin to talk, of our lives, how things are with us. After a few minutes it is almost like the days when he lived at home, as a boy, and we were close.

He dumps another load of thatch, pauses, and says, "I was talking to a teenaged boy, a friend of ours, about things that are troubling him. I told him that he won't always think the way he does now, and I thought to myself how you used to tell me that and I didn't believe you. I thought I would always stay the way I was." He laughs softly. It is a pleasant sound. All of the intervening years between us have vanished.

He briskly strides off with the old wheelbarrow he gave me long ago. I look around the garden, now almost iridescent in the moonlight, with the long shadows, and it occurs to me that the garden has wrought another of its small miracles, as befits a pair of serious gardeners moving mulch by moonlight.

> *All admit that in a certain sense the several kinds*
> *of character are bestowed by nature . . .*
> —Aristotle

I used to drive by a plot that was prepared each spring for planting. The soil looked rich for Cape Cod, as if costly loam had been imported from elsewhere. Empty bags of fertilizer and bales of peat were strewn about. Tools leaned against the fence, suggesting no want of dynamic industry and good intentions.

After a few days rows of spinach, peas, and other spring crops poked green shoots through the earth, like advance troops awaiting reinforcements. Then nothing happened. Gradually weeds took over unopposed. The tools rusted against the fence. The garden died in its infancy.

Year after year the same little spring tableau took place, almost like a stage setting for an uncompleted play. I never saw or knew the gardener but suspect that in other areas of endeavor he or she failed to follow through and their personal life was largely a tangle of good intentions and unfinished projects overgrown by figurative weeds.

A certain type of person is attracted to the idea of gardening. There is the romantic notion of being self-sufficient and supplying the home table with food grown by their very own hands from their very own garden. This is a compelling notion for the susceptible. Often they buy expensive equipment and a fashionable shed to store the extensive paraphernalia. They happily pay outlandish prices for the newest, best, and biggest items featured in slick mail-order catalogues offered by entrepreneurs who bought their name from somebody else's list and will sell it to another; we have all become objects of commerce.

These would-be gardeners usually do prepare the soil and plant in the spring, "as soon as the soil can be worked," just as the experts advise. But the pioneering spirit that inflames them soon burns out. The garden reverts to weeds and desolation. By late fall, among the weeds, may persist a forlorn or ravaged cabbage that never made it, a diseased pepper or two, the pitiful misshapen remains of what tried to become an honest cucumber.

"To hell with it," says the exasperated gardener. "I'll have another go at it next year." Usually that is an end to it, although the person always refers to and thinks of himself or herself as a gardener. They may subscribe to gardening journals and newsletters. Often they are impressively knowledgeable about all phases of gardening. I know one who has not attempted a garden for twenty years but he is up-to-date on gardening developments and keeps his equipment at the ready. He always has the same explanation for not planting. "The soil is resting this year," he says.

Every garden has a unique blend of character and personality. Character is the physical makeup, its composition and fertility, the location, amount of sunlight, rainfall, and other amenities. Personality is largely conferred by the gardener, reflecting his or her own aesthetics, gardening know-how, energy level, techniques, intended use of the garden, and other individual and perhaps mysterious or imponderable forces.

Look at a garden carefully and you can tell much about the person who tends it. It becomes a kind of Rorschach test, often revealing more about us than we care to make public. We leave our fingerprints behind. Some gardens are exquisitely laid out, some mathematically planned, some a spontaneous jumble. Some are planted scientifically, others by whim or afterthought. Regardless of method, the odds are strong that the rest of the gardener's life follows much the same lines.

I critically study my own garden with dismay. I, too, am revealed. The perceptive observer would know that it represents minimal planning; happenstance and circumstance play a larger role than forethought or design. I do not recommend it as a way to run a garden or a life. I should get a grip on myself and reform but it is now late for that. Tolerance, I tell myself, like charity, begins at home, or at least in your own garden.

And so it criticized each flower
This supercilious seed;
Until it woke one summer hour,
And found itself a weed.
  —Mildred Howells

I have struggled all morning to contain an explosion of chickweed and purslane that resisted containment. Both are formidable garden warriors. They entangle their roots with those of the new carrots and it is easy to pull out baby carrots inadvertently along with the weeds. Rarely am I able to remove entire weeds. In a couple of days they are back, thicker than ever; weeding seems to give them new vitality and determination.

More unwanted growth awaits me each day. Purslane and chickweed are the worst; they are everywhere. Quack grass grows rampant among the rhubarb along the fence. There are dandelions, plantain, crabgrass, vetch, pokeweed, pigweed, nettle, and others. All volunteers, of sorts.

Weed seeds are in the manure and compost I use, in droppings of birds, blown in by the wind, and carried down by rain. Millions are in the soil itself. Each disturbance of the earth brings dormant seeds to the surface to germinate. The purslane and chickweed are so persistent that when weeded they need only touch the ground to recover. Let the least bit of soil cling to the roots and the plant resurrects itself. Chop up the roots and you have dozens or hundreds of new plants. Let them go to seed and the battle is lost. There is an adage: one year's seed, seven years' weeds!

I accidently left a closed cold frame over a bare patch of garden soil and the intense summer sun beat directly on the glass, creating a fiery buildup of heat inside, but still weed seeds in the earth germinated and grew into a thick tangle, the roots plunging more than a foot deep in search of water. Vegetables lack such hardiness and commitment. They would have failed to germinate or died as seedlings. Weeds know they have a job to do; they will not be denied.

I rather like weeds. I admire their spirit and pervasiveness. With their inherent toughness they are like many self-made people; they thrive on adversity. They are barbarians, untamed, relentless fighters. Weeds are survivors. They strike in a hundred places at once. Destroy one or a dozen and two dozen or two hundred spring up. Get rid of one variety and another takes its place. Or several. They never give up.

Tenacity and self-confidence are the great strength of weeds. They have been on earth hundreds of millions of years. After the sideshow of man is ended, they will probably still be around covering the mess we left behind, helping heal the wound we call civilization, preparing the way for the next drama to follow. Weeds should not be written about only by agronomists or whatever weed specialists are called, but by poets and philosophers as well.

Weeds are everywhere. They are universal. They cover blood-soaked battlefields, cemeteries, ancient trade routes, buried centers of commerce, and unknown cultures. They take over abandoned projects and failed dreams. They grow among the ravages of Appalachia, in Normandy, Jonestown, Hiroshima, and "Plimoth," Massachusetts. They grow in dried river beds and crusted clearings that were lush tropical rain forests. They are the first life to return to exhausted soils. They mercifully cover our mistakes and infractions of natural law. They are time's great eraser. They give absolution to greed, ignorance, arrogance, and folly.

A weed is more in the eye of the beholder than the object itself. Webster defines a weed as "a plant of no value and usu. of rank growth." Of rank growth? Probably. But no value? No value to whom? One person's weed may be another's flower, dinner, livelihood, or life-sustaining medication. Self-interest largely determines what is a weed. Weed extracts keep many people alive. Digitalis, a powerful heart stimulant and diuretic, comes from foxglove. A morning glory is a decoration on the trellis but a nuisance among the tomatoes or beans.

Crabgrass, a garden menace, was the first grain grown by man and is still used as cattle forage in the South. Chickweed, dandelions, and plantain are found in salads and cooked as greens, excellent sources of vitamins and minerals. Dandelions have been employed as tonic, laxative, wine, diuretic, and the roots ground as a coffee substitute.

Growths that we curse as weeds may have helped feed ancient man. They or their ancestors must have been among early plants that bound new soil particles together with their roots. They absorbed carbon dioxide and provided oxygen to help purify the atmosphere and probably had a hand in forming the essential ozone layer that protected fragile new growth and emerging life forms from the unshielded fury of the parent sun.

Many of today's weeds were brought to America by the Puritans and other early settlers who considered them indispensable as herbs, for food, and medicinal purposes. When no longer useful they escaped their garden confines and became wildly successful on their own, their status lowered to weeds— unwanted growth, the most commonly accepted definition of a weed. Today so-called weeds are found from coast to coast. Millions are spent yearly trying to control them.

In the United States there are 1,775 kinds of weeds, according to the Weed Science Society of America, more than half coming from Europe, Asia, and tropical America. They were brought intentionally and accidentally, in pockets and packets as seed for food crops, clinging to clothing or the fur of animals, hidden in ship ballast dumped on these shores, transported by wind and water, part of the restless earth migration of plants and animals. Most of our present food crops are tamed weeds.

Weeds are considered enemies because they compete with

more desirable plants for water and nutrients. They may crowd out or suffocate food plants, or even poison them. They can harbor pests and disease. They may grow tall to block out sunlight and keep vegetables from developing. Certain weeds can poison people, cause rashes and allergies. They can disrupt existing harmonies and habitats. Japanese honeysuckle, an aggressive import, will crowd out desirable native land growth. That beautiful menace, loosestrife, can take over wet areas.

The virtues of weeds are seldom sung. Their roots reach different depths to bring up nutrients used by other plants. Plunging weed roots searching for food and water break up subsoil, opening paths for worms and other soil organisms. They aerate the earth, enabling soil to "breathe" and water to penetrate deeply. They improve the soil's tilth and heart. Some weeds are used as insect repellents in biodynamic gardening. Others are brewed as "tea" or incorporated into compost to stimulate soil organisms. Farmer Bagley believed weeds, in moderation, had a place in the garden.

Weeds (by our definition) help feed millions of the world's hungry. They harbor not only pests but also their predators. A weed patch, unsightly by our cultural values, may be a rich habitat providing food and shelter for many of the creatures that share the earth with us. Wild asters and goldenrod, both weeds, provide my bees with the nectar and pollen that enable them to live, reproduce, and pollinate my garden. Weeds provide food for the wild bees and insects that make modern agriculture possible. They are a forgotten link in our dollar economy.

Many weeds have unappreciated aesthetic value. Even the lowly chickweed has an exquisite bloom, a tiny five-rayed flower once known as starwart. Most wild flowers are simply weeds with pretty faces to attract insect pollinators.

I am especially fond of bouncing bet, also known as soapwort and, in England, as London's pride because its fragrant flowers masked the gamey odors of Elizabethan London with its lack of sewers and infrequent baths. It has been used as a soap, bleach, water softener, tonic, and medicine for every-thing from syphillis to promoting perspiration.

The seeds were brought to America about 1600 by the col-onists. Later the plant was grown along inland canals as a ready source of soap for use on barges. It is said to be more fragrant at night than any other weed. *Green Immigrants* asserts that bouncing bet was so named because the flower suggested the backside of a laundress, with her numerous petticoats and skirts pinned up and bobbing ruff revealed as she scrubbed clothes in a tub of suds.

Clair Haughton, the author, also pays tribute to dandelions, asserting that "every part of this ancient herb is useful in our modern world—its leaves, its blossoms, its roots, the latex in its veins, the very air it exhales. Finally it offers our children a legacy of laughter. Generations have picked bouquets of its golden flowers, spent happy hours twisting curls from its stems, and told time on dandelion clocks by blowing at its fluffy seed heads. Perhaps the dandelion's most delightful gift to human-kind is centuries of laughter."

A more sinister view of the dandelion is presented by the late naturalist-philosopher Joseph Wood Krutch, who saw dandelions as representing a potential new direction in evolu-tion. Dandelions, he explained, belong to a group called "com-posites," which cast their seeds upon the winds without any kind of plant or insect union or help. "They proved that sex is *not* necessary." He called this "devolution," and speculated that it may represent progress for nature because it is more effi-cient. He further theorized that flowers may be on their way out and that other organisms, including man, ultimately may take this path. Sex, he said, may be a thing of the past.

The primary function of weeds is to keep the earth's surface from drying out and to prevent erosion. Weeds flourish where vegetables and flowers will not grow. Some seeds will grow in almost any soil, regardless of how poor it is. Weeds are sometimes called censors of the soil because they lose their viability sooner in bacteria-rich earth than in poorer soils, and indicate soil deficiencies. Certain weeds grow in soils lacking some nutrients or with an excess of others. There is probably no soil too impoverished to support some desperate growth called a weed.

In the garden I do not want weeds. Outside the garden I generally try not to interfere with nature's designs. In the garden I must work constantly not to be overwhelmed by nature's determination to have her way with weeds. They are her first line of defense. She tries to protect that which I do not want protected. We work at cross-purposes toward the same goal. We both want to cover bare soil but go about it in different ways with different ideas about what goes where. My way is more chancy. If I plant parsley I may or may not get parsley. I am sure to get weeds. My garden, to nature, is a passing annoyance.

I am never allowed to forget that a garden is an artificial contrivance imposed on nature. She does not tolerate this impertinence lightly. She resists my domesticated, pampered seeds arranged in neat alignments, cooperating reluctantly, by sufferance alone. Weeds are her primary protest, a rebuke for the arrogance a garden represents. Weeds wipe out not only gardens but faint-hearted gardeners as well, doing a bit of "weeding" on their own.

Weeds owe much of their success to the remarkable staying power of the seeds. Most remain viable for five years or more. Witchweed can remain dormant in soil for up to twenty years and will not germinate until after two. Many weed seeds must undergo freezing to germinate. An experiment was begun at Michigan State Agricultural Station in 1870. Seeds of twenty common weeds were buried in bottles and dug up and tested at five- and ten-year intervals. Thirty years later half of the seeds were still viable. After nearly a century three of the original twenty were alive.

In one study more than 158 million viable seeds were found in a single acre of land. A single witchweed can produce 500,000 seeds in a summer, mullein 250,000, pigweed more than 100,000. Seeds floating down an irrigation ditch numbered more than 1 million every twenty-four hours. Efforts at weed control have not been too successful. Weed killers, like pesticides, remain in the soil, sometimes for years, disrupting natural balances. Everyone is familiar with the herbicide Agent Orange used in Vietnam. It caused more lasting misery for people than damage to vegetation.

To wipe out weeds is like attempting to still the mighty pulse of the ocean or halt the silent beat of time. Weeds are forever. They may be agents of eternity itself. Science is unable to explain their longevity and persistence. A scholar calls it simply "genetic vigor," another name for the life force.

Vegetable seeds, unlike weeds, require pampering. Even with the best care they may fail to germinate or grow, as if they know they are thwarting nature's design and are reluctant to be part of such a scheme. Vegetable seeds dramatize a natural law: the perversity of all living things. Weeds obey a more powerful command: the will of all living organisms to survive and reproduce. Those two rules dominate every garden.

Everyone has seen a single weed, often crabgrass with its relentless creeping tentacles, growing through a hairline crack in concrete or asphalt. It is a fitting image, possibly a postscript, to a world being increasingly paved over. It is also a metaphor of the life force, nature reasserting herself in the mysterious scenario of life. Weeds may be censors of civilizations as well as of soils.

Who makes the ultimate decision of what is useless and must go among plants? Man has never yet succeeded in eliminating a single unwanted species of plant, as he has animals. Nature has abolished many plants. Nature alone decides what is useless or unwanted in the plant kingdom through the mechanism of natural selection.

The chickweed and purslane are more or less under control for the moment. I have finished weeding the carrots and onions. Both look deceptively weed free. Onions require special care because their shallow roots are so easily disturbed; they are extremely sensitive to weed competition. There is less disturbance if the roots are soaked before weeding.

I personally enjoy weeding, especially by hand. Working down close to the plants and soil seems more personal. Hoeing or cultivating with a tiller is mechanical and detached, the latter noisy as well. I particularly like to weed when I am troubled or have a problem. Perhaps it helps me get rid of the weeds in my own life.

Now 'tis spring, and weeds are shallow rooted;
Suffer them now and they'll o'ergrow the
garden.
                                        —William Shakespeare

I drive by John's garden, where it once grew, and now it is covered by weeds. John would never have tolerated weeds. They would have choked the "'tatoes." Weeds were like trees, a menace to be wiped out. There are many changes now but the weeds hold special poignancy. They are a reminder of the fragility and transience of all human endeavors. John was a kind of weed himself in a tidy, cultivated garden of growing conformity. He was, in the end, out of place, a symbol of a vanished past.

He was a neighbor of sorts. He lived at the foot of the hill and we were at the top. He was the first gardener I knew when we moved to Cape Cod. Knowing him did not come easily. Our first contact was abrasive. I knocked on his door, introduced myself, and asked if he could tell me where I could buy firewood. He glared at me. "No!" he roared and slammed the door. Welcome to the neighborhood!

John was, like his house, old and weather-beaten. Almost invariably he had a stump of a pipe clamped between toothless jaws. The pipe was always at a jaunty angle, suggesting a plump Popeye.

His speech was peppered with mysterious references to *her*, *she*, *he*, *him*, *they*, and *them*. No one had a name or point of reference. All of these indefinite pronoun personages seemed to be mixed up in his mind and indistinguishable in his speech. I was never sure who did what to whom or where. Usually John referred to "they," a who or which that emerged as an anonymous villain. Occasionally identification was aided with a slight nod of head and pipe, suggesting some indefinite compass point where the outrage occurred.

Before we became social I would walk past his place, to and from the marsh, on the lower dirt road. Around the house were piles of old lumber, doors, pipes, rusting washing machines, and other dump salvage. John later revealed that he had brought home the wooden doors to build a fence "so they can't gawk in here when they go by." I must have been one of the gawkers, a "they."

His garden was beside the house, adjacent to the road. It was huge. Usually he was working in it when we passed. He was in his late seventies but had amazing energy. Every year he enlarged the garden. Later I asked what he was going to put in it. The answer was typically laconic: "'tatoes." He had a fixation with potatoes. Most of that enormous garden was in potatoes. God knows what he did with them.

Behind the house was a steep embankment. John would take wheelbarrows of sand from the face, wheel it several hundred feet to the front of the property, and dump it over a slope adjoining the road. Day by day, year by year, the bluff became steeper, the garden larger, the road narrower. I always called "hello" when we passed. He was weeding the 'tatoes and pretended not to see or hear.

'Tatoes were not his only obsession or phobia. He also loved to cut down trees with a chainsaw. Not one tree remained on his property. Then he began ranging up and down the narrow dirt road whacking down every tree on both sides.

I expected explosive protest from the neighbors. Nothing happened. Not one word. That amazed me. I did not yet know how things are, or were, on Cape Cod. Before the new people came, bringing new ways with them, idiosyncrasies were considered a personal matter. Live and let live! If it does not kill you or cost you money, mind your own business.

All day, from my garden on top of the hill, I heard the whine of the chainsaw below. It was as if John had declared a blood vendetta against the trees. Evenings, after the chainsaw was sheathed for the day, I walked past his house. He was chopping away at weeds among the 'tatoes with his hoe. "Hello," I called. No reply.

There was a new stack of wood for the stove. Most people do not burn pitch pine in wood stoves because it causes heavy creosote buildup in chimneys. Creosote held no terrors for John. He later confided that he used one wood stove but had four more in the basement. "When everybody was taking theirs to the dump, I kept mine. I brought some back from there. You should never throw things away. You never know when they'll come in handy."

After we became social he revealed that when he built his house thirty years earlier there was not one pine tree between his lot and the bay. "Now you can't see anything. Nothin' but trees. They all grew up at once. They're no damn good. No use to nobody."

"What have you got against trees?" I asked.

He did not answer, the fate of most of my questions. He was four-square for progress. He would have liked the entire earth plastered over with asphalt and concrete.

I learned from others that John came to the Cape as a young man, first working as chauffeur and yardman for a wealthy family. Then he became a carpenter. Almost everyone on Cape Cod then was a carpenter or fisherman or both. After a few years he quit building. He did nothing except look after his garden and bring home castoffs from the town dump, the extent of his civic participation. I have no idea what he and his wife lived on. Many people here seem to make out without visible means of support. This was true even before welfare became a way of life.

John and his wife had a son and daughter. After the children left home he had a large addition put on the house but did none of the work himself. Why not? I asked. He gave me a long sideways look and puffed on his pipe, which was out. No answer.

I had heard that a cottage next to his house belonged to him. It was charming but had been vacant for years. It needed paint, the stucco facing was cracking, tattered blinds hung in the front windows facing the road. It looked forlorn and unkempt. The cottage was set back behind a row of trees that had somehow escaped the wrath of John's chainsaw. I asked why he left it vacant.

"It's hers."

That meant his wife. He never called her anything else. "But why doesn't she sell or rent it? Why just leave it empty?"

"I don't know what's in her head. She don't tell me nothin'."

Shortly after that, possibly as a result of our conversation, he went on a new rampage with the chainsaw. He cut down every tree around the cottage. Previously it had looked wistful and charming, if forlorn, as if it harbored a romantic secret. Now it looked barren and forsaken. The unshielded sun attacked it with new ferocity. Paint began to flake off. The blinds looked more shredded than ever. Even the foundation seemed to be sinking, as if in despair. With no shade, weeds began to appear.

One day an old car was parked in the weed-covered driveway. Soon the tires went flat. The body began to rust through. Weeds grew tall around the house and car. The derelict vehicle made the cottage look more abandoned and forsaken than ever. It was, in retrospect, almost an omen.

I return to the time before John made peace with me. The sand embankment behind his lot kept being dug out and getting steeper. The garden now invaded the road. John showed no sign of weakening in his determination to enlarge the garden. He still ignored my greetings, pretending not to see or hear me. But he obviously kept an eye on me. Our next-door neighbor, Polly, said she had mentioned to John casually that her bird feeder had disappeared from the yard. "Can that feller across the road be trusted?" he replied. I was still suspect.

John began to soften toward me after we met at a local trailer camp where the owner kept horses and we both went for manure. He drove an old red sedan with the back seat and trunk cover removed so he could fit in barrels of manure. I offered to help him load. He curtly refused. "I don't need no help!" He struggled with the heavy galvanized cans alone. I had insulted his Yankee pride; help is a sign of weakness.

Instead of backing off I charged recklessly forward. Would he like to help load my pickup and we could drop the manure off at his garden and not mess with the cans? He blinked as if I had slapped him and sucked noisily on his dead pipe. "I've got all I want," he said, got in the sagging red sedan, and creeped off.

A few days later I was working in the garden. Out of the corner of my eye I saw the red sedan drive by. I pretended not to see it. We had changed roles. John drove to the end of the road, turned, came back, and stopped. He ambled toward the garden. Without greeting, he pointed across the fence. "Tomatoes!" he said.

"Tomatoes," I replied.

"Where your 'tatoes?"

I was being tested. Had I said I did not grow potatoes he might have returned to the red sedan and driven off. I pointed toward the far end of the garden. He entered the gate and went to the potatoes. For several minutes he studied them, sucking on his pipe but saying nothing. Then he inspected the entire garden. His only comments were to name the vegetables under observation. I followed him. We stopped in front of the beets.

"Beets," he said.

"Beets," I replied. "Do you grow them?"

"She don't like them."

"I'll give you some."

"That girl across the street," he said.

"What?"

"She still live here?"

"Yes," I said, assuming he was referring to Dawn. She lived across the road with her two children.

"You ought to get rid of some trees," he said. "Too much shade. When I came here there wasn't no trees. You could see everybody. Ought to cut them all down."

He stayed a few minutes longer and departed with the beets. No thanks. No farewell. He simply turned, walked to his car, and drove off. That was it. Apparently I had passed inspection. He probably thought anyone who had a garden could not be all bad. Especially if they grew 'tatoes.

He would occasionally stop by and inspect the garden. We always had trouble communicating. I could never figure out the various shes, hers, hims, and theys. I did know that Polly was always "she."

One day John made an astonishing overture: "You want some leaves for your garden? Go see him and tell him I said to give you some leaves."

"Who, John?"

"Him."

"The road supervisor?"

He nodded. The pipe whistled. "Him."

Next he told me about a cache of seaweed to be had. Seaweed is always scarce. John was getting almost maudlin.

He became part of the pattern of daily life. We visited back and forth in our gardens. When I passed his place, walking to or from the marsh, he would stop his perpetual weeding to show me some new planting or innovation. Once it was a new watering system, operated from a shallow well he had drilled just for the garden and a pump salvaged from the dump. Black plastic pipe, also from the dump, snaked along the ground to water the 'tatoes to be grown in the new addition being built from the embankment.

The next home improvement was a fence made of the salvaged wooden doors. They were strung together vertically beyond the house hiding his dump treasures, a wild juxtaposition of sizes, colors, and styles. Passersby no longer could gawk in. John was proud of the door fence. "Maybe I'll grow vines on the outside," he mused.

We met frequently at the dump, at the manure pile in the trailer camp, in town. Once he arrived at my garden with a brown paper bag which he thrust at me. "'Tatoes," he announced, turned abruptly, and drove off as if embarrassed by so sentimental a gesture. Social had turned into something akin to friendship. Gardens will do that. I suspect he was lonely.

Each year John's garden became bigger. It now encroached on the drainage ditch beside the road. The sand bank was so steep that it threatened to collapse. Almost no trees remained on the lower road. I did no more than grumble to Peggy about John's depredations against the land. A bag of 'tatoes, some leaves and seaweed had neutralized me. Live and let live! I was becoming one of them.

The cottage next to John's house remained vacant. It was more rundown and dejected looking than ever. Suddenly I stopped seeing him in his garden. He no longer dropped by to visit. His garden looked neglected. There were weeds. One day I ran into him in town. He had lost weight. For once the pipe was not clamped between his jaws. He did not look him-self. He was pale and moved unsteadily. Neither of us men-tioned his health.

Several weeks later we met again in the market on Main Street. I was startled by his appearance. He was gaunt. The pipe was still missing. He was uncharacteristically pale. He had new false teeth that were incongruously white and shiny against his withered flesh. I asked how his garden was.

"Don't have none," he said, still smiling, the false teeth gar-ish in the fluorescent light over the meat counter. "Don't have no energy."

"Do you have tomatoes, John? Can you use some? I have plenty."

"He gave me some two days ago. Then she gave me some more yesterday." He nodded vaguely in the direction of these benefactors, or possibly where he last saw them. I had long ago stopped trying to identify the phantom people in his life.

"Then you don't need tomatoes?"

"Besides, I've got trouble down here." He pointed to his pants, now much too big for his shrunken frame. The waist was gathered in folds by an old leather belt several notches too long, the end dangling from the tarnished buckle.

"I'm passing blood," he said.

"Have you been to a doctor?"

He shook his head negatively, still smiling and revealing the white artificial teeth. I had trouble reconciling him with the John I knew. "Those fellers are all alike," he said.

He went into a lengthy tale about his old sedan that had stopped running the previous day. A mechanic installed a new alternator. John drove one block and the car stopped again. It turned out that the only problem was a loose wire all the time. In his mind, doctors and mechanics, "those fellers," were all the same. Incompetents and thieves. He seemed more con-cerned about his car than passing blood.

"You'll go to the doctor now, won't you?" I said.

Again he shook his head, still smiling, the false teeth gleaming in the fluorescent light. "No, I think I've lived long enough."

A few days later I drove past his place. He was sitting in a chair in the yard, staring at his former garden, now largely gone to weeds. He seemed to be in a reverie. At least he did not raise or turn his head. I was tempted to stop or call to him but sensed that it would be an intrusion. I wonder now what thoughts occupied his mind that day as he gazed at the desolate remains of his garden. He was still staring ahead as I drove away.

I saw him just once more. "She" suffered an accident and was hospitalized. John was too weak to care for himself. I was delivering Meals on Wheels and his name appeared on my list. I knocked on his door. After a long time he answered. It was shocking to see him. He was skeletal. Death was in his eyes but his spirit was undaunted. "I don't want that goddamned meal," he croaked. "Take it back!" He slammed the door, just as he had the first time I called to ask about firewood. Perhaps he felt humiliated to have me think he was on the dole. He must have gone hungry that day out of pride.

The next I heard he was dead. We had moved to a nearby town by then and I was busy building our new home. I had lost touch with him. Only by chance I learned of his death. I had missed the brief obituary in the local paper. I suppose it was like most obituaries; it told what he did, not what he was. Who really totes up the balance sheet of a life?

I drive by John's old place and am startled by the changes. The dirt road is now blacktopped to serve a nearby development. The enlarged garden has been pushed back for road drainage. The fence of salvaged doors is gone. The old house has been painted and the dump castoffs carted away. Nothing is left to gawk at. The ravaged embankment in back finally collapsed; a few weeds have taken root at the base.

The cottage next door had a brief revival. It was repainted

and the derelict car removed. In place of the car was a sleek power boat on a carrier. The torn blinds in the windows were replaced by bright curtains. There was even some landscaping. The cottage looked optimistic and cheerful. Pine seedlings were trying to replace the trees that John so conscientiously cut down. Then, suddenly at night, fire destroyed the cottage and there is now only charred earth where it stood.

I have a hard time absorbing these changes. I concentrate on what was once the garden. In my mind I see rows and rows of lush green 'tato plants and John whacking away with his hoe, pretending not to see or hear me. The vision passes quickly. No trace remains of the garden that once existed. Only the weeds.

> *Diseased Nature oftentimes breaks*
> *forth In strange eruptions.*
> —William Shakespeare

A small garden mystery awaits me: One of the tomato plants is drooping ominously, its leaves turning yellow. I quickly look at the others. They appear healthy. That is reassuring. The ailing plant offers many possibilities ranging from the insignificant to the fatal. The first question is what is the problem? Second, what is the remedy?

An odd thought crosses my mind: How would Richie Dunn have handled this crisis? Why do I think of him now after all these years? I have not seen Richie since I was a youngster in Kansas. It must be some kind of unconscious connection . . . the bottles, the catfish, those lush untroubled gardens . . .

But a more immediate concern: What to do about the sick tomato? I can get rid of it, treat it, delay and watch developments, ignore it. It could be as serious as fusarian wilt, the dreaded "yellows," a contagious fungal disease, or a simple lack of nitrogen corrected by a shot of fertilizer. It could be something in between, a combination of somethings, or several somethings at once. It could be temporary or terminal, manageable or unmanageable. What to do?

Disease is one of the biggest problems in gardening. Like pests and adverse weather, it is part of the game. A garden is always in some kind of peril; each plant has a multitude of enemies. They can come singly or in combination. Disease can bring pests and pests can cause disease. Weather can encourage or cause either or both. The various foes can kill outright, weaken, cut or delay production, or lead to distorted plants and produce. Nature is as ingenious in dispatching as in creating.

Read a list of all the threats and you may never take up gardening. Fortunately, most never materialize. Those that do usually have the grace to come singly, a couple or few at a time. Rarely do the same enemies strike in successive years or hit the same crops. Most can be controlled. Some cannot. Gardening, as noted before, is not for the frail of spirit. Neither does it require wild optimism or a perpetual stiff upper lip. Odds are good that seeds planted will grow and produce. Courage!

I never gave the problem of lurking threats great thought until I read a book on plant protection. It was unnerving. How does anything survive? A single tomato plant is subject to nine different pests and twenty-eight diseases were listed. I was lucky not to know this until I had grown tomatoes successfully for many years. Knowing too much can be as dangerous as knowing too little.

Experience teaches that chance plays a role in every garden. A Cornell University College of Agriculture bulletin states that: "Even the best cared for garden has problems. Some are inconsequential and often cannot be attributed to any fault of the gardener. Occasional plants suffer or even die from unknown causes. Adverse weather such as high temperature, too little or too much rain, and high winds can cause poor growth, blossom drop, and plant damage. . . ."

I take comfort in this. It gives scientific respectability to garden failure, at least to the role that chance plays. All of us are subject to forces over which we have little or no control. There are misfortunes that defy logic, analysis, and textbook cures. Each garden has its own eccentricities, secrets, and mysteries, just like the gardener in charge.

These garden unknowns may vary from year to year, month to month, week to week, and even day to day. From garden to garden. Even when everything is done by the book and conditions appear ideal, all known factors must come together at the right time in the right combination. And still, as Cornell Agriculture points out, there remains the element of chance.

Seed, soil, and weather must be right and compatible. Each crop must be treated individually, its specific requirements met for optimum growth. What works for one crop may not work for another. What works one time may not work the next. Gardening is that complex and unpredictable. Adversity is always at hand, always ready to strike, awaiting its moment. But the other side of the coin is the life force. Nature is not implacable. She will often negotiate. She destroys only to renew. Nature is rarely unreasonable. She, too, is pursuing self-interest.

I study my drooping tomato plant. What is the real wonder here? That one plant is ailing or that all the rest are healthy?

While still new to gardening I tried to learn the various diseases plants are subject to. It was a Herculean task and I soon gave up. Then I tried to memorize disease symptoms and their causes. That was more hopeless. Each symptom may have many possible causes. Even experts are often baffled, able only to say, "It could be . . ."

I finally settled for learning that there are three primary causes

of disease: unfavorable environment or physiological disturbances; fungal and bacterial ailments; and viral diseases. But
the same major obstacle remained: So many ailments have similar symptoms. My limited knowledge did not change the odds
of chance; it did not reduce the number or character of the
threats.

Nature invented an infinite variety of sorrows that can afflict
garden plants. The list includes such colorful and fascinating
names as blast, pink root, scab, leak, bitter rot, cracking, tip-
burn, damping off, black scurf, clubroot, blackleg, blight, sooty
mold, ghost spot, hollow heart, etc. The length and variety are
quite disheartening to the garden idealist and positive thinker.

I personally have not encountered most of these destroyers
but respect their menace. They are as sinister as they sound,
ready to strike if they are present and I falter. Almost every
crop can be attacked by many ailments. They can affect every
part of every plant—root, stem, leaf, flower, seed; they may
strike one, several, or all parts progressively or simultaneously.

I once kept files with illustrations that graphically portrayed
a melancholy procession of plant cankers, pustules, lesions, distorted roots, shrunken stems, stems girdled with black streaks
and leaking sticky vascular fluids, yellowed splotchy leaves,
greasy black foliage, mold, blotches, blisters, rotting fruit, etc.
They were morbid pictures. You would not want them on your
walls unless you have serious problems that go beyond the garden.

Most disease, once established, is irreversible, particularly
that caused by bacteria, fungi, and viruses. There is no choice
but to compost the afflicted member and let heat kill the pathogens. Better, burn it. Such plants must be removed promptly
before they infect their neighbors. That is the primary concern
with my ailing tomato. Is whatever it has contagious? Could it
wipe out the entire crop?

I never bothered to learn specific symptoms of most garden
diseases. There are too many symptoms, too many possible

causes for each symptom. Giving an illness a proper name does not reduce its menace once the threat is recognized. It is enough to determine that a plant is dying or too weakened to produce and should be dispatched at once.

As an aid in prevention it is helpful to know how disease is spread. Fungi are transmitted by wind and other agents, the plantlike spores swept from plant to plant, even by hard splattering rains. Bacteria and viruses are carried by human hands, insects, garden tools, and machines; smokers can convey bacterial disease from tobacco on their hands. Viruses can be carried in seeds, ready to invade plant cells and work their mischief.

We are warned repeatedly that pathogens are more easily spread about on wet foliage, urged to buy disease-resistant seed varieties, get rid of afflicted crops at once, disinfect tools and machines used on ailing plants, rotate crops, and practice garden sanitation to discourage weeds and disease-bearing insects.

Gardeners are advised to take specimens of ailing plants to their local county agricultural extension service for analysis. But sometimes it is difficult for the most knowledgeable agents to examine a dead specimen and assign a specific cause of death. It may not be that important anyway; no death certificate is needed. An autopsy is only of academic interest in most cases. The specific reason for many plant fatalities can never be determined. R.I.P.!

Insects are probably the primary vectors of disease. They may carry pathogens or wound plants so disease organisms can enter the exposed tissues. An average garden harbors a rogue's gallery of disease-bearing pests. Some are specialists in their choice of plants. Others, as we know, attack several crops. Aphids dine on just about every garden vegetable. Not all pests directly transmit disease organisms; some are content merely to eat the leaves or suck out the juices, weakening the plant so disease can take hold.

These garden foes themselves face a formidable enemy: the so-called balance of nature. An estimated 90 percent of common garden pests are subdued by natural controls—weather, diseases that cut them down, plant defenses, or their own predators.

Biological warfare accounts for most pest mortality. A frog, with its nondiscriminating appetite, will eat 10 pounds of insects during a single summer month, devouring four times the capacity of its stomach every 24 hours. Lady beetles consume 50 plant lice, or aphids, a day and lay 1,500 eggs in two months; their larvae dine on 25 aphids daily, along with other insect eggs.

Other players in this lethal garden tableau include daddy longlegs, also known as "harvestmen" because of the time of year they appear; praying mantids; parasitic wasps; spiders; and birds. A flicker breakfasts on 2,000 ants. A yellow warbler may devour 10,000 aphids in a day. A barn swallow can dine on more than 1,000 fleas, mosquitoes, and other insects per day. Many birds eat their weight in various insects daily. It is really a pretty rough world out there; everybody seems to be eating somebody else. We glibly speak of the balance of nature. But eating one another is about what it comes down to.

I finally decide that my sick tomato plant is a victim of the most innocent disease category—an unfavorable environment, or physiological imbalance, as the experts have it. It does not have the morbid symptoms usually associated with viruses, bacteria, and fungi. I am also inclined toward this theory because of the recent erratic weather, a long rainy spell followed by intense heat which could stress plants. If the afflicted tomato was already weak from some other trauma it would have less resistance than its fit neighbors to adverse weather.

Another possibility is that it is responding to not getting the right nutrients or not in the proper proportion; those yellowed leaves could be trying to tell me something. Again, a weakened plant would respond more dramatically to duress than its stronger kin. Yellowing leaves are a symptom of nitrogen (N) shortage. Phosphorus (P) and potassium (K), the other two major soil elements, have their own deficiency symptoms.

Trying to diagnose plant ailments by NPK symptoms alone can be tricky even for the skilled. No one element may be wholly responsible. Often the cause of poor growth, discolored leaves, or other symptoms is complex and no single factor wholly responsible.

The problem may not be in the soil at all but caused by cold temperatures, hot winds, drought, too much rain, or mechanical injury. Any or all of these and other insults and injuries can produce symptoms similar to those of soil deficiencies. Insects and soil-borne diseases also may disrupt a plant's normal functioning to give the appearance of nutritional disturbance; many unrelated problems mimic deficiency symptoms.

Even that is not an end to it. Cornell cautions that poor growth may be traced to oddities such as leaking gas mains, lack of sunlight, drainage problems in the subsoil, or even invading large tree roots. Bafflements and deceptions abound in the best ordered and most conscientiously maintained gardens.

So what to do about my ailing tomato? I could give it a nitrogen cocktail in the form of manure tea and see if it perks up. But what if I am wrong in my judgment? Any delay could cause problems. The plant could be in the early stage of something serious, just as a person may feel rotten or look frail before displaying morbid symptoms. But I dismiss that. A garden has troubles enough without paranoia.

My experience is that once a plant is weakened, as this one obviously is, it does not develop or produce normally; it also may invite pest attack or invasion by pathogens which could infect other plants. I have plenty of other tomatoes, plus volunteers standing by. Why take chances?

Reluctantly I pull the drooping patient from the earth and compost it. A postmortem reveals no problem with the roots. None of the terrible things that could have happened down there out of sight took place. At least not so far as I can determine. Into the bin it goes. Problem resolved. Mystery remains.

Once more I think about Richie Dunn. Did he ever have to deal with a sick tomato? I doubt it. I knew Richie when we lived in Kansas one summer. No one called him anything but Richie. Everyone liked him. He was black, very old, without teeth, deeply wrinkled, and gray. He was bent almost double with rheumatism. He never complained although he must have been in pain. He asked the world for nothing, took little, and gave much. He was always smiling and cheerful.

Richie and his wife, Emma, whom he called, for reasons unknown to me, "old high engine forehead," lived in a shack near our house. Between the properties he kept his garden, an unfenced lush oasis of corn and almost every known vegetable.

The corn towered over my head. Richie sold two dozen ears for a quarter and invariably threw in an extra. This might have been personal gallantry, good public relations, a neighborhood marketing strategy, his kind heart, or some reason known only to him. It was wonderful corn: sweet, tender, never a defective ear or worm.

Nothing Richie Dunn grew was blemished by insect, disease, or mysterious cause. He would not have known the meaning of soil deficiency or imbalance. NPK would have been a foreign language. That Kansas earth, speaking its own language, was rich and black, once virgin prairie with topsoil two feet deep. The only fertilizer Richie ever applied was the occasional extra catfish he caught in the nearby river. In parched Kansas every moving body of water, regardless how insignificant or apologetic, is a river; even dried-up baked stream beds are rivers.

Perfection was not the only unusual feature in Richie Dunn's garden. On his nearby fruit trees, which produced magnificent cheeries, peaches, and apples, hung unexpected ornaments—whisky bottles filled with water. The bottles dangled from strings tied around their necks. Cars driving down the adjacent highway would slow and almost sail off the road as startled drivers ogled the sight of trees festooned with dangling whisky bottles that looked almost like strange growing things.

Why did Richie Dunn never have blight, rot, pustules, lesions, mold, splotches, blotches, blisters, pests, problems with the weather, compacted earth, soil imbalances, seeds that failed to germinate or that produced sick plants, uncooperative or hostile microbes, viruses, or fungi, physiological disturbances, and all the rest? I ponder this as I inter my failed tomato.

Droughts that decimated other gardens passed Richie by. His crops were impervious to that blazing sun and searing Kansas heat. What was the answer? What was his secret? I refuse to believe it was the catfish fertilizer or chance alone. I prefer to think it was the whisky bottles.

Somewhere deep within his unconscious, he understood the hexes and voodoos that bedevil all gardens, those of scientists and artists, novice and experienced. Those bottles dangling from fruit trees, in that baked land of a long-ago summer, neutralized or repelled the evil spirits and unknown and unnamed adversities that vex Cornell's experts and hover over every garden, waiting to strike and overwhelm art and science alike.

> I want live things in their pride to remain
> I will not kill one grasshopper in vain
> Though he eats a hole in my shirt like a door.
> I let him out, give him one chance more.
> Perhaps while he gnaws my hat in his whim,
> Grasshopper lyrics occur to him.
> —Vachel Lindsay

Morning is the best of all times in the garden. The sun is not yet hot. Sweet vapors rise from the earth. Night dew clings to the soil and makes the plants glisten. Birds call to one another. Bees are already at work.

234 · WILLIAM LONGGOOD

This is a time to inspect the latest growth. A time to pull a few weeds and gather ripe vegetables. There is sweetness in the air, the sound of insects, a soft rustling of wind bearing the salt tang of the sea.

I like to get into the garden every day during the growing season, and even in the winter when possible. I feel a loss of continuity otherwise. In only a couple of days during the growing season a garden can get away. Weeds take over. Vegetables get too large to be edible. Insects multiply and do irreparable damage. Disease can start and spread. Plants may suffer for want of water or attention. Any number of things can go wrong. Even a brief daily inspection prevents many problems. Not visiting the garden every day is like not seeing a friend regularly and losing contact with what is going on in his or her life.

The first stop of my morning inspection tour is the spider who lives in the cucumber cage. His web is in the center, among the climbing vines, supported by long, stout silken threads like guy wires. The web would be almost invisible among the leaves were it not for pinpoints of dew that glisten in the morning sun. I have to be careful when gathering cucumbers not to disturb the spider or damage his web. He is, after all, a desirable guest, or tenant.

My spider—I have become possessive about him—is still asleep in the center of his web. At least he appears to be asleep, although he may be only resting, waiting for breakfast to show up, or even digesting his last meal. Many careless passersby are ensnared in the lethal gossamer trap, a procession of unlucky grasshoppers, beetles, flies, moths, butterflies, bees, and wasps, pests and allies alike; he too, is not discriminating in his tastes.

The spider methodically wraps his helpless victim in silken threads until it looks like a mummy. He casually injects venom into the creature to dissolve its internal organs and after leisurely sipping the juices he casts out the lifeless hulk and awaits the next meal.

I admire the delicacy and beauty of the web, the elegant efficiency of this garden executioner, despite the toll of my bees and friendly wasps. I also respect his life-style. I assume he is a male, living a carefree bachelor life, because of the late hours he keeps, sleeping away most of the day, and his rather untidy housekeeping, often leaving bits and pieces of his meals stuck to the web. He is missing a leg, suggesting a misfortune in a sexual encounter, possibly driving him into bachelorhood. He is lucky to have escaped with his life and gets about quite well with his remaining seven legs. That is one more than insects have to start with; even handicapped, he (an arachnid) is a leg up on them.

I have read that male spiders are smaller than females, less aggressive, especially in sex, not so ill-tempered or treacherous. The male is said to be less conscientious than the female in spinning and maintaining his web. I am not aware of any imperfections in design or construction, not being an expert in such matters, but have noted a small tear that goes unmended. He seems content enough with what he has, an enviable trait.

When not sleeping or resting in the sun he occasionally takes a stroll as if to check out the neighborhood and stretch his remaining legs. He never seems to go beyond the cucumber cage itself, as if believing that your web is your castle or, if he is a philosopher, living the axiom that the longest journeys can be taken without leaving home.

I have become fond of my spider tenant. We live harmoniously. I consider him an excellent neighbor and companion. He is never in arrears, paying his rent by disposing of pests. He never complains about the accommodations or intrudes on my privacy. He does not bid me to have a good day, tell me to take care or think positively. He does not furtively tap into a computer my personal life or finances. He does not have a phone-answering machine or try to sell me insurance. He does not discuss politics or religion. He does not debase the environment and takes only what he can use. He is a welcome addition to the garden and my life.

I often look at the spider in his web and wonder what, if anything, is on his mind. Much has been written of late about cognitive animals. Do they think? If so, what, and how? Is it thinking as we know it, considering possibilities and making choices? There is no clue from my spider; he seems implacable.

Is he really asleep, dozing, or, possibly, observing or contemplating the pageant of life around him, preferring to be a spectator rather than take an active role? Are his dreams, if any, of fat beetles, juicy grasshoppers, and passionate, passive lady spiders? What thoughts may occupy that little spider brain as he basks in the sun's early warmth, unaware of my presence, or indifferent, without fear, as I check him out on my daily rounds?

Spiders are among the more fascinating creatures in nature. They represent some 400 million years of evolution, making them one of Earth's earliest inhabitants. Thus, my companion is of an old and distinguished line. Spiders and birds are considered the most effective natural controls of insects. I consider myself lucky that my spider took up quarters among the cucumbers, despite the loss of an occasional bee or wasp.

Spiders are widely feared but, in fact, are shy and rarely bite people; the venom of most spiders has little effect on warm-blooded creatures. Only six of some three thousand known types of spiders can harm humans, among them the brown recluse and the notorious black widow. My spider is not one of the dangerous ones, so I have nothing to fear from him.

Spiders are said to have the largest brain for their size of any invertebrate, so I do not consider it unreasonable to speculate that my spider has a few thoughts, or even insights, as he observes life from among the cucumbers.

My spider is a common garden type, bearing the generic name orb spider, the kind most people are familiar with. He anchors his web from one side of the metal cage to the other, but any other supports would do as well, and stations himself in the center of the web; this is known as the "free zone," away from the sticky filaments that trap his victims.

About half of one fly a day is said to supply sufficient energy for daily web building and maintenance but I am not able to verify this. My spider appears to live for the day, never putting anything aside for the future. If this seems improvident it also suggests that he is content to live for the moment or hour and let tomorrow care for itself. He also knows that if things get bad enough he can eat his web and respin it the following day, a kind of crisis management that I hope my spider is spared.

A web is all-important for a spider. It is home, source of food, and means of finding mates. A spider is almost blind, having only eight dim eyes compared to some 6,300 in each of a bee's two compound eyes, so he must largely sense the world rather than see it. Tiny hairs covering the entire body enable him to feel the slightest vibration of the web. When I rummage among the vines for cucumbers it must feel like an earthquake but I assume my spider accepts this as the price of his tenancy; certainly he never protests.

Most spiderwebs look more or less alike to the uninitiated but they are said to be as individual as fingerprints. Each spider has its own unique method of forming its web, a kind of creativity. One spider can be told from another by the way it spins and joins the threads. This has been established by computer studies on the thousands of intersecting points in a single web. Each web is a small masterpiece by a skilled craftsman. Spiderwebs may have been the inspiration for the earliest cities, with their central hub, concentric circles, and avenues and boulevards radiating from the hub.

The size and complexity of the web are determined by the amount of silk available, which depends on the food supply. This must take a bit of planning and problem solving, no great challenge, I should think, for the brainy spider. I never actually caught my spider spinning, although I peered in often, hoping to see him making a patch or putting on an addition. As I noted, he did not appear to be an overachiever or even grabby, for that matter.

The number and strength of the threads are largely adapted to the type of prey expected. A finer web, with more closely spaced threads, is needed for flies or mosquitoes. Coarser and stronger strands, widely spaced, are for grasshoppers and larger, more vigorous game. Some spiders in the tropics spin webs so strong that they are capable of catching birds. My spider spun the most flimsy and delicate of webs, suitable for only small game and his modest aspirations.

Spiders can spin as many as seven different types of silk for different purposes. No single spider can form all seven but all are said to spin at least three. The silk is formed in glands in the abdomen and dispersed as threads through spinning organs known as spinnerets. The silk is a protein that hardens when exposed to air. The threads are so elastic and strong that they are used in optic and surveying instruments and have other industrial uses. So far as I know, my spider was never in the work force.

A spider, prudently, never moves without leaving an attached safety line behind. If he falls he simply reels himself back. The finest silken threads are used by young spiders, shortly after birth, as a means of travel. Millions have been seen floating down with these flimsy filaments; possibly my spider arrived by this method.

Some spiders are predatory, stalking their food. One, forgoing a web, uses a sticky lasso or bola-like glob on the end of a line which he hurls to trap victims. Orb spiders do not go in for this type of thing. They are passive hunters, content to let prey come to them. By the intensity of the web vibrations they seem to know what they have snared. A bee, because of its stinger, is dangerous and may be left until it is has exhausted itself struggling to escape. A fly poses no threat and can be dealt with promptly. The victim may be wrapped in silken threads, a spider form of food preservation, and left for dining later.

Courtship for a male is a perilous undertaking, as my spider possibly discovered. If he goes seeking a mate, he remains discreetly in the web parlor of his intended, tentatively plucking the threads, as if saying, "Is your husband home? . . . Is it safe? . . . Are you in the mood?" He is skittish with good reason.

The female is not to be trusted. She will sometimes lure a suitor, exciting his lust with a false display of receptivity, and suddenly lunge and devour him, making the unlucky fellow her dinner instead of the father of her children. Male spiders, like their counterparts among all species, including humans, perform various antics to attract attention and create interest; lust has many expressions but a common goal.

Even if the female gives the proper response her suitor risks all. She may change her mind, consider his technique flawed, or suddenly feel the need of a snack. Ardor may turn abruptly into a fatal embrace. The male spider does not appear to fear or flinch from these hazards. His sizable brain does not seem to serve him well in amorous adventure; that, too, is hardly unique to spiders.

If the act is successfully consummated the male beats a hasty and well-advised retreat. Behind he leaves a sack of sperm that the female utilizes at will, sometimes long after the mating takes place. This gives the female time for second thoughts, one of nature's more inspired ideas.

A female can lay up to three thousand eggs but the average

is closer to a hundred. She can give birth any time of year. Most orb spiders, if all goes well, live about a year but that takes a bit of luck, a commodity not always in great supply.

My particular spider remained with me for several weeks over the summer, living his bachelor life. He was a handsome fellow, black with strikingly beautiful yellow markings on back and belly. There was no suggestion that he was impressed with his appearance or concerned with his image. He did not look the least sinister or display hostility or animosity for my kind.

He never seemed to resent my foraging for cucumbers. He never moved or appeared to be distracted from any reflections or meditations he may have been engaged in. I tried to interrupt or disturb him as little as possible, respecting his privacy and presence as he did mine.

We had an undeclared pact of live and let live, each of us going his own way. He moved with grace and speed when necessary, not impeded by his missing leg. He appeared well adapted to his life situation, which I consider an admirable trait; his life and past otherwise remained his secret.

My spider lived in his web among the cucumbers until fall when a visitor from the city went out to look over the garden while I was getting dressed. I followed him out a short time later. He looked triumphant, crying, "I found a big spider in the cucumbers. But it's all right. I killed it."

I looked at the cucumber cage. Both spider and web were gone. Later the visitor left and I went about my chores.

Now I am terrified at the Earth, it is that calm
  and patient,
It grows such sweet things out of such corruptions,
It turns harmless and stainless on its axis, with
  such endless succession of diseas'd corpses,
It distills such exquisite winds out of such infused
  fetor,
It renews with such unwitting looks its prodigal,
  annual, sumptuous crops,
It gives such divine materials to men, and accepts
  such leavings from them at last.
                                                    —Walt Whitman

On a fall day a few years back I was driving my old Jeep pickup when I saw an elderly couple raking leaves. I introduced myself and asked what they did with the leaves. The man pointed to an embankment and said, "Throw them over there."

"Have you been doing that long?" I asked.

"Years and years," he said.

"Then what do you do with them?"

"Don't do nothin'."

"Do you want them?"

He looked at his wife for guidance.

"What do you do with them?" she asked suspiciously.

"Use them in the garden," I said. "For compost."

"Are you one of those organic gardeners?" she asked, as if encountering a new and suspect species.

I never feel comfortable when described that way. It sounds as if I belong to some kind of cult or club. Rather than make an issue of it I said I guessed I could be called that.

The couple hesitated, then conferred. They had an obvious dilemma. The worthless suddenly had value. Was it not crazy to give away something of value? After lengthy deliberation she said I could take all the leaves I wanted but not to leave too big a hole where they had been. Over the next few days I removed several loads of leaves. Those under the top layer were beautifully composted into rich crumbly leaf mold. Black gold! Broken-down leaves are one of the most valuable additions to compost; they contain up to 5 percent nitrogen along with other minerals and improve soil texture.

I kept asking the woman if I was taking too many leaves. At first she said, "Take all you want." Then she started asking questions. How do you make compost? What does it do? Why don't you just use bought fertilizer from the feed-and-grain? I tried to answer her questions honestly. With each forthright reply I could see that beautiful leaf mold slipping away.

I was forking leaves into the truck when the woman walked over and asked me to look at her garden. We passed several small cottages. She explained that every summer she and her husband moved into a converted chicken coop on the property and rented their house, along with the cottages, to "summer people."

"That's how we get along," she said. "That and the garden. My husband keeps wanting to sell the cottages and move to Florida but I tell him to forget it. They're the goose that laid the golden egg. Some of them have been coming back for ten years or more. They're like family. But I don't like to get too friendly with them. Then you can't raise the rent so easy."

We reached a tiny plot of ground behind the main house. "That's the garden," she announced. "You think that compost would help?"

I assured her I thought it would. The garden was little more than dead sand. I marveled that anything could grow in it. But I recall an agriculturalist in Israel, in the Negev, telling me that anything can be grown in any medium, even rocks, "if you have enough chemicals and a little water." The woman said she did not take much care of the garden anymore as she once did. "I'm getting too old. My husband don't care about it. He just likes to sit and watch TV."

I told her that I did not like to take without giving something in exchange. I would be glad to turn her garden and dig in some leaf mold. She nodded and, without expression, said, "That's all right."

I spaded the garden, which was not much of a chore, dug in as much leaf mold as it could handle, and added lime to counteract the acidity of the leaves. When I went to report that I was finished, she called from another room, "That's all right."

The following summer I dropped by several times with garden produce. Each time the woman or her husband accepted it with identical words: "That's all right." Once I asked her how the garden was doing. "It's all right," she said.

I would like to report that the couple started a compost heap, using their leaves, and lived organically happy ever after. But they went right back to throwing the leaves over the embankment. I was never very successful in enlisting converts to my various causes. I never proselytized very hard. I was never convinced that what worked for me would work for others. Each of us, it seems, must find salvation in his or her own way.

It is easy for me to link salvation and compost. Compost has an almost mystical quality. It is made up of anything that is or was alive and is biodegradable—straw, spoiled hay, grass clippings, animal remains, manure, garbage, flesh, table scraps, etc. A compost heap represents immortality. Nothing dies as such. All living things complete their cycle and return to the pool of life. There is neither beginning nor end, only the inexorable turning of the great wheel: growth, decay, death, and rebirth.

The history of the earth is written in a single handful of fertile soil. It is the culmination of countless natural forces converging to form the organic cover that sustains the fragile web of life. It is the story of creation itself, a microcosm of the parade of minute forms and organisms that hacked at solid rock to transform it over hundreds of millions of years into the rich

humus that produces the food we eat and makes possible the
oxygen we breathe. Soil is the only true capital we have. We
have a hard time remembering that money is merely a symbol
of wealth. The only real bankruptcy is an exhausted soil no
longer able to sustain life.

Soil is a mixture of minerals, organic matter, oxygen, and
water inhabited by a living community. It swims and breathes;
it is alive. It is a working union of untold trillions of particles,
each encased in an invisible film of water, each a tiny world in
itself dependent on the other minute worlds surrounding it.
Everything is in balance, all units interacting in a physical,
chemical, biological interchange, soil, air, water, plants, and
animals composing a great symphony of mutual need and
assistance.

Who and what populates this world of darkness in the top
few inches of earth? Fertile soil is an interlocking rich ferment
of yeasts, molds, fungi, algae, bacteria, viruses, actinomy-
cetes, amoebas, protozoa, and other microorganisms, many
bearing strange names and exhibiting odd behavior, all dwell-
ing in some kind of harmony or accommodation, offspring of
the original settlers and architects of soil, helping produce
enzymes and acids that build new soil.

They range in size and shape from amorphous dots to weird
convoluted forms seen through a microscope as balls, rods,
corkscrews, and indescribable configurations. Some multiply
at a fantastic rate, living less than a half hour and dying to
enrich the earth with their bodies. Peter Farb, author of *The
Living Earth*, observed, "We live on the rooftops of a hidden
world."

Helping cultivate the subterranean universe of soil are myriad springtails, millipedes, mites, maggots, nematodes, fierce
shrews, beetles, moles, ants, spiders, solitary bees, wasps, and
earthworms, the latter known to Charles Darwin as indispensable builders of soil. Some soil inhabitants are predators, almost

all are prey. Some assist others to live. It is a world of symbiosis, mutualism, commensalism, and parasitism.

The various creatures and organisms loosen the soil so it can breathe and water can flow among the particles, enabling the inhabitants to perform their vital chores. About half the space in our underground metropolis is open, occupied by air and water, providing the dampness necessary for the work to continue. The soil community forms the base of the so-called biotic pyramid that supports all life above.

Each soil organism is a specialist in breaking down organic matter so it is available to plants. Together they form what amounts to a marvelously complex miniature factory. Here the essential work of life takes place. Unusable nitrogen is processed so it can be "drunk" by the probing roots to feed the plants above. Carbohydrates are broken down and digested for energy to synthesize cell tissues. Dissolved rock forms vital mineral salts.

Step by unseen step, miracle by miracle, the organisms of earth build and enrich their habitat, which we employ for our use. There is constant exchange between organic and inorganic, chemical and biological, life and death. Here we have the greatest wonder of all, that dead matter becomes the stuff of life. Nature recognizes no boundary between life and death.

Soil, air, and water are never separated. They work together in an unending interchange, a great symphony of mutual need and aid. Four chemical elements, lifeless by themselves, make up the bulk of all living matter: carbon, hydrogen, oxygen, and nitrogen.

Dr. Barry Commoner gives a lyrical description of how these four elements enable us to live: "They move in great interwoven cycles in the surface layers of the earth, now a component of the air or water, now a constituent of a living organism, now part of some waste product, after a time perhaps built into mineral deposits or fossil remains." Our lives end. The matter

246 · WILLIAM LONGGOOD

of which we are composed goes on forever in different forms, perhaps in different bodies, in different lives. Atoms that are a man today may have belonged in the past to a cockroach, a bird, a worm, a shell, a tree, a grain of sand.

> Observe this dew-drenched rose of Tyrian gardens
> A rose today. But you will ask in vain
> Tomorrow what it is; and yesterday
> It was the dust, the sunshine, and the rains.
> —Lucretius

Chlorophyll forms in leaves. Photosynthesis fuels plants. Algae bloom in ponds. Lichen, moss, and fungus grow on rocks and earth. Yeasts and molds float in the air. Drifting spores seek anchors. Spat attaches itself to shells. Seeds split and take root. Sperm and egg make union. Ovule receives pollen from stamen. Rain falls, snow melts, winds fuel weather. The earth flowers and fades.

Viruses and bacteria promote health and disease. Soil organisms break down organic substances into humus and make nutrients available to plants. Galaxies of microbes perform their mysterious rites. Atoms split and reform. In the sea minute plankton are eaten by fish, which are eaten by larger fish and are, in turn, themselves eaten in an ever upward progression as the pyramid narrows to the top where man positions himself, laying waste and wanting.

Compost is nature's own invention for recycling her spent energies. It is the great driving force of soil and life. It is to these restructured organic wastes and discards that soil looks for its own food and renewal.

The gist of organic gardening is that life cannot be bought in a paper bag. That was the essence of Sir Albert Howard's experiments that led to organic gardening, which is based on the use of compost. Sir Albert was a British subject doing agricultural research in India in the early 1900s. He was disenchanted by the destruction of soils from the use of chemical fertilizers, soil and erosion, and the spread of disease among plants and animals.

He found that when he grew grains as the Indian peasants did, in soil enriched by plant and animal remains, cattle rarely contracted hoof and mouth disease. He became convinced that the ills of soils and animals had common cause in the "NPK mentality."

Soils, he held, were unbalanced by chemicals and starved for organic nutrients. He believed that the illness of plants and animals was their protest. Compost became his medium of returning to the earth the nutrients taken from it. His was a revolutionary message: Feed the soil, not the plant.

Sir Albert held that NPK fertilizer "mined" soil by using up organic matter with its microorganisms and trace minerals without replacing them. Soils became progressively dry, crusted, and subject to wind and rain erosion. Plants produced as much bulk as ever with only three major soil components, NPK, but their composition was changed. They lacked their former resistance and were attacked increasingly by disease and insects. This led to ever heavier doses of NPK and pesticides. The soil was not only starved but poisoned as well, a progressive debasement of the earth.

The agricultural establishment has been slow to accept the findings that brought Sir Albert knighthood. An exception was Dr. William Albrecht, former chairman of the department of soils at the University of Missouri School of Agriculture. He demonstrated with experiments that by increasing soil fertility it was possible to give plants 100 percent protection from insects without use of sprays. At the same time adjacent plants grown in infertile soils had 100 percent attack.

He observed that protection against disease and insects begins in the soil where the "lowly microbes" produce substances which are moved up through plants, to animals and to man at the top of the biotic pyramid. Instead of poisonous sprays to protect plants, he advocated restoring fertility to the soil. He testified before a congressional committee investigating the use of cancer-causing chemicals in foods that he believed many diseases in humans could be traced to deficiencies in soil where their food was grown.

Raw organic matter is converted into compost by a series of specialists, one wave of microorganisms taking up where the last left off. Fungi break down the tough woody tissues of cellulose and lignin, then bacteria move in, different ones doing different jobs. The pile decreases in size and heats up. When it cools, insects and burrowing animals, including the invaluable earthworms leaving their rich castings behind, take over.

The pile is composed of successive layers of vegetable matter for carbon, manure for nitrogen, soil with its microorganisms, (usually in that order), and just enough water to moisten the whole thing. Sir Albert made piles six feet wide, ten to thirty feet long, and five feet high. Mine are more modest.

The first time I made compost I could not believe it would work the way Sir Albert described. But, sure enough, after a few days it was too hot to stick my hand in. A properly made pile generates about 160°F within days and then settles down to around 130 degrees.

When it starts to cool off after a couple of weeks, the pile should be turned. It will heat up again and cool again. Turn it and provide some kind of venting to give the microbe work force the oxygen needed in the process of decomposition, keeping the heap damp at all times. In about three months you will have rich crumbling compost to enrich the garden, a complete fertilizer with all major and minor soil nutrients, plus any unknown elements it may contain.

What goes into compost is as important as the pile-building technique. Some materials break down faster than others by providing the soil organisms more high-energy nourishment. The higher the nitrogen content the faster decomposition takes place. This is known as the c/n (carbon-to-nitrogen) ratio. Barnyard manure has a 14:1 c/n. Sawdust, which is slow to break down, is 500:1. The more carbon present, the more nitrogen is needed for decomposition. The greater the diversity in materials, the richer the finished product.

Nature makes compost a little differently than we do, slower, but the idea is much the same. Leaves and plants fall to the ground to decompose, mixed in with the droppings and urine of animals and, finally, their nitrogen-rich bodies. Nature takes about five hundred years to build one inch of topsoil; we destroy it in minutes.

When farmers spread manure directly on the earth to break down, along with decaying organic matter, they are largely copying nature but call it "sheet composting." Turning under a green cover crop of rye, clover, or the like is known as "green manuring," a valuable soil-building method used by organic gardeners, mimicking but speeding up nature's process.

A properly made compost pile does not attract rodents or other scavengers. The finished product has a sweet, earthy smell and bears little resemblance to the raw materials that went into it. Compost is not completely broken down but rather becomes granular, giving soil organisms something to "chew" on. The organisms gradually transform rough compost into humus, which is less fibrous than compost.

Humus is the final product, a rather mysterious substance. It does not itself feed soil organisms, Peter Farb points out. He describes it as a "biological dead end," explaining that it is the *process* of humus formation, not the material, that releases energy, minerals, and carbon dioxide for plant growth. Eventually it oxidizes to little more than air and mineral salts that went into it, and newly formed humus replaces that which vanishes.

I am no longer as conscientious about following Sir Arthur's formula for making compost as when I began gardening. There is no proper layering. This and that goes in as it becomes available, followed by the occasional shovelful of manure and earth. Rain alone provides most of the moisture. I rarely get around to turning the heap or properly venting it; lifting compost is hard on the back. Instead of having compost in three months, my heaps take a year or so to break down. This is of no concern to me. I am in no hurry. My microbe work force toils at its own pace.

I pay a price for this indifference to good form. An improperly made pile does not generate the heat necessary to kill pathogens and weed seeds. I may reintroduce both when the compost is dug into the garden. Sir Albert would be appalled. I do not recommend my system, or lack of system.

In the beginning I enjoyed thinking I was recycling nutrients and replenishing the soil. As my technique deteriorated, this illusion faded. Often at night I merely dump the kitchen scraps on the pile, intending to cover them with earth or manure in the morning. Usually it is not necessary. My little friends of the night eat the banquet before it can be covered, let alone composted for return to the soil. A small furry body occasionally slithers past as I approach the bin, disturbed in its nocturnal meal, to vanish in the darkness. Once a skunk was dining in the bin when I approached and I almost dumped garbage on him in the darkness. When I take kitchen leavings out at night now I am aware of the possibilities.

I do not begrudge these creatures, my neighbors, this repast. They share my life, why not my compost?

It's a very odd thing—
As odd as can be—
That whatever Miss T. eats
Turns into Miss T.
      —Walter De La Mare

I came to this kind of gardening by chance. When we moved into our new home in New Jersey in the mid-fifties, one of our first acts was to buy a few packets of vegetable seeds, a bag of chemical fertilizer, a bottle of insecticide, and spray gun. Were these not the essentials of gardening? We had great expectations as we chopped up the hardpan in the yard, primarily compacted clay from backfill crushed down by a bulldozer. It took a pick to break the surface. We worked in fertilizer, planted the seeds according to instructions, watered them, and eagerly awaited the harvest.

Eventually a few pitiful shoots emerged. We blasted them with poison from the spray gun. Despite our expectations and efforts, all promptly died. I just didn't have the touch. To hell with gardening!

The following year I started researching food chemicals for the newspaper. I wrote a series of articles but the paper refused to publish them ("They would scare people to death!"). (Not to mention our advertisers.) Later I wrote *The Poisons in Your Food* (Simon & Schuster, 1960), the first major book on food chemicals. That was a long time ago. It was a new and startling idea that the food supply was not completely safe and fully protected by the government. I was naive.

Years of research opened new worlds to me. I not only learned a different way of growing food but, more important, came to understand that I had a large measure of control over my own health and well-being. That, too, was a new idea. I had thought that sickness and health just happened. "You are what you eat" took on new meaning. We are all like "Miss T."

252 · WILLIAM LONGGOOD

Much of my education had come from extensive expert testimony during congressional hearings on food chemicals. That led to a 1958 change in the food laws, calling for a ban on cancer-causing chemicals and opening the floodgates for other chemicals with the "tolerance" concept.

The "Delaney Amendment," banning carcinogens from foods, has never been fully enforced. The Environmental Protection Agency has identified only sixty-six of three hundred pesticides used on food as known or suspected carcinogens, according to a recent report by the Natural Resources Defense Council (NRDC). Permitting the use in food of "weak" carcinogens that someone has decided are "safe" is another accommodation to industry. Cancer experts generally believe that no chemical that causes cancer in any animal has a place in the food supply.

Among those testifying before the committee was J. I. Rodale, founder of *Organic Gardening and Farming*, now *Organic Gardening*. He was a disciple of Sir Albert Howard, the patron saint of organic gardening who linked soil health with that of animals and humans. Almost no formal research has been done on this vital connection. Why? Unfortunately, chemicals are more profitable than is health protection.

Only a small percentage of the nation's food supply is tested for contamination from more than 2 billion pounds of pesticides used annually in the United States alone. Many pesticides banned for use in the United States are sold abroad and come back to us in imported foods.

Rachel Carson was concerned about two hundred active ingredients employed in pesticides. Now there are more than six hundred and pesticide use has doubled since the appearance of *Silent Spring* in 1961. Fewer than a thousand inspectors oversee the nation's entire food supply, and only 1 percent of all agricultural products are tested for poisonous residues. Testing, when done, reveals the presence of only about half the pesticides in use, many of them violently toxic. By the time illegal contamination is detected, the food has probably been consumed.

The Food and Drug Administration, in charge of food safety, openly admits that most pesticides are inadequately tested for properties that cause cancer, birth defects, and other health hazards. Many of these substances remain as residues because of the tolerance concept that small doses of poison are safe. No one knows the cumulative effect of repeated small "safe" doses over a lifetime.

In addition to pesticide residues, processed food is laced with some three hundred non-nutritive additives, including sweeteners, colors, preservatives, extenders, conditioners, etc. Even if each is "safe" by itself, no one knows the effect when they combine with the other chemicals we ingest; we are all part of a vast chemical experiment.

The official line is that there is only "negligible risk." What is negligible? Negligible to whom? We all differ biologically in our resistance to chemical insult, the most vulnerable being the young, old, weak, and allergic. Children are considered six to twelve times as susceptible as adults. "The average child receives four times more exposure than an adult to eight widely used carcinogenic, or cancer-causing, pesticides in food," according to the NRDC, which supports Mothers and Others for Pesticide Limits, headed by the actress Meryl Streep.

"As a result of this exposure to only eight pesticides during their preschool years alone, as many as 6,200 children may develop cancer at some time in their lives [and] . . . three million children may be exposed to 'neurotoxic' pesticides, which can cause nervous system damage, at levels above what the government considers safe," states the NRDC.

As many people are learning, the safety of our food supply depends primarily on guesses, incomplete information, and official optimism.

The second year we were in our new home I decided to experiment. Was it really possible to grow crops without artificial fertilizers and pesticides? I was skeptical. Compost was

virtually unknown. DDT was a garden-farm-household sta-
ple. *Silent Spring* was well in the future. I was chided by my
colleagues at work, but indulged by my bosses, when I cam-
paigned in articles against massive aerial sprayings of DDT. A
cheerful if skeptical colleague observed that I was the best friend
a gypsy moth ever had.

I broke up the compacted clay in back of the house with pick
and mattock, inch by inch, a foot and more deep, and worked
in huge amounts of cow, horse, and chicken dung, grass clippings, broken-down weeds, decomposed leaves, peat moss, and
anything biodegradable I could lay hands on. I went along our
suburban road chopping down weeds for the new compost heap.
My neighbors thought I had lost my marbles. I took the leaves
they would have burned and piled them to decompose.

That concrete-like clay gradually became soft, friable soil
that you could dig with your fingers. Even the first year I was
able to grow vegetables without the use of commercial chemicals. What a thrill! Our modest garden was a kind of neighborhood wonder. Having it was a big thing for me, the beginning
of a new way of life, a different way of looking at life. It helped
bring a new awareness about beginnings and endings and the
great cycle that welds everything together in an interlocking,
interdependent, and indivisible world. It all begins in the soil. . .

*God forbid that I should go to any heaven in which
there are no horses.*
—Edwin Markham

Courtesy ads appear now and then in a local paper
offering free horse manure, accompanied by some enticement
such as "Come and get it!" and a phone number. Usually these
offers are disappointments. The manure is impossibly far from

where it can be loaded, it must first be raked up and then carried through an electrified fence, it is of poor quality, full of sand and unusable, or has been sprayed with pesticides.

If piled and accessible, often there is a problem with the bedding. Sawdust and wood chips take forever to break down. Used without being composted they make soil so porous that it dries out quickly and prevents firm root contact with new plants. The high carbon content requires so much nitrogen for decomposition that it can cause a nitrogen deficiency in the soil.

Peggy says my standards are too high and I expect too much. Perhaps. But one must draw the line somewhere. With me it is manure. My good friend Ed Wallace, from newspaper days and now long dead, claimed after a trip to Japan that everyone needs some symbol of perfection in his life. Manure may fill that role for me. I consider myself a connoisseur of manure, a manure elitist, if you will. There is compromise enough in life without lowering your standards on manure.

I personally like manure. I never feel so affluent as when bringing back the occasional load of high-class dung. When we moved here and I was preparing the new garden, Stu brought a pickup load of horse manure as a garden-warming present. I never had a more welcome or thoughtful gift.

For most of us who garden without use of packaged fertilizers, manure is a primary source of nitrogen. It is relatively abundant, often free, and usually available if you are not too particular. Cow manure is generally preferred to horse dung but more difficult to find and expensive to buy; it costs a small fortune where I live and little is to be had at any price. The family cow, once a domestic mainstay, has virtually disappeared, another casualty of progress.

Cow manure contains less nitrogen than horse and is considered "cooler," less likely to "burn" delicate young roots. Fresh horse manure is hot. Left unturned in a pile it will billow out clouds of steam and even reduce pockets to ash. It can be used as a heat source in hot frames. I like to work it directly into the soil in the fall and let it decompose over the winter. Otherwise I use it in compost or let it break down in a pile.

Manure actually does vary in quality. The healthier and better fed the animal, the better the manure. Dung is composed primarily of water, undigested bits of food, digestive juices, and a large population of bacteria, those "wretched beasties" of their discoverer. Along with nitrogen, manure contains phosphorus and potash. Urine is also high in nitrogen and potash, an excellent aid in the composting process. In fresh manure nitrogen is still soluble and subject to loss through oxidation.

An average horse produces about eighteen thousand pounds of manure a year, compared to twenty-seven thousand pounds for a cow with its multiple stomachs and complex digestive process. About half the total weight of manure is lost while rotting, making the dry residue richer in concentrated nutrients. In some parts of the country, near feedlots, manure is considered a pollutant.

When I started gardening, cow and horse manure were plentiful and of high quality. People were delighted to get rid of it. Now there is competition for available supplies as more converts turn to organic gardening. The quality is usually poorer and there may be a charge. Often, though, there is an unexpected bonus: the people you meet when getting manure. Manure, too, has many dimensions.

Soon after moving to Cape Cod I found an excellent source of manure, the trailer camp previously mentioned. The old man who ran it had bought horses for his grandchildren, and after they were grown and gone he kept the horses as pets, or possibly out of sentiment. The old man was gruff, known as difficult and tight-fisted, but he loved his horses. Animals can bring out the best in some people, just as sentiment can be elusive and take odd forms.

The old man bought bedding of expensive straw. The horses

were fed the finest Canadian hay, itself high in nitrogen. The manure was dumped next to the stable where it was easy to load. It was partly broken down, almost perfect compost when I got it. The old man was particular about who got the manure; one misstep and you were through.

I took no chances. Frequently I brought my benefactor baked goods as tribute. The old man had trouble breathing and always stood bent over a table, braced on his elbows, listening to a police scanner, as many local people do. He never looked up, as if afraid he might miss a crime. He never acknowledged the pies, cakes, or homemade bread. I would deposit my offering on the counter. Without raising eyes or voice, he would flatly say, "There's manure out back."

That was our entire communication. Eventually he died. The horses disappeared. The camp was upgraded. No sign of the horses now remains. Even the old man's rundown trailer is gone, replaced by a fancy new unit; nothing holds still.

My next source lived a free-wheeling style, surrounded by a wonderful clutter of abandoned vehicles, broken machinery, and unfinished jobs. He would do a bit of welding when in the mood or desperate for funds. He kept three horses for tourists to ride, if they found him, a pair of donkeys as pets, some pigs, free-ranging chickens and caged rabbits, which I suppose he and the young woman who lived with him ate. Manure abounded. So did the stench. The proprietor welcomed my taking the manure. He would open the broken corral gate so I could scoop droppings directly into the pickup. He even consented to weld a cracked brass planter for me.

The horses were kept in a precarious lean-to built of scrap lumber from the dump. The donkeys were stabled in a makeshift structure adjoining the house. Manure was heaved out of the donkeys' quarters, forming an organic ramp for them to get in and out. I was always cautioned not to take the ramp.

The manure I could have was in a soggy patch in the corral. It was saturated with urine, compacted by hooves, and had an awesome odor when disturbed. Peggy closed the windows when I returned with a load of that ripe manure. It is a disservice to language to call it manure; it was pure and simple shit.

Shit has an advantage over manure. High-class horses are often fed toxic substances to kill flies in their manure, and their stalls may be routinely sprayed during warm weather. Real genuine shit contains no poisons. If there are no worms in well-rotted manure, turn elsewhere; look for pure shit.

My source of shit also eventually vanished, as everything does here, sooner or later. He said the town was getting too built up and fancy for him. He was a local character, another endangered species as rustic habitats are progressively suburbanized and the world becomes more conforming. His former place is now tidied up, no longer an affront to the fastidious, the lot subdivided and a new home in place.

For a while I got dung from registered Morgan horses that lived in a posh stable with green wall-to-wall carpeting. I expected great things of that elegant manure but the soil microbes indicated no class awareness. The Morgan manure went to pot when the bedding, in an apparent economy move, deteriorated from straw to sawdust. It was also moved for storage far from the stable for aesthetic reasons and I ceased to find worms in it. I am forever being overrun by progress.

When we had our first garden in New Jersey, cow manure was available from a nearby dairy, a huge truckload costing only a few dollars delivered. I made compost of it combined with rotted leaves. Every fall I saved great quantities of leaves in a large pen made of felled saplings from the garden clearing.

Collecting the leaves was an autumn ritual. Bret and the neighborhood children would hide in the leaves I threw into the pen and pop up to "scare" me, shouting and laughing. I remember Katie. She was only three and almost lost in a red snowsuit, muffler, and stocking hat. Katie was perched on the top rail of the leaf pen, crying because she was too little to dive into the leaves like the others. I still see her, swathed in her red snowsuit, clinging to the rail, tears rolling down rosy little cheeks, and the others shouting and laughing at my pretended fright as they popped up among the leaves like so many elves.

That was many gardens and compost heaps ago. Katie probably has children of her own by now, but she remains my prisoner in time; I refuse to let her go or grow up. As I unload the latest acquisition of horse manure, inferior to the great manures of the past, I think about the leaf pen and Katie and the children and the bountiful supply of cheap cow dung.

That was all part of a world that no longer exists. But a garden, like a person, has many facets. It endures. It holds many memories. That may be its immortality, bolstered by manure and compost. Manure is the driving force of compost as compost is of soil. It is the transition and link between that which was and will be, what scientists refer to as the nitrogen and carbon cycles. For those so inclined, manure, at its best, may represent that totem of perfection that my departed friend Ed said we all should have in our lives.

I wish to speak a word for nature . . .
—Henry David Thoreau

A turtle turned up in the garden today, one that I put there last spring and then forgot about. I had rescued the creature and brought it home to feast on insects. There was some risk in this: Box turtles are known to dine on crops as well as bugs, as likely to eat our insect allies as pests.

I brought the turtle home with still another misgiving. It might consider me high-handed for interrupting its journey, making forced labor of it, however good my intentions. In my defense, I found the creature crossing a busy road. It could have been run over.

I could have deposited it at the side of the road, not disrupting its migration and overcoming my own need to meddle and interfere with natural processes in the name of good works. The turtle would still have been at risk. Box turtles, rescued from traffic, are as likely as not to turn and resume their perilous trip as if disoriented or suddenly changing their mind, often a fatal misstep. I used to see many turtles that had been run over by cars. I rarely see one now, perhaps because there are fewer turtles to be run over.

Recently I read about a turtle that had its shell crushed by a car. A kind and inventive veterinarian repaired the damage with epoxy resin, the type used to patch holes in rusting vehicles, and sent the patient on its way, one of the happier applications of modern technology. If I were a turtle I would not count on such benevolence as a regular thing.

My guest, or prisoner, is classified as an eastern box turtle, as opposed to its western kin. Each is appropriately named for the area it lives in. Only minute differences separate the two, primarily the pattern and color of the shell; both are about six inches long, fully grown.

Box turtles, which include many subspecies, are well named, having a hinged lower shell that closes tight against the upper shell when the head is withdrawn, forming a tight, protective "box." The hinge muscle is so strong that a man cannot open it with his bare hands. My turtle has a handsome segmented brown and yellow shell, typical of its kind. It has bright red eyes, indicating that it is a male (females have brown or yellow eyes). It appears well adjusted, or did when found, and in sound health.

I tried to research box turtles in local libraries but there is surprisingly little material available, most of it of a scholarly or technical nature. I did learn that turtles have a fine history. They appeared some 250 million years ago (185 million according to a second source) and have outlasted the dinosaurs. Turtles apparently knew something the dinosaurs did not know, or were not exposed to the same planetary upheavals or environmental stresses.

Eastern turtles, like mine, may live 100 years or more in the wild, about double that of their western relative. The reason for this discrepancy was not given. Turtles are said to outlive all other animals. A box turtle in Rhode Island was marked and released early in the 1800s and was recaptured 129 years later, still in prime health.

Records for longevity are understandably hard to come by. It used to be common to find turtles roaming about with dates carved on their shells. Often they went back fifty years or more. The custom of carving dates, or the finder's initials, on turtle shells seems to have passed, along with the turtles. The turtle I found had no date or initials.

I read about a tortoise, a relative of the box turtle, that lived 189 years. It survived two forest fires, was run over by a car, and finally succumbed when stepped on by a horse. This suggests that the turtle clan is likely to be around for a while unless catastrophe intervenes. I do not know how they will ultimately handle the greenhouse effect, acid rain, the vanishing ozone layer, weather disturbances due to forest destruction, worldwide pollution, and other effects of man's stewardship of the earth.* Will turtles still be around when our kind is gone, as they outlived the dinosaurs, watching futuristic lichen and mosses taking down the World Trade Center?

For all that science has learned, box turtles remain largely a mystery. Intense study has given little insight into the reptilian personality. Turtles appear to be imperturbable but are reported to have an active enough sex life, although they breed just once a year. Some females, it is claimed, can store sperm and do not need to mate annually. This would seem to enable them to be more choosy about their partners.

---

*Even now turtles are said to be disappearing throughout the world, and some scientists view this as a symptom of a deteriorating world habitat for all life.

The male suitor makes a fine macho display. He bites his intended, rears up on his hind legs, head thrown back triumphantly, before lunging to mount his mate. The female's high-domed shell accommodates the male's curved lower shell during copulation. This seems cumbersome in theory but apparently works out well in practice. A method used effectively for 250 million years (or even only 185 million) cannot be too flawed. I like to think that my turtle, during his confinement, has not lost his erotic urges or the knack of executing them. I had not considered that possibility when I brought him home.

In late spring or early summer the pregnant female digs a shallow hole in the ground and lays three to six eggs which she covers with earth. Neither parent faces up to family responsibilities. Both take to their heels, he immediately after mating, she after laying eggs. Both parents then continue their solitary ways. Turtles are not encumbered by family or social obligations, which may or may not contribute to longevity.

Baby turtles emerge in late summer and are on their own. The first six months are the most perilous. Young turtles resolve the problem of food by not eating until the following summer. If lucky, a few of all those born survive. Turtles have strong jaws and no teeth; their primary food is insects and slugs.

Some species of turtles, curiously, start off as carnivores and end up herbivores, and others, including box turtles, become omnivores. This progression, I assume, is due to physiological change rather than any mellowing philosophy. Certain turtles have a taste for poisonous mushrooms. They eat them with impunity but anyone eating the turtle's flesh is poisoned, a kind of posthumous revenge that does not help the turtle.

Turtles have suffered heavy mortality from people, both as food and as mystical symbols of eternity. Sailors once took them on long voyages for protein in soup. Indians devoured many, and used them in ceremonies, burying the live animals with their dead. I do not know if this helped the dead Indians. Certainly it did nothing for the turtles. Ancient people believed the world was held aloft by a giant turtle, a rather pleasing image.

Box turtles pose baffling questions for behaviorists. They are so diverse in habit and habitat that it is difficult to draw general conclusions. What is true of one species in one place may not be true of another elsewhere. What is true of one individual may not hold for others of the same species.

Box turtles, as a rule, live in an area not much larger than a football field and may spend their entire lives there. They move slowly, unlike the green turtle that whips along at 20 miles per hour. It must take a box turtle a long time just to learn his territory. Most turtles do not seek adventure or conquest but are content to remain within their small domain, without excitement. They are not overbearing. They may be lonely and welcome company.

The picture of the usual resident stay-at-home turtle can be deceiving. Some are wanderers, forever on the move, going from place to place, an aberration that has been noted in an ongoing study of box turtles at the Massachusetts Audubon Society's Wellfleet Bay Sanctuary. Bob Prescott, the director, said his people have reached few conclusions. "We get mixed signals."

Why are some box turtles residents and others roamers? he asks. Is it to assure genetic diversity? Bob, who takes a cosmopolitan view of life, postulates that the resident turtles keep the home fires burning, while the roamers may go from one territory to another to give the stay-at-homes a hand sexually, if needed, or to fill in if there is a vacancy.

"We are not sure," he says. "We have tagged one-hundred-and-thirty box turtles since 1985, some with radios, to track them. Some stick around. Others show up once and are never seen again. We see some individuals who are aggressive. Others are not. Some will defend their territory. Others won't." Turtles pose the same puzzles as people.

Like so many other creatures, turtles have been hunted and

badgered almost to extinction. Box turtles once abounded in Massachusetts. Now they are of "special concern," a last perilous step before they are "endangered." It is illegal to make pets of them, which I gather is the same as captives. I did not know this when I brought the turtle I found home. Their plight promises to worsen as development further deprives them of their last places to live and earn an honest living.

With open land disappearing, where is there for these creatures to go? Will they end their days looking through fences blocking their way, and crossing heavily trafficked roads, a journey too often never completed? When planning new housing developments and shopping malls, consideration is rarely given to who or what is being displaced, made homeless, or wiped out altogether. The tragedy is that so few care.

Good intentions, like indifference and cruelty, can be another threat to wild creatures. I learned this from a sad personal experience. Several years ago I found another box turtle gazing through the garden fence from outside, as if trying to figure out how to overcome this obstacle in its way. I also put it in the garden to eat pests and then forgot about it. In the fall it was caught in the merciless blades of a rototiller and crushed. I should have learned my lesson. I did not. Instead I captured and imprisoned the second turtle.

I rediscovered my latest captive guest by chance while clearing out dead squash and cucumber vines, a first step in getting the garden ready for winter. The turtle apparently had fared well enough. It seemed to have eaten sufficient insects and plants to keep up its strength and spirits. It was pressing against the fence from inside, as if trying to escape, as its predecessor had tried to get in from the outside. To a turtle a garden fence must be baffling; there are no fences in nature.

The creature would have a hard time making it through the cold months in confinement. I could, I suppose, convince myself that it would be safe in the garden, at least protected from predators. The same argument can be made for zoos and other places of animal detention. I leave it to the philosophers to decide which is better: a natural death or an unnatural life.

I release the captive outside the fence. He takes off at once toward the meadow nearby. His pace is lively for so small a creature. Maybe he is afraid I will change my mind. He departs with not so much as a backward glance at his summer quarters, or what could be thanks for restoring the liberty I had deprived him of.

Where will he go? I do not know if he is or was a wanderer that I interrupted in his rounds, possibly en route to take over a vacated territory, give a friend a hand, or just examine the possibilities. Mayhaps he was a homebody, merely checking out his small domain when rescued or captured. What mischief did I unwittingly cause? Did I save him from the peril of traffic only to disrupt his life pattern?

The occasional turtles I see all seem to be ever on the move. Do they have a destination or wander wherever chance takes them? Are they seeking the ideal place to settle down, some turtle El Dorado? What propels genetic diversity? Is it a search for self-fulfillment, whatever that is for a turtle?

Are they driven by some internal restlessness, like so many others who roam the earth, always looking for more and better, for greener pastures, juicier insects? Perhaps their odyssey is nothing more than the search for other turtles, the perfect mate, the idyllic life that may lie just beyond the next hill or fence or across the fatal highway.

With sex to distract them only once a year, and briefly then, what occupies turtles in their migrations? Do they catch a few meals on the run, doze in the sun, and that is the whole of it? Once dispossessed, it must be hard to relocate. The old neighborhood would probably be changed, possible gone altogether; things move swiftly nowadays, for both people and turtles.

My turtle, released, is out of sight almost at once in the ground cover and underbrush. I sit in the old metal chair, warm from the late afternoon sun, and consider our brief relationship. Why did I bring it home and make it captive? By what right did I disrupt its journey? It seems to be our nature to interfere in the lives of other creatures. We control, manage, manipulate, disrupt, and kill for our convenience, amusement, or profit. Possibly the kindest thing we can do for our fellow creatures, most of the time, is leave them alone and let them work out their destiny by themselves.

A startling thought occurs. I would like to be very rich. I would buy a huge tract of land never to be disturbed. It would be just for animals. No multiple use, no limited access, no fire roads, no scenic views, no wilderness trails, no research, no studies. No nothing. It would exist solely for the creatures of the earth to live on in their own way without external interference. But where does the money come from to fund my little fantasy?

It is late, time to go inside. Still I linger. I am thinking about the turtle, now on its own. What will happen to it? Will it find a place to snug down in proper reptilian fashion when cold weather strikes?

Come spring, perhaps, it will meet a lady turtle, possibly the widow of the one killed by the rototiller at my hands. They will give birth to baby turtles. He will become the local stay-at-home resident. But that is unlikely. A new housing development is scheduled to be built in the meadow where the turtle was heading. He will be dispossessed again, or killed. Already orange stakes outline what will be a forty-foot-wide asphalt road. Every day I await the roar of a bulldozer crunching into the soft earth with its exquisite covering of grasses, mosses, blueberry, beachplum, and other native growth that provides living quarters and food for many small animals. Soon it will be gone, all gone.

We, too, like the turtles, have spent much of our lives running and hiding from progress but always it manages to find us and we must flee again. Now there is nowhere to go. At last it has us cornered, our backs to the wall, or the doomed meadow, and its deadly work goes on with crushing finality.

I wish my little turtle friend well, a safe journey and happy ending, wherever chance, nature, or destiny takes him, whether as resident manager or wanderer. I hope he does not hold against me the wrong I did him. Do turtles hold grudges? It is late now. The sun is losing its warmth. I go inside still thinking about the turtle and my own little fantasy about protected land just for animals.

The dream persists. Wilderness is virtually gone, nature desecrated, creature habitats corrupted or wiped out. Why not a few spots on this diminished earth left alone just for animals?

The great business of life is to be to do, to do without, and to depart.
—John, Viscount Morley

I pick four celery worms off the carrots but find only one on the celery. A few diehard squash bugs linger on the zucchini, stalked by a daddy longlegs who seems in no hurry to strike. A half-dozen tardy caterpillars are on the bush beans, and an itinerant late potato beetle lurks on the eggplant.

I am not sure what all of this adds up to. It could be the full moon but I prefer to think it is the balance of nature reasserting itself as it seeks new equilibrium in keeping with the passing season. The balance never seems to stabilize. It is always in motion. Who is ahead? Who is behind? Who keeps score?

A squash bug appeared on the bathroom window screen last night. It is late for squash bugs, and bathroom screens not their usual habitat. I blame it on the full moon. Peggy, taking a more earthy view, says it was trying to get to the zucchini already in the freezer.

When I picked a few peppers this morning I found that the

marigolds that were supposed to protect them had themselves been eaten. Pam, who knows many of nature's secrets, particularly those of flowers, suggests that with all the diddling about over the years perhaps marigolds are no longer what they once were.

Everything seems slightly askew. Lily is on full-moon wild time, disappearing for unaccounted hours and reappearing as suddenly and mysteriously as she left, pursuing her secret life. She has bolstered her appetite of late, apparently bulking up for winter.

Summer is winding down. Butternut squash have climbed the back fence, making their annual break for freedom, some caught in the wire mesh in absurd shapes. New zucchini turn up misshapen in odd configurations. Young cucumbers, not to be outdone, are caricatures of themselves with round bottoms and pointed heads.

I like to think there is a sound scientific explanation for these antics, that it is a trick the cooling nights play on heat-loving plants, but they, too, may be responding to lunar pulsations or other cosmic forces known only to them.

The tomato plants are producing but the leaves are starting to yellow and a couple of plants are already dead. I have noticed that when plants are giving out they often make a final desperate effort to reproduce themselves, sending forth the most pathetic little nodes. This is especially true of tomatoes. I have come to think of the drive for immortality in any species as "making tomatoes," trying to leave something of themselves behind. The reproductive factor.

There is so much of recycled nature in a garden that I do not know how it could fail to affect one's life view, to give a sharpened sense of mortality. Every living thing has its own time and season, each, in turn, moving along, completing "the business of life," to make way for the next, the remains going into the compost heap to provide for that which follows.

When we are not exposed to the daily phenomenon of growth

and decay, life and death no longer play a dominant role in our thoughts and we lose that which gave those who preceded us the sense of reality that comes with plunging one's hands into the soil and tending the green shoots that respond to the life force which the earth harbors and the sun and rains beget. We lose a sense of earth's rhythms and its poetry, which help give meaning to existence.

The most triumphant growth in the garden is Al's Special, a tomato plant grown from seeds given me by a doctor friend who got them from a patient of his. The plants were astonishing from the start, huge green fountains that produced torrents of medium-size perfect tomatoes, large cherries, really. I have grown them every year since, but only one or two plants because of the space they take. Al's Specials show no sign of faltering, defying the changing season, pouring forth tomatoes, as if trying to give heart to their failing companions.

This year I tried an experiment, planting a few crops by the moon. Legend holds that it influences growth. Plants that produce the desired or eaten part aboveground (tomatoes, corn, etc.) should be planted in a waxing moon, that period of increase between a new and full moon. Plants that produce the eaten or desired part belowground (root crops) should be planted in a waning moon, after the full moon and before the next new moon.

This is ancient lore once practiced by farmers but scoffed at by scientists. Many plantings are calculated in terms of zodiac signs. The few supervised scientific experiments showed little difference, and my own modest experiment reveals the same result. Maybe I shall try again. As Dr. William Albrecht, the Missouri University soils expert, said, "Faith must take up where science leaves off."

I have trouble realizing that another gardening year is almost over. Soon it will be time to start thinking about putting the garden to bed. That is an apt phrase. The garden is literally closed down for the season, to rest, covered with a blanket of mulch or green manure to protect the soil from beating rains and driving winds, to sleep away the winter and in the spring to bear new life.

I am not ready to think about fall or winter. The days are still hot, the nights only starting to cool. The fading plants mourn their loss as the days grow shorter and life ebbs. Even weeds outside the garden, now turning brown and forlorn, concluding their own life business, share my disbelief and dismay that another gardening season is coming to a close as summer begins its long journey in pursuit of the retreating sun.

Not all is work and purposeful endeavor in the garden. Of late I have been playing a little joke on skunk. Every night he tunnels his way under the double gate to the west where I unload manure. The following morning I fill in the hole and at night he digs his way in again to get to grubs in the manure and mulch, and this has become a kind of game we play. Once he uprooted a young butternut squash in his grubbing but I do not hold that against him.

A few days ago, instead of filling the hole, I put a heavy metal grill over the spot where he comes up inside the gate. That night skunk dug as usual but came up against the grill. The same thing happened the following night and each night after that. Skunk did not give up but must have wondered what was going on.

This afternoon I saw him crossing the yard near the beehives. He is always disheveled but today he looked worse than ever. He was the most disreputable, woeful-looking skunk I ever saw. He also appeared to be in a temper, snapping his tail and not looking at me for our usual friendly greeting.

Enough is enough. I have tormented skunk beyond endurance. Tomorrow I shall remove the grill so he can get back to his regular diet. But I shall continue to fill the hole each day so he must dig his way in at night. I do not want to spoil his character by letting him think he does not have to work for a living. Skunk, like the rest of us, must realize that there is no free lunch—or gratis nocturnal repast for grubs either, for that matter.

> *Songs Spring thought Perfection*
> *Summer criticizes;*
> *What in May escaped detection,*
> *August, past surprises,*
> *Notes and names each blunder.*
> —Robert Browning

The late summer garden has a tranquility found no other time of year. This will continue until season's end. The frenzied growth of spring and early summer is past, its vitality largely spent. The last plantings are in. The older plants have made their stand. The strong and resolute survived, the weak and unlucky perished. The record is more or less written, the design complete; nothing remains now but to complete the harvest and tote up the final score. I have come to think of this time as the August doldrums, an affliction of matter and spirit alike.

A mature garden is much like an old person. There is no longer a consuming drive to produce or succeed. It is possible to sit back and relax. One makes peace with the situation at hand; expectations have been realized, compromised, or dashed altogether. The resolutions and hopes of spring are the triumphs and disappointments of the August doldrums.

In early summer a different mood prevails. It is more upbeat; there is a subtle intensity. Plants compete for water, nutrients, space, and sunlight. Insects are numerous and active. Life and growth are rampant. The place jumps. Plants seem to double in size overnight as they reach for the vernal sunlight.

This is deception on the plant, of course. It believes it is
fulfilling its destiny, seeking species immortality by reproducing itself. In the end it, like its companions of summer, will be
ruthlessly whacked down and eaten. So much for immortality.

With summer's end activity slows and almost ceases. The
surviving plants could be saying to themselves, Why knock
ourselves out? Why all the commotion? Why this mighty striv-
ing to be number one? We all wind up in the same pot anyway.

I like the feeling that there is no longer a need to push. This
is my favorite time of year. The metal chair, my seat of inac-
tivity, invites me to sit and relax in the warm sunlight, to become
part of the doldrums about me. There is little to do. Only late
spinach and winter crops are still to be thinned, a chore to be
put off as long as possible. Mulching the carrots and leeks for
winter can also be delayed until the critical hour before the
first freeze. Even the weeds contribute to the serenity by not
multiplying quite so aggressively.

I have served notice on the butternut and pumpkins that
there is no longer a sense of urgency. They, too, can knock off
and contemplate past achievements. I cut off the vines with
new blossoms so remaining energies can go into forming fruit
already set. Some of the vines I chopped off had brilliant orange
trumpet-shaped flowers that quickly collapsed, as if brought
down by an assassin; they look desolate atop the compost.

I wonder idly if the remaining plants "look" over at their
fallen comrades and brood about the futility of their lot. Sooner
or later that will be their final destination. Or are they of ster-
ner stuff with a more positive outlook and do not dwell on
ultimates and final destinations?

Even in its dotage, or maturity, the garden continues to yield
heavily. The most modest plot, we know, can produce muni-
ficent returns. Our immediate neighbors, here only for the
summer, have a postage-stamp garden that provides them with
fresh produce during their stay with a small surplus to take
home, a bit of summer by the sea transferred to Manhattan.

They also take the family cat that must renounce the freedom of summer for city life inside an apartment. Each year this transition is made. Nubba is a stoical and adaptable cat, accepting urban bondage with the same equanimity as her owners.

The garden follows its seasonal progression. The early broccoli was allowed to go to flower to help provide the bees with fall honey. The bees need all help possible to get through the winter. Late kale and other plants that will overwinter have already embarked on their new careers.

The potato vines have died down but the tubers below will not be harvested until the weather cools. Only an occasional beetle lingers before taking cover to sleep away the winter and make sure of next year's progeny. The pole beans never quite made it to the heavens but topple over their tripods, a bean reproach for my not providing them with longer poles and a more worthy challenge.

Fall cabbage and broccoli are dispersed throughout the garden in an effort to outwit the wily maggots. The peppers, now red and full of vitamin C, never quite lived up to their early promise but my expectations may have been more flawed than the peppers.

Birds by day and skunk by night search for juicy grubs under damp mulch covering the potatoes. They hurl the thatch aside, unearthing the biggest and best spuds, it seems, and exposing them to sunlight that turns potatoes green, toxic and fit only for compost. It is nip and tuck whether the sun or I will get to them first. Robins are especially vigorous in searching out the grubs. The garden feeds a large and varied clientele.

The onions have formed huge balls, the tops fallen or pushed over to force late growth into the bulbs. They will be picked and placed on stacked screens to dry in the sunlight, then bagged or braided for winter storage in the root cellar.

That is hyperbole. The term "root cellar" is more imposing

than the reality. The so-called root cellar is a small corner of the basement, walled off and insulated on sides and top with a window for ventilation and temperature control. Potatoes, onions, shallots, winter squash, cabbage, and pumpkins will keep until spring. The potatoes, onions, and shallots remain resolute until some inner voice commands them to heed the life force and sprout.

We will continue to have fresh produce until the cold comes, but some plants are already gone. The celery went to seed during the prolonged hot spell with no rain. The rhubarb, so vigorous in the spring, the first garden offering, is dying off; once-tender stalks are now limp ropes sprawled on the ground, the juices running backward into the roots for winter survival. We have a good supply of rhubarb in the freezer. Rhubarb is the only vegetable that replaces fruit in the diet; it is especially tasty cooked and mixed with yogurt and honey.

Volunteer tomatoes, potatoes, and butternut squash grow out of the compost, their foliage keeping the pile from drying out. Last spring we had a leftover flat of basil that looked pitiful. Instead of disposing of it I planted the block of root-bound seedlings directly into the compost. Those crowded, unhappy plants grew to enormous size, outdoing their cosseted siblings in the herb bed. Each time the basil is disturbed it releases its fragrance, as if showing appreciation for a chance at life.

Volunteer tomatoes are everywhere, even among the onions, as if seeking their protection. The weeds never give up, even this late in the season. They seem especially attracted to the young carrots, which may represent a kind of weed gentrification or social climbing.

I read recently that Charles Darwin, in one of his many experiments, cleared a 2 × 3-foot patch of earth and "exactly 357 weeds reared their heads, and out of this number 295 were destroyed, primarily by birds and slugs," demonstrating, to him, balance in the struggle for existence. Once more nature was pitting one life form against another, playing her endless game in which there seem to be neither losers nor winners.

Time now saved from diminished garden chores is spent in the kitchen as we put up the bounty of summer. Every day we harvest something that must be canned or frozen. Vegetables have little regard for our ability to use or put by only limited quantities at a time. Some days we are almost inundated, particularly by beans. Most of the beans we need have already been put up. Those still coming in are primarily for the table or to be given away.

The tomatoes were late ripening again this year. Only a couple of weeks ago we picked our first tomato, a kind of garden landmark, and celebrated with cheese-lettuce-tomato sandwiches on homemade sourdough bread. Only now are the tomatoes coming in quantities suitable for canning.

I know of only one local garden that produced tomatoes earlier this summer. It is in a hollow and everything grown there is ahead of us in the spring and gone earlier in the fall, done in by the frost seeking lower places. Helen tends the garden but Bill takes satisfaction in having early tomatoes. He has lofty standards for Helen's garden and it had better measure up. I suspect that the first tomato they harvested this year may have been premature. He conceded that it was "a bit underripe" and his lips seemed to pucker as he discussed it.

Tomatoes are the measure of most gardens. If all else fails and tomatoes are plentiful the year is considered a success. People who grow nothing else often put in a few tomatoes. I read that patio containers have become popular with urban apartment dwellers with any kind of balcony or sun exposure, and they are probably an improvement on those supermarket imposters.

As we go about our canning chores I think about living in New Jersey and the marvelous peaches we put up then. They were grown by Mr. Packer, an old-fashioned grower like Farmer

Bagley, also displaced by development. He used to grow and sell those wonderful peaches for $3 a bushel, the price of a small bag now. The peaches had their skins removed, were halved into jars, bathed in hot syrup, and processed in the ancient graniteware canner that Peggy inherited from her old granny and we still use. The peaches in their jars were works of art. Peggy likened them to canned sunshine.

The canning season and late summer garden are inseparable in fact and memory. All gardens of the past merge together in retrospect, part of the invisible interwoven threads that link us to our past. The sun, then as now, is deceptively warm as the days start to cool. A slight breeze stirs the plants now winding down from their labors but does not ruffle the serenity of the garden's fading community of life.

Suddenly there is change. Plants that appeared vigorous and verdant only a few days ago are languishing, as if overwrought or stressed beyond endurance. Heat, wind, drought, and spent energy have made their mark. The August doldrums exert a toll.

Even the beans have lost their rich green. Squash leaves are mysteriously shriveled. Pepper plants sprawl on the ground as if beseeching help. The dill has gone to seed, the lacy ferns of spring now the brittle stalks of August. The tops of late onions look bedraggled, unmindful that their glory is not above but below.

Change came during a three-day storm when I could not get out to oversee the garden. It was the first serious rain in weeks. The mauling the plants took from the winds cannot alone account for their dispirited look. Something else happened, some secret communication from nature that summer is winding down.

The calendar, of course, denies this. It proclaims that summer still has almost a month to go, time enough for late crops to ripen and transplants to take hold before winter strikes all down. But there is this mysterious change of mood.

The remaining days of summer will be warm, even hot, but they will not be scorchers. We have passed the season's zenith and are now going the other way. It is time to complete the harvest, to savor what is left of summer, and to make my own transition to the season to follow.

I especially like to work in the garden after dinner this time of year, doing such tasks as still need doing. The coolness has moved in after the waning heat of day. A faint breeze blows off the sea. Most of all I enjoy the tranquility and solitude. Sweet earth smells rise. The plants no longer are in neat alignment but have reordered themselves in a tangle of yellowing foliage.

The garden is relaxed, its work done for the day. There is still growth but not the pace imposed when the sun beat down relentlessly. This, perhaps, is the time for the late garden to consolidate gains made, to gather strength for tomorrow's remaining effort.

Often I do nothing but sit in the chair and feel evening coming or watch the sun set in a burst of brilliant hues, savoring these fleeting moments. The light grows softer and softer. The first stars appear. The insect chorus gains volume. Mosquitoes attack. Reluctantly I go inside, leaving the garden to itself and the coming night.

> *One heard the musical voice of the garden, whose loveliest hours revealed their joyous soul and sang of their gladness.*
> —Maurice Maeterlinck

W hen I take the kitchen middens from the latest canning session out to the compost before going to bed, the orchestra is in full chorus. Night vapors and scents from the earth mingle with the fragrance of honeysuckle nearby and basil growing in the compost. They merge into the rhythmic pulse of night. The sky is a great amphitheater of stars. Only the rim of the full harvest moon, a solid disk of molten gold, is visible over the horizon.

I gaze at the Milky Way, bathed in light traveling 186,000 miles a second, taking 900,000 years to reach Earth. But such figures have no real meaning to me. I only know the garden is awash in a sea of distant light, perhaps cast by other worlds long gone. I am lost in the magic of night. Wonderful things must be happening. The stars are so many candles. The golden dusky lantern of a moon rises out of the sea itself. I linger to enjoy the nocturnal concert.

Is it not only fair that the performers serenade me by night when I feed them by day? Do I not pay a price for this melodic tribute? I listen, enraptured, to the huge chorus that I sustain and, like the cost-conscious paymaster of a symphony orchestra, say "Do we really need so many players? Could we not do with fewer to feed?"

The musicians are in excellent form tonight. The company is made up of crickets, katydids, cicadas, grasshoppers, and others, perhaps, that I do not recognize. Artists all! Already they have tuned up. The maestro has given the downbeat. The program is under way with a scraping of ridged wings and file-like legs, a resonance of clicks, buzzes, chirps, and trills. They saw and rasp away, the sounds amplified and vibrating in insect bodies on the night air. The faster the tempo, the higher the pitch. I have read that the insect song is in the key of C-sharp but some say it is more varied. I would not know.

Such a multitude and diversity of rhythms, beats, notes, and themes. There is point and counterpoint, solos, duets, quartets, the full chorus. Melodies are passed back and forth, improvised upon, repeated, given individual interpretation, and refined. Who composed and arranged this evening's concert? There are, I assume, standing ovations and encores, jealousies and bruised egos in such a gathering of artistic talents and temperaments.

A succession of musicians has played over the summer, beginning with tree frogs, plaintively announcing spring. Following were the snowy tree cricket, the narrow-winged tree cricket, the jumping bush cricket, katydids, cicadas, and grasshoppers, some residents, others itinerants, guest artists, as it were. Each player has his own song and beat but these change as the season progresses and players come and go.

The most acclaimed performer is the snowy tree cricket. For the technically minded, it saws its wings, with their file and scraper arrangement, back and forth to produce sound waves that vibrate up to five thousand times a second, which we hear as short chirps. This distinguished soloist is said, by entomologists of fine ear, to make the insect world's most melodious sound, likened by one to a tiny muted trumpet. The snowy tree crickets alone play in unison, their song heard almost a mile away.

In ancient China the greatest cricket singers were kept in resplendent cages for their music, like songbirds, and they had exotic names like Golden Bell, Spinning Damsel, and Child of the Weaver Shuttle, and were sold for large sums of money. Some Chinese even now keep crickets for their music.

Almost every schoolchild learns that by counting the number of chirps heard in fifteen seconds and adding 40, you get the approximate temperature in degrees Fahrenheit. The warmer the night, the more chirps. I have always intended to test this but never have. I would do it now, this night, but carry neither watch nor thermometer so am unable to verify the snowy tree cricket's scientific accuracy. I accept tonight's reading, whatever it is, on faith.

The katydid also makes music with its rasping wings. Folklore holds that frost will follow six weeks after the first katydid song is heard. Katydids, with their shiny green oval wings, are members of the grasshopper family. Rubbing the forewings together twice says "Katy." Three times announces "Katy did." Four times proclaims that "Katy didn't." Why are they called katydids? Why not katydidn'ts? How did their song evolve? Did the first players have more crude instruments?

The cicadas, briefly, add to the chorus, a throbbing, buzzing, vibrating sound made by contracting muscles that control two drums in the abdomen. Grasshoppers contribute a more grating, less musical note than crickets. They rub the files on their rear legs across ridges along their wings, almost like fiddlers. So what if the grasshopper's song is a little scratchy, not so melodic as that of the more talented cricket? He makes up in volume and enthusiasm what he lacks in technique. Is it the music or what it stands for? Intention or execution?

These various performers were the first musicians on earth, producing what one writer called "the first animal sounds ever heard on our planet." Males make the music. Their song is assumed to attract mates, but why does it continue long after mating takes place?

The concert gains poignancy and urgency as summer nears an end. But here we have a communications problem. Female crickets and katydids are notoriously hard of hearing. They have their ears on their front legs, the only insects said to hear with their knees. Do they give themselves to the finest player or the one nearby that they hear? Does this not say something about love? Do they listen with their hearts or their knees?

Love has many songs. There are calling songs ("I would like to make your acquaintance"), courtship songs ("I am here"), and staying-together songs sung during mating to keep the female occupied so she does not nibble away the male's sperm packet before it enters her body ("Are you listening?").

The male tree cricket has glands on his back that the female gnaws on while absorbing his sperm. This has been called "the first box of candy." Another cricket has no song but lets the female chew away his wings to keep her occupied during copulation to assure absorption of his sperm. Love is indeed a many-splendored thing, both in and out of the garden.

What a whirring, drumming, and strumming of wings and legs proclaiming insect prowess as the mighty macho chorus sings of devotion, debauchery, and deceit in the cause of fleeting love. What a boasting of unproved virility! What lies and duplicity besmirch those tender raptures? All of the little music makers, those winged troubadours of night, obey the same command imprinted in their being by an unknown power. Who wields the baton they play to? What master conductor is on the podium?

Does every player find a mate? That seems unlikely with so many suitors. What happens to those unlucky bachelors whose love songs arouse no answering lust? For them there is no tomorrow, no second chance. Soon the air, already cooling, will chill. The chorus becomes slower. Fewer remain to serenade the darkness. The cold descends. Only a smattering of brave and defiant voices linger. Killing cold strikes. The concert is over. Amour is dead for the season.

But not yet. Throughout the night the chorus still plays, melodic and wistful, steady as an unseen metronome pacing the darkness. It is fascinating that the individual performers, each singing his own song, the melody and beat changing with locality and time of year, create such atonal harmony, such rhythmic beauty. The song of the cricket alone is considered "bewilderingly complex." A renowned entomologist described the sequence of insect music as "the season's program."

Dr. Howard Ensign Evans, a Harvard entomologist, has this to say about crickets: "I do believe that an intimacy with the world of crickets and their kind can be salutary—not for what they are likely to teach us about ourselves but because they remind us, if we will let them, that there are other voices, other rhythms, other strivings and fulfillments than ours."

Professor Evans observes that "it is good to slacken our pace now and then and listen to the patterns of sound that fell on meadow and forest millions of years before there were men to hear them; patterns that in their simplicity and repetitiveness suggest the heart beat of life itself or the ticking of some cosmic clock." Nathaniel Hawthorne said of the tree cricket's song that "if moonlight could be heard, it would sound like this."

This night, with its concert, is not given to music alone. There is a dazzling light display as fireflies respond to the seasonal urgency to procreate. The songs and signals of love are all around me. But behind the beauty and the insect chorus lurks perfidy. Treachery and base strategies are afoot, or awing, in the unending search for food and mates. Life is the ultimate trophy to be won, death the consolation prize of the loser.

Fireflies are among the more visible and romantic performers in the great nocturnal drama of survival. They use flashes, as crickets use song, certain birds display, and man dissimulates, to find mates, each species having an individual flashing pattern to make sure it breeds with its own kind, nature trying to maintain her concept of order. But all is not what it appears to be. The darkness abounds with intrigue as firefly femmes fatales mimic the flashing patterns of other species, devouring amorous males who report for assignation. There are all manner of signals, countersignals, flashes, lures, traps, betrayals, and murders.

The duplicity of fireflies has no known parallel in the entire animal kingdom, according to scientists. But are not courtship and death closely allied throughout nature? A sobering though as I linger amidst the majesty and fragrance of the night with its multiple mysteries, gentle luminescence, and treacheries.

Suddenly I am aware of a strangeness. Something has happened. There is a slight shift in the night breeze, a freshening. But there is something else. There is a pause, almost a break in the symphony. In that moment some subtle transformation takes place.

I know at once what it is. I have experienced it before. In this instant summer has ended. It gives the lie to the calendar.

What do calendars know of such matters? Nature has made her intention clear. The warm days and nights to follow are mere ritual. Another season is ready to take stage. The orchestra picks up again but seems to have a different tempo, a new rhythm, an undertone of melancholy. The music says, "Summer is over . . . Summer is over . . ."

Do the musicians know what has happened? There seem to be fewer chirps. I sense sadness in the chorus. Much still remains to be done before the season's program ends. The concert continues. I go toward the house, silhouetted by its own gentle luminescence that intrudes on the darkness, and leave behind the sweet exhalations of earth, the treacherous fireflies, and the songs of a summer night.

> O cricket from your cheery cry
> No one would ever guess
> How quickly you must die.
> —Basho, 17th-century Japanese poet

> *Most of the luxuries, and many of the so-called comforts, of life are not only not indispensable, but positive hindrances to the elevation of mankind.*
> —Henry David Thoreau

A visitor studies the garden intently for a long time and finally comments that it is "busy out there." That perplexes me. It is midday. Nothing moves. "Busy?" I say. "Yes," she replies with an indefinite wave of the hand. "Lots of things going on. You know what I mean. Busy!" I try to see the garden through her eyes, as a stranger. It is rather like looking at

someone you know intimately and suddenly seeing them in a
new way.

She is right. It is "busy" out there. A lot is going on. Not
activity but a clutter of contraptions, tools, and materials. This
clutter, this "busyness," is the garden's mechanical or physical
life-support system, as compost and manure sustain it biologically; together they make the garden possible.

Seen through the visitor's eyes there is disorder everywhere.
Strewn about are plastic pails, stacked bales of peat moss, a
steel drum for manure tea, watering cans, two cold frames long
overdue for paint and glazing, stacks of old screens for protecting tender seedlings from the sun and for drying onions, the
compost bin, compost-sifting screen, piles of manure, plastic
windscreens, an old table with sink for washing vegetables,
and numerous plastic milk crates bearing warnings of terrible
penalties for failure to return to this or that dairy promptly;
the crates are handy for collecting vegetables and make fine
impromptu footstools or seats.

There is more disorder: hoses snaking along the ground,
scattered bricks used to anchor plastic during windstorms, bird
bath surrounded by geraniums, rolled fencing the peas grew
on, galvanized cans containing wood ashes and rabbit manure,
tomatoes spilling over their cages, some now tilted with the
weight of the bearing plants, and raised beds placed more by
whim than design. Propped against the fence are tools I neglected
to put away.

More unsettling to the orderly eye are scores of sticks, poles,
metal rods, and stakes thrust into the earth and leaning at different angles; there must be a hundred or more. They were set
out to mark newly planted rows, warn of tender transplants,
or remind me to water this or weed that. There are so many
in such disarray that they could be some kind of weird volunteers sprouting from the earth and frozen in a wild dance.

I see them now through the visitor's eyes. She was being
charitable. The profusion of markers looks more berserk than

busy. They represent a sort of system I evolved to signal what needs doing. I once considered painting them different colors to designate various tasks to be done, another of my inventions that never got off the ground.

The "busyness" is emphasized by the late season. Much of my untidiness was formerly concealed by early summer's lush growth, but as plants died off or were removed, my transgressions against order were starkly revealed. The markers remain, a profusion of tilted broom and mop handles, broken fishing rods, aluminum poles, stakes, pipes, and laths. I no longer remember which stood for what or if the chores they were to alert me to got done.

The visitor sees these various items as so many unruly objects. To me almost every one has personal meaning. Every garden has its own history. The gardener alone knows what each irregularity signifies, as a historian can rattle off battles and significant events. A patch in the fence recalls a rototiller mishap. A sagging gate was victim of a miscalculation in backing up the truck. New fence posts, higher than others, replaced some that rotted. The older a garden is, the more adventures encountered, the more wound stripes it is likely to bear. All may add to the general sense of disorder or enhance its personality.

Most of the garden's physical support system, except for the tools, came from the town dump. Astonishing finds used to be available for the discerning picker. The problem was not to be overwhelmed, not to take more back than you brought and to take only what you could use at the time, not what might prove handy at some future date. Alas! The golden days of dump picking are over. The dump is now a sanitary landfill, everything usable or unusable covered immediately by a bulldozer. Euphemisms pose their own dangers.

Nothing is changed, really, except the antiseptic title. We now bury what we used to burn and pollute the earth instead of the air. The old dump was, at least, a kind of community recycling center. The landfill represents pure waste, the ultimate repository of America's once-great wealth. When a society finds it more economical to waste than to conserve its natural resources it is in mortal danger.

Every civilization that ever existed ultimately collapsed. We may be the first to bury ourselves under own wastes. A society can be measured by what it throws away. Archaeologists use the dump sites of ancient civilizations to determine what kind of people they served. What will future archaeologists say about us?*

Every gardening book worth its compost devotes at least one section to tools. The list is usually extensive, depending on the tastes and purse of the writer. The more expensive the book, generally, the more expensive and elaborate the tools and equipment considered necessary. An illustration may show a toolshed, doors ajar, revealing equipment neatly hanging from hooks at the ready, the shelves a tidy arrangement of supplies.

What would Thoreau have thought of such displays? The only tool he referred to in Walden, as I recall, was a hoe to cultivate his beans. I assume he had a shovel to turn the earth and possibly a rake to smooth it but I doubt if he went much beyond those basic implements. I can imagine a pithy aphorism directed against those who complicate their lives with excess gardening baggage, something to the effect that an honest hoe in the hands of an honest husbandsman is all that is necessary to cultivate the soil of the earth rather than the furrows of commerce.

Garden tools have become so expensive that Thoreau's advice to simplify our lives with fewer possessions makes sense, if only economically. The more equipment one has, the larger the structure necessary to house it. An entire barn or garage can be devoted to storing the machinery alone considered necessary to gardening today.

*The local dump-and fill recently became a "transfer station"; we now send our wastes elsewhere for burning and some recycling.

My own tools are relatively simple, but Thoreau would likely have had an aphorism for me, too: "An honest tiller of the soil can use a single hoe for both the soil and the spirit." The damning truth is that I have not just one but several hoes (all for the soil). Most were salvaged or handed down but a few, admittedly, I bought. Hoes are a weakness of mine. I have a variety of shapes, including one that is a hook and another a small triangle designed to work in close to the plants.

Nothing seems to excite the imagination and stir the creative juices of inventive gardeners like hoes and weeds. Almost every garden catalogue offers some revolutionary style of hoe possessing miraculous powers. Do I need it? I ask myself. Can I do without it? Economics and Thoreau usually keep me in line.

In a moment of inspiration I had an idea for a revolutionary hoe with miraculous powers but it never got beyond the usual idea stage. I learned long ago that it is better not to put home-made miracles to the test.

I am as impressed by the few tools necessary to garden as I am by the number I have accumulated. Most hang in the toolshed, only rarely or never used. I have no recollection where most came from or why I kept them. I am not sure what a couple are for. I tend to use certain favorites again and again. Tools have a personality of their own, a proper feel. If a tool does not have the right feel it hangs unused. Most of my favorites have gone through a succession of handles.

Garden tools have a special meaning. They represent one of the great milestones in human evolution, when man began to grow his own food. The first tool was probably a pointed stick to scratch the earth and plant a seed, a revolutionary act that may mark the real beginning of civilization, the transition from hunter to farmer and the first settled communities. Then he learned to attach a shell or sharp stone to the stick and he had a primitive hoe and progress was on its way.

A hoe is still the basic gardening tool, as it must have been for ancient growers. I usually leave a hoe propped near the gate for impromptu use. My favorite was once used to mix concrete and still has mortar clinging to the handle. Other favorite tools are a rake with one missing tooth but perfect balance, a round-nose shovel for digging, a six-tine pitchfork for mulch and compost, and a heavy four-prong potato rake for unloading the truck of manure or thatch.

I like to have two of the tools I use the most frequently, an indulgence that I justify with my own kind of rationalization. Much time can be wasted looking for a misplaced hoe, rake, or shovel—a problem not covered in gardening manuals.

The toolshed, with mouse as curator, houses a wheelbarrow and garden cart, the latter a bargain that came as a kit from a discount store. I could get along nicely without the wheelbar-row, which is seldom used now and has a flat tire. I keep it because Bret gave it to me long ago. That is the trouble with sentiment; it takes up so much room.

The overburdened toolshed also contains a freewheeling assortment of watering devices, posthole digger, sledgeham-mer, ax, mattock, fork, crowbar, and on the floor are bushel baskets, tarps, bags of mineral supplements, and a rusting shovel and fork awaiting new handles. A shelf holds rotenone powder and "gun," along with odds and ends. Generations of mouse families have been raised in the containers on the shelf. In the potting shed, which forms the back of the toolshed, are trays with small hand tools, stacks of pots, flats, row markers, twine, and other essentials of gardening.

The only power equipment I own is the small tiller men-tioned previously, but it is used sparingly. The tines revolve so rapidly that they pulverize the soil. This can interfere with solid root contact when transplanting, and small seeds tend to get buried too deeply and lost when planting. A small tiller is not as easy to use as the ads claim; it must be pulled backward to dig into the earth, and like most machinery, it is noisy; it also tends to break down frequently.

The tiller, when working, does its job with commendable vigor and enthusiasm and saves many backache units (BAUs), my measure of garden tasks. It is especially useful for cultivating and chopping manure or compost into the soil but I flinch from the way it attacks the earth. Nature, the ultimate gardener, eschews such violence. Despite the tiller's advantages, it has no personality, a shortcoming of all machines, one not encountered with hand tools.

Every gardener can list the equipment he or she considers necessary or important, based largely on personal experience, philosophy, style, taste, finances, time available, expectations, and what a garden represents for its keeper. Voltaire bade us tend our gardens but, unfortunately, did not tell us how or which tools to use.

Fall

Just after the death of the flowers,
  And before they are buried in snow,
There comes a festival season
When Nature is all aglow.
            —Author unknown

Fall made a stealthy appearance during a rainy spell this week. Officially it arrived at 4:46 yesterday morning but had already announced its presence in innumerable small ways: in the lighter air after summer's humidity, the diminishing heat of the sun, the fading foliage, morning fog, and clear night sky. The moon has a clarity and brilliance present no other time of year, transforming the garden into a frozen sea of light. The days are noticeably shorter, the nights cooler.

Most of the songbirds have departed and the mornings are strangely silent. I no longer sleep with one foot outside the covers. Lily does not want to stay out after dark. The garden chorus has reduced volume and slowed tempo. Peggy is potting plants that will come inside for the winter, a seasonal rite that alone makes fall official for me.

The garden is singing its September song. Plants that are

exhausted or dead go into the compost, joined by others that are still in good heart but have no time to mature. In the end everything goes into the compost, all of the yesterdays and todays that give life to tomorrow's gardens.

On this early fall day the garden is trying to reconcile the change from summer to autumn. The air is warm but there is a haze which the sun has not yet burned off. The foghorn at the ocean cuts through the overcast. Bees fly lazily about. Bumblebees buzz ferociously in the thyme. There are good earth smells. Traffic noise from the highway is finally muted after summer's frantic search by tourists for relaxation and escape from problems. Tourists are as much a part of the cadence of the seasons here as the weather and tides.

The garden foliage is turning yellow but the surrounding pines remain brave and resolute, as green as ever. Only a few leaves have turned on the sturdy oaks. Trees and people have much in common. Both are pawns of invisible forces over which they have no control. Perhaps this year the trees will declare their independence and refuse to shed their leaves or needles upon command. Why should not trees rebel against the tiresome cycle of events that rules them, just as gardens resist the discipline imposed on them, and as people try to break their unseen bonds?

When Bret was in his early teen years he said to me, "I'm tired of doing all the things I have to do."

"What are the things you have to do?" I asked.

"I mean like having to get up in the morning and dress and eat breakfast and go to school."

I saw his point. It does get tiresome living by rhythms established for you and not by your body, rhythms that violate individual biological clocks to conform to rigid rules imposed by society's conventions. "Why don't you take a day off?" I said. "Why go to school? Why not stay in bed all day and sleep and eat? Defy the world!"

"Can I?" he said eagerly.

"Of course."

"All right, I will."

But he never did. I asked him why not. He said, "Oh, I would get too far behind. Besides it wouldn't change anything. It would only be putting off everything for a while and I'd have to do twice as much then."

I had no answer for him then nor do I now. I, too, am caught in the invisible web that encompasses all living things. I, too, respond to a silent command on this fall day, just like the trees, the seasons, the tides, the tourists, and the plants. Like the garden, I am in a state of transition, accommodating to the changing season. A new self emerges, my fall and winter self; I am molting and casting aside my old skin just like some developing insects shed their old, confining forms.

My summer self was more extravagant, outgoing, and even optimistic. My fall and winter self is more withdrawn and contemplative. I take my mood from the garden. I look forward to "hibernation." This new fall self would confront the unanswered questions and unresolved dilemmas that my summer self ignored or pretended did not exist.

The garden, as my new self takes over, is an oasis of peace. The great discipline that governs all things prevails. It submerges little rebellions and mutterings of protest. It gives purpose and order to the flow of days. It protects me from relentless and unseen pursuers.

In an imperfect world where so many things are wrong and we can do so little about them, it is reassuring and comforting to have one small area where we can exert some measure of control and make it much as we want it to be. The garden, on this new fall day, another birthday just past, is my safe harbor, my port of embarkation as I sail into the uncharted sea of old age.

There comes a point in human affairs, at least garden affairs, when expectations and baseless optimism give way to the real-

ization that certain things will not be. The reason is less important than the emerging reality. That which has not been done
in the garden probably will not get done. It is a time to pause
and take stock of what I did not get around to. The list of tasks
undone is depressingly long and familiar. But things that never
get done are also part of gardening.

Once again I did not paint the cold frames or reglaze the
glass. I did not cover the compost to prevent nutrients from
leeching out. I did not rototill the entire garden to work in a
top dressing of compost and manure and expose buried insect
eggs and sleeping insects to reduce next summer's assault. I
did not get around to planting a green manure crop to take root
before cold weather sets in.

The garden is both forgiving and generous. It will overlook
my misdemeanors. It demands almost no attention this time of
year but continues to produce like an old friend repaying a
debt of gratitude past its time of need.

I look at the earth and think about the thousands and thousands of insect eggs and sleeping animals snugged down there
awaiting next summer's garden. They were more conscientious than I. For them the stakes are higher. My oversights and
delays pass almost unnoticed. Their failure to get eggs into the
earth on schedule, or to take refuge themselves, would be fatal.

How do they know they are the final generation of summer
and it is time to go under? What is the triggering mechanism?
The weather had not changed perceptibly when they prepared
for winter. Are they aware of the great responsibility they have
to keep their link in the chain of life unbroken? Do they count
on the sloth of gardeners like myself not to expose their eggs
or disrupt their winter slumber?

I marvel anew at the complex web we call life as I contemplate the creatures of the garden, most now out of sight. They
do not seem to be going much of anywhere, evolutionwise, as
far as I can see. The cockroach, it is said, has not changed in

250 million years. Did it take as its motto, "If it's not broken don't fix it"?

The others do not seem to be making visible progress, according to their biographers. On the other hand, I do not see that my own kind is doing so well either, according to what I read in the papers. Evolution could afford to move at a leisurely pace when the world was more static. Now, with man speeding up changes in the earth and technology altering everything almost overnight, evolution had better crank up or it will be left behind.

The new season advances ever so slyly in its annual pilgrimage. The earth gradually cools, to be followed by chilling frosts. Once-vibrant plants turn apathetic and then become dormant. It is all gradual, slow, dignified, an inevitable process without malaise, scruple, remorse, or sadness. For the garden there is no artificial life-support system at this time to generate false hope or rejuvenate deadened desire, no clinging to that which is forever past. There is no altering or denying this reality as fall deepens and the weather becomes steadily cooler.

A few flowers remain, visited by bees stoking up for winter, transferring pollen to ovum, "brides and their bridegrooms, meeting in the wedding chamber," as Carolus Linnaeus wrote in his epic taxonomy of plants, an anthropomorphic description that shocked his eighteenth-century peers, upsetting them more by noting that "the nuptials are celebrated openly before the whole world." My late-blooming flowers unabashedly seek their own immortality as the season winds down.

The sun drops progressively lower in the afternoon sky. By mid-winter it seems to hang perilously and then sink slowly into the sea. The sun is a crimson ball of fire that will surely scorch the earth and set the sea to boiling as it dips beneath the horizon.

Year after year, from the study window overlooking the garden, my lookout post on the world I oversee, I watch the sun swing back and forth, nadir to zenith, and then reverse itself, like a mighty cosmic pendulum. This daily progression, summer to winter, winter into summer, reminds me of a series of still photographs. From my fixed station I can almost measure the daily movement of the sun in feet and inches. Each evening the sun moves this many more feet toward spring or fall. The setting sun and moon are in the same sky as we begin to prepare for the winter not yet in sight.

> *There is something in October sets the gypsy blood astir.*
> —Bliss Carman

It is early morning when I arrive at the beach parking lot. Stu is already waiting in his red pickup. "Are you ready to go?" he calls. His face is ruddy from the early morning chill and he is in high spirits. Stu is always in high spirits.

We stop at the entrance to the beach where the blacktop ends, put the vehicles in four-wheel drive, and let some air out of the tires. From here we cannot see over the dune but there is the salt tang of the sea, the smell of fish, the gurgle of incoming waves. The sky is marvelously blue.

We go in pairs in case either vehicle breaks down or gets stuck in the wet sand. Stu is more experienced with this kind of driving so he leads the way. We follow tracks left by fishermen. The bay is flat and iridescent with only tiny waves lapping against the shore, last week's storm forgotten, that wild fury now a gentle murmur.

An elderly couple sit on beach chairs, huddled in blankets, staring at the deep. They nod imperceptibly to us. They are probably retirees newly moved here or visitors. They squint in the sunlight as they gaze steadily out at the vastness of the sea, perhaps contemplating their own abyss within.

We leave the couple behind and continue down the beach. We have about two hours before the incoming tide could trap us, time enough, with luck, to extricate ourselves should either vehicle run into trouble.

We drive about half a mile, barely skirting the waves. Sharing the beach with us are gulls, plovers, and the fleet sandpipers racing back and forth with the waves in the endless game they play with the ocean, a kind of timeless ballet engaging birds and sea.

High on the beach, at the foot of the dunes, are rotting timbers washed ashore long ago, parts of stricken ships that were beached or broken in the surf and driven up on the sand to be covered and uncovered by countless tides in the eternal pulsations of the sea. The area, offshore, is known as a graveyard of ships, thousands of unlucky vessels having gone down on the shoals.

There is the corpse of a gull, dead fish, shells of horseshoe crabs and remains of other small marine disasters, and debris washed in by the tides. In a one-week survey Seashore rangers found 5,829 artifacts on five lower Cape beaches, 80 percent of them plastic.

We pass several fishermen. Many spend the entire night on the beach surfcasting, apparently unmindful of the cold. They never seem to get discouraged if they catch nothing, pulling in empty lines and casting again and again, ever hopeful. For many the act of fishing is more important than catching fish. Some give their catch away or throw it back into the water, finding in the act their own interchange with nature.

The air on this early October morning is cool, almost cold, with a stern, bracing quality. The only sounds are the waves and the crunch of tires in wet sand. Ahead is our destination, an enormous buildup of seaweed washed in during last week's storm, collected in long windrows as high as my head. It bears the briny scent of the sea and is a deep green, made up of many varieties but primarily eel grass. This is a bit of luck. Seaweed seldom collects in such huge quantities, and then it is soon covered by sand or washed back to sea. If it remains for any length of time it starts to decompose with a foul odor like methane gas or a corrupted cesspool. During the tourist season the towns dispatch crews to bury or remove it.

Stu discovered this cache while reconnoitering the beach and generously alerted me. Usually we have to gather the stuff in small amounts, a forkful at a time, along the wrack line. Visitors to the beach, probably city people, often seem puzzled when they see us collecting seaweed and ask what we do with it. We tell them it is for the garden. They nod but look skeptical; the idea of having a garden seems foreign to many.

Seaweed has been extensively studied but no one knows exactly how it works in gardens. It was used by the Romans to grow crops some two thousand years ago. Modern·research has found that it improves soil, promotes germination, mitigates transplant shock, boosts yields, discourages some fungi, and helps control certain predators, including flea beetles and aphids, while attracting ladybugs; it strengthens root systems, increases photosynthesis, helps plants absorb trace elements, and enhances resistance to frost. All that and free! When available.

Seaweed has about the same amount of potash and nitrogen as an equivalent amount of cow manure, at least fifty minerals, including all major and minor plant elements and acids that improve soil texture, as well as vitamins and hormones that encourage and control plant growth and promote yields. Seaweed helps make up for the poverty of our seashore soil.

It is only to gather this wonder substance that I bring a vehicle on the beach, disrupting the harmonies of nature and the peace and reflections of those who come to escape the clamor and pressures of daily life. Often I prefer to buy it as a liquid extract and use it primarily to give new transplants a gentle boost.

Seaweed has the advantage over manure of being weed and disease free. I let the pile rest so rains can wash off much of the salt, and then rototill it into the earth in the fall for decomposition over the winter. It can also be broken down in compost. Either way it makes soil black and rich. I have used it as mulch but it tends to dry out and blow around unless covered by a heavier material.

Seaweed has served seashore communities in many ways. Early settlers used it for insulation, piling the stuff around the foundations of their homes, which had no basements. A friend of mine found it in the walls of his two-hundred-year-old house much as fiberglass is used now; he simply transferred it to his garden and tilled it in.

In early days some Cape Cod towns regulated the amount of seaweed individuals could take in times of scarcity. The only restrictions now are those imposed by nature and the rules governing beach access for vehicles.

For all its virtues in gardens, bathers consider seaweed objectionable floating in the surf. Lifeguards often have to rake the beaches they oversee in the morning, one of the less glamorous aspects of the job. The only quarrel I have with seaweed is the broken fishing line caught in it that gets tangled in the rototiller's tines.

Before we start to load I take time to marvel at our surroundings. Everything is of a part: land, sky, water, seabirds, the fresh morning breeze, the sun still pale and withholding its warmth. There is the rhythmic murmur of waves breaking on the shore, ever advancing and retreating as they have for millions of years, the shriek of gulls outraged by our presence on their turf, or surf, and properly so. This is their realm. We are the intruders. The tire tracks and our presence are the only visible violations of a timeless world where land meets sea.

We back the pickups, red and blue, to the huge mounds of brilliantly green seaweed, button our jackets tighter against the chill, and use pitchforks to load. The seaweed is mounded so high that we can stand on the lowered tailgates to work. The seaweed is heavy with salt water washed in on the night's tide and already has a strong odor when disturbed; it will have to be composted without delay.

We keep a watchful eye on the incoming tide. Each new wave washes slightly closer. We had counted on two trips this morning but will get only one. We have but a day or two to remove the seaweed before it is covered by sand from the tides or the sea reclaims it as food for its own. Or, possibly, the town will send out a crew to bury or remove it. We work steadily together, loading first one vehicle, then the other.

Most of the time we do not talk. Words have little place here and violate the sense of timelessness that nature imposes. But once Stu pauses and looks up to exclaim, "Isn't this great?" "Yes," I say, "great!"

The third day comes a frost, a killing frost . . .
—William Shakespeare

*W*inter has made it clear that it is on the way. We had our first frost, not a killing assault, to be sure, but a frost nonetheless. It showed that it meant business by injuring the plants so they sagged. They must be aware that there will be no more growth for them this year, or ever again, for that matter.

When we awakened, the frost lay white against the garden like spun silver, every plant painstakingly coated by a master painter. The crystals glistened in the morning sun, refracting the brilliant light in many colors and shadings. Nature, ever an extravagant but impatient artist, is soon bored with her creations and eager to change them or get on with another project. Within minutes the frost vanished, leaving the earth its customary seasonal brown.

All around us is the glory of autumn, the deciduous trees, and especially the few maples, radiant in multihued splendor. The oaks try to join the fall foliage festival but the best they can manage is to look drab and forlorn. Everything seems to be waiting.

Nighttime temperatures sank into the thirties with the frost. To prove that it is not to be taken lightly, the cold sent the thermometer plunging two degrees lower the following night and most of the remaining plants drooped ominously, anticipating the final blow, signaling that the end is near.

Broccoli is one of the few crops not intimidated by winter's early visit. It has a resolute personality. Broccoli is an irrepressible optimist and continues to think positively as the cold moves in and more susceptible plants of negative outlook fade or succumb. This is an admirable quality in man, woman, or vegetable but, in truth, I find broccoli a little too bouncy for my tastes, even a little depressing. I suppose it is all a matter of reality, and one reality is probably as good as another if it serves its possessor well. Reality, after all, is where it takes you.

This year I put the fall broccoli in late but with its upbeat temperament it managed to head before the cold came and will continue to grow, if at a slower pace, for the next few weeks, providing fresh broccoli for the table and some to freeze. This is especially fortunate because we lost most of the early planting when the weather turned suddenly hot and the plants went to flower without heading. Even then, the broccoli found a silver lining, exulting in the explosion of yellow blossoms that fed the bees and cheered the summer garden.

I am surprised that Prince Charles did not mention any conversations he had with broccoli. Perhaps it was some delicacy on his part, a respect for private communication. I have never personally talked to a broccoli, or even a broccolo, but have eavesdropped on their chats and overheard other vegetables discussing them. There is considerable resentment and envy because of broccoli's hardiness and increasing popularity as a nutritional source.

Broccoli is rich in iron, calcium, and vitamins A, B, and C. It is a member of the cabbage family, related to cauliflower. In England it is called winter cauliflower. Webster describes it as "a large hardy cauliflower," which I consider a bit of a slight and do not altogether go along with. Broccoli can stand on its own without family connections.

Historically, broccoli has been around long enough to prove its staying power. It was grown by the Romans some two thousand years ago but did not become popular in the United States until the 1920s, which may reflect more on American tastes than on broccoli. Nutritionists and cooks have made such a fuss over it in recent years that it is now found in many home gardens.

Broccoli is easy to grow and has few pest or disease problems. The biggest menace I have encountered is root maggots, but they usually attack only the early crop and can be managed with collars, floating row covers, or other precautions to keep the flies from laying eggs at the base of the stems.

Broccoli is forgiving about soil conditions, as befits its plucky disposition, thriving even in our sandy soil. It likes plenty of organic matter, moisture, and mulch to keep the roots evenly cool and moist. Its only display of temperament is a dislike of extreme heat or cold.

Broccoli that is heading should be cut while the buds, or flower clusters, are still tight and have a dark green luster. Even after the heads are removed the plants develop numerous edible bonus sideshoots. Broccoli is really quite determined, although this may be aided by positive thinking. The sideshoots continue to form until the plant is cut down by excessive heat or cold.

Along with being tasty, nutritious, and easy to grow, broccoli is among the most versatile of all vegetables in food preparation; with fresh or frozen on hand, a quick and delicious meal can always be whipped up.

Broccoli can be served with seasoning, butter, and a dash of lemon or cider vinegar, in casseroles, soufflés, salads, soups, enchiladas, pureed, baked, hot or cold with a mayonnaise sauce, and, for those of such tastes, layered with chicken or other meats in a white sauce, or sour cream for the brave and defiant. Fresh raw broccoli makes a delicious appetizer served with a dip or in salads. My own favorite is fresh out of the garden prepared as a salad.

PEGGY'S BROCCOLI SALAD

1½–2 lbs. fresh broccoli (4 cups when ready to cook)
1 small red onion, peeled, trimmed, and cut into ¼-inch cubes, about 1 cup
3 tsp. Dijon mustard
4 Tbsp. lemon juice
¼ cup olive oil
¼ cup parsley, chopped fine
salt to taste

1. Trim off and discard rough stems and core of broccoli. Cut remainder into bite-size pieces, enough to make 4 cups.
2. Boil water, enough to cover broccoli. Let cook 5 minutes or until crisp-tender. Drain. Put pieces in salad bowl. Sprinkle with onion cubes.
3. Put mustard in mixing bowl and add lemon juice, stirring rapidly with wire whisk. Add oil while beating vigorously. Add desired salt and parsley.
4. Spoon dressing over broccoli and serve hot, lukewarm, or cold. Yields 4 servings.

> *No warmth, no cheerfulness, no healthful ease,*
> *No comfortable feel in any member—*
> *No shade, no shine, no butterflies, no bees,*
> *No fruits, no flowers, no leaves, no*
>   *birds,*
>   *November!*
>   —Thomas Hood

*W*hat is more desolate looking than a November garden in the rain? A writer, whose name I neglected to note, aptly described such a sight as "having an atmosphere of its own, composed of weak sunlight and that wet collapse which a dying garden exudes." The October garden was tired but not without hope. This one recognizes that it has entered its final season. It has found something beyond hope. Acceptance.

From the study window I look down on the vegetable corpses with dismay. A miasma of melancholy seems to rise from the ruins of summer. Perhaps I am thinking about my own November. I feel an urge to spare the fallen plants the indignity of public suffering and resolve to give them, without further delay, decent interment in the compost bin, as if becoming a new part of the life cycle would confer a cheering plant immortality on them. But I do not move. I continue to stare at the stricken plants and contemplate my own sense of loss at the death of summer.

The garden is silent now. The summer chorus is stilled, the songs of love and hope hushed. The musicians have perished, gone underground, or found shelter to await the coming of spring. Most have died and left behind some part of themselves, returning to earth that which they took from it.

November comes by its reputation for dreariness honestly. It is a churlish, sullen month. For the first time we look into what an old newspaper clipping I hold refers to as "the cold and angry eye of winter." It is the grayest, cloudiest month of the year, with rain, clouds, or snow blotting out the sun 50 percent of the time. November is one of the wettest and wind-iest months of the year. Some of the worst storms in the Northeast have occurred during November, including one in 1898 that sank 202 vessels off the New England coast.

At night now, when I take kitchen scraps to the compost bin, I listen in vain for an echo of the music of the departed musicians of summer. The moon looks cold and alien as winter readies its hand. I no longer tarry to savor the sky and that sweet sense of mystery and sadness that belongs to summer nights so quickly gone.

> *The wind one morning sprang up from sleep,*
> *Saying, "Now for a frolic, now for a leap!*
> *Now for a madcap galloping chase!*
> *I'll make a commotion in every place!"*
> —William Howitt

The wind is kicking up its heels today, shrieking, howling, striking the house with great hammer blows. Through the study window I see the garden being pummeled unmerci-fully. Pails and screens are hurled around. A row of bedrag-gled winter kale whips about like a chorus line gone berserk.

Wind is a fact of life here. It almost never ceases to blow on this peninsula sixty-five miles at sea. Unobstructed ocean winds stunt the tough little pines which regulate the height and veloc-ity of ground winds, setting their own terms on how much protection we shall have. Wind and trees are forever locked in unresolved dispute.

When we came here the ceaseless wind bothered me. Now I am used to it. When it does not blow I find myself listening for it, wondering what is wrong, almost uneasy.

Wind is especially hard on the garden. It dries out soil and plants, causes erosion, and can lower temperatures, slowing growth. During storms it can literally whip plants to death or so weaken them that they succumb to disease or insects. It is particularly hard on the sensitive eggplants and cucumbers. Beans have been ripped out of the earth and stripped of leaves, peppers bowled over, and other shallow-rooted plants set back, their maturity delayed.

The frisky wind has overturned cold frames and smashed glass covers, knocked tripods of pole beans askew, and tilted tomato cages, uprooting plants. A particularly vicious wind tore a storm window off the house, its replacement now reinforced with duct tape already ripped into shreds.

Gale-force winds (39–54 miles per hour) are not unusual. Some are in the storm range (55–74). I have not been here during a hurricane (75 plus) but have read how those of the past drove mountainous waves that wreaked their fury against the shore and civilization's puny outposts. Experts say we are overdue for a hurricane of 100 mile-an-hour winds. The future holds many threats. Ten thousand years from now, we are told, Cape Cod will be covered by ocean, making real estate here a risky investment.

The winds we live with day by day have many moods and tempers. The winds of summer, when I work in the garden, carry such diverse sounds as the whine of traffic from Route 6, tolling church bells, the whinny of horses at pasture, dogs barking, bird songs, the music of insects. In fall, winter, and spring we are buffeted by winds of force and authority; nor'easters are especially dreaded, often lasting for days, giving our small world a forlorn drenched appearance and causing human spirits to sag. The wind in such a tempest may bear the breath of an odorous broth composed of dead fish, salt spray, fog, rotting seaweed, and the abiding mystery of the deep itself as mighty waves crash against the shore, reclaiming waterfront properties for the sea, distressing homeowners and chambers of commerce.

Most old-timers here are knowledgeable about the wind,

strategically sheltering their gardens. They have lived with untamed ocean winds all thier lives, reading them as city people do newspaper weather forecasts. They sniff the air knowingly and exclaim, "We're in for a spell of weather." Or a cursory, "Rain's comin'." The sky may be cloudless but by wind direction and some inner wisdom they know that rain or change is imminent; often they best the official forecast.

Bill keeps tabs on the weather with a variety of wind vanes he makes of copper, lined up in a row. He gave me one in the shape of a rooster. I enjoyed watching chanticleer try to figure out what the erratic winds were really up to. It whirled crazily, undecided which way to head, and finally collapsed or had a breakdown under the congress of conflicting winds, hanging bent, immobile, and confused on its spindle. Bill reinforced the copper rooster but I have not yet returned it to test its newly installed valor in confronting the swirling winds that assail our hill and garden.

Occasionally, around midday in the summer, the air is fairly still, a lull between the offshore breezes of morning and the cooling onshore winds of afternoon. Such moments of calm are rare. The oak that grows beside the kitchen window where we eat is almost never motionless, threshing wildly in storms, lashing the house violently as if protesting the intimacy forced upon it.

The only protection the garden has against the battering wind is the ring of trees. But they pose a dilemma. If I leave too many they shade the plants. Cut them and I lose my protection. Tree windbreaks, planted during the dustbowl days of the thirties, were found to blunt the wind's force, sending aloft vertical columns of air up to twenty times the height of the barrier. I take my chances by leaving the trees.

Wind is the principal limiting factor in most seashore gardens, the one element over which there is little control. Often the plastic windscreens I erect are knocked over and sent reeling as the wind mocks my efforts to divert it.

The sound of wind is one of my early memories, sighing through the open loft of a Kansas barn as I lay in sweet-smelling hay from adjoining fields. In a stall below was Jimmy, a stallion described to me as "an Indian horse," so wild that no one had ever been able to ride him except my cousin Mel, who was wild like Jimmy, a dozen years older than I.

A few years later Mel died in an accident, on ice skates, part of his wildness, not yet thirty, and he was buried close to where he had ridden Jimmy the Indian horse. The gravesite was under a tree on a hill overlooking a river, and I remember the wind moaning over the grave as the coffin was lowered into the ground.

I have heard and felt many of the winds of the earth, the keening wind of the Midwest prairie, the unnerving Mideast desert sorocco, gentle winds stirring a temple-like Pacific forest; I have experienced a tornado that brought down a stone church. Often now I awaken in the night to hear the wind-driven surf throbbing against the shore.

I think of the great winds that sweep the earth in response to its vast weather engine powered by the sun, coursing endlessly between poles and equator, concocting storms, spawning dust devils, pollinating plants, broadcasting seeds, propelling airborne creatures, cooling bathers at the seashore, drying clothes on lines, and teasing and resisting the strictures of civilization.

The same winds that girdle the planet may once have sighed through the loft of a Kansas barn and moaned over the grave of my cousin who died at an early age, and now they playfully fling pails and scatter screens in a garden located on a peninsula extending into the sea.

Impulsively I resolve that tomorrow I shall return the copper rooster to his outpost to keep tabs on the nomad sea winds that buffet this weary old globe as it spins endlessly through space churning up new winds to accommodate the pageant called life.

Winter

For iron Winter held her firm;
Across her sky he laid his hand;
And birds he starved, he stiffened worm;
A sightless heaven, a shaven land.
                              —George Meredith

W̲inter has struck. Real winter, not the calendar event, which lies ahead. It arrived at its own pace and time. All day there was a feeling of change in the air. The morning was mild but the sky overcast. There was a brooding sensation, the tension of an electrically charged atmosphere.

Morning breezes gave way to gusts. By late afternoon the wind gained velocity and shifted to the northwest. There was, at first, a slight chill. The sky became increasingly gray. The temperature dropped suddenly. By dark it was freezing. During the night the cold struck with savage fury, driven by shrieking winds. By morning the birdbath was frozen solid, the ground seared by cold, the grass brittle to walk on.

The day remained cold, below freezing, but the sun was bright and the house deceptively warm from solar radiation. Lily kept crying to go out and almost immediately was back screeching to come in. That night the temperature plunged again, and again the following night, the third time in succession, like an assault force battering down the enemy with repeated attacks, each picking up where the last left off.

From nature's point of view, I suppose, this change is not as abrupt or severe as it appears to me. For weeks the days have been mild, the nights progressively chilly, gradually cooling the earth in preparation for the coup de grace of our brief Indian summer.

Now the garden is ransacked by the vandal winter. Several plants survived the early frost and the first assault of serious cold, the irrepressible broccoli, kale, a few beets that never got picked, some heads of cabbage, the remaining celery, and a row of parsley. All but the kale finally succumbed to the repeated blows of cold, the tissues ruptured by the freezing and expansion of their own juices, a kind of biological treachery imposed by winter.

The kale, although sagging slightly, remains a rich green and will survive the winter, usable through spring until it goes to flower, sending the bees into ecstasy. The beehives have been insulated for winter, entrances reduced to keep out mice and other would-be lodgers looking for snug quarters. The bees are already in their winter cluster with the queen protected in the middle, served by the faithful few who will live until spring when newcomers take over.

Several bees flew around me as I winterized the hives. When I went into the house one had clung to my clothing and beat its wings frantically against the glass to escape. I trapped it in a container and released it in front of the hives. It went unerringly to the right one and scurried through the entrance, disappearing without as much as a farewell wave or thank you.

The garden now wears its winter coat. When I applied mulch a week ago it seemed strange to be preparing for the cold on such a lovely day. Carrots and leeks are under huge mounds of thatch to be dug as needed. Lettuce grows in a cold frame and will be harvested through the first of the year. The last potato beetle of the season had found the last potato plant and was ravishing it alone; the tubers, having yielded their secrets, are stored in the root cellar along with other produce.

Shelves in the root cellar are lined with colorful jars of processed tomatoes, dilly beans, pickles, relish, jams, and jellies. Other vegetables are in the freezer. Drying herbs hang from the kitchen beams lending a festive touch along with their fragrance. Dried flowers on a tray exude their own aroma while awaiting conversion into potpourri.

When the temperature started to tumble, Peggy rescued large clumps of fresh basil, chives, parsley, and dill which now rest in glasses of water over the kitchen sink. Those edible bouquets retain a brilliant green while their fallen comrades lie prostrate and brown outside. The indoor herbs will last a week or more. Some can be rooted and transplanted to pots of soil and grown for winter use.

Before the killing cold struck, some tomatoes were still turning a hopeful red. We picked a few in time and they ripen on a windowsill. A border of impatiens around the herb bed remained to thrust straight up, proud and haughty, defying the calendar to the end. Then the cold came. The garden seemed to be taken by surprise, as if never sensing impending disaster.

The cold hit without warning. News accounts claimed it was some kind of record for the date. We always seem to take comfort in statistics, as if they help mitigate the impact of adversity or give an extra dimension to unexpected triumph or good fortune. There may be some kind of perverse pride in enduring the coldest, hottest, largest, shortest, most, least, or some extreme never confronted by previous generations. I have noticed the same kind of perverse pride or satisfaction in very old people upon learning that their contemporaries have died, the ultimate victory in the ultimate competition in a competitive society.

There is no solace for the garden. The morning after the first cold wave struck, the flowers still had their color, although somewhat faded, the edges of the blooms a bit shriveled, a startled expression on their flower faces, as if death had come as a shock, a final terrible awareness of the end. It reminded me of the face of a beautiful young woman I saw on an autopsy table in the Bellevue morgue during my newspaper days, horror and surprise still etched on her face after she plunged to her death following some private disaster.

Following three days of intense cold and piercing winds, the weather has turned warm again. The sun shines almost hot against the deep russet leaves of the oak beside the kitchen window as we eat lunch. The windows are open. The cold-frame cover is again raised. Heat once more radiates from the earth. But now we know that this latest return to Indian summer is not to be trusted. We have lost our innocence. Gradually, by degrees, the cooling will go on with brief reprieves of warmth, possibly even an occasional hot day, until the cold comes to stay.

The zucchini, after producing a couple of final baby squash before being struck down, were dispatched to the compost without the honors due them for performing so valiantly. The broccoli, those fallen optimists of summer, have also gone to the compost. Unpicked cabbage and celery await disposal, along with the ravaged peppers. Some tomato plants still have green fruit clinging incongruously to blackened vines, like ornaments no longer camouflaged by the rich green foliage of the season past. The pole beans, after their usual late rally, succumbed, the green teepees now bare tripods entwined with dead vines in counterclockwise mortality.

The garden appears lifeless, although life still pulsates in the earth below, now slowed as the creatures burrow down for winter. The eggs and larvae of next year's pests and their predators are settled in until spring, like opposing armies that recognize an undeclared armistice and go into winter quarters. When the weather moderates, they will resume their perennial combat and begin new campaigns in the unending struggle for survival and advantage.

I think of the multitudes of soil residents and countless millions of seeds of vanished plants slumbering out of sight in the chilled earth as the drama of winter unfolds and casts its spell downward. The microorganisms will continue to perform their strange antics, multiplying and reducing their legions, until the penetrating cold eventually overtakes them and the bloody battleground of summer is at peace, stilled by the truce of winter.

In today's warm sunlight the impatiens look curiously battered, their haughty pride now gone. Marigolds and petunas in the window boxes remain as leafless dry corpses. Sunflowers, those stately sentinels of summer, are reduced to withered black stems supporting shriveled seed heads bowed like penitents at prayer. Rhubarb plants adjoining the herb bed sprawl on the earth in grotesque submission, as if they had never known vibrant life, their once-crisp stalks now so many lifeless ropes, summer soldiers cut down by the advance troops of winter, and our disrupted Indian summer lingers as a transitory and imperiled visitor awaiting its imminent doom.

Nothing that is can pause or stay;
The moon will wax, the moon will wane,
The mist and cloud will turn to rain,
The rain to mist and cloud again,
Tomorrow be today.
—Henry Wadsworth Longfellow

*W*e awaken to find ourselves prisoners of fog. The fine droplets of moisture form such a dense blanket that the garden is invisible from the house. I can see only the ghostly outlines of fence posts near the gate. To the east the overcast is so thick that there is no horizon. We could be inundated by the adjacent sea itself. All sounds are muffled, absorbed by the fog.

Nature, the artist, in putting on this fine performance, is unmindful of the inconvenience to me. I had planned to gather thatch this morning but now am forced to wait until the fog lifts. Never mind, nature says. Why all this busyness and hurry? I put on a splendid show for you. Fog is part of my ongoing poem. Relax and enjoy it.

It is sound advice. What difference whether I gather the thatch this morning, this afternoon, tomorrow, or ever for that matter? If I do not get the thatch something else will turn up. Nature is not that parsimonious or selective. She seems more interested in her poem than the product.

Look how I take care of you, she says. I blot out your garden so you cannot see all that you left undone and that needs doing. I provide you one stirring performance after another. Do you appreciate my gifts? Do you take time to enjoy them? Must you be blind to my artistry because you are inconvenienced?

A foghorn cuts through the overcast. It is from the offshore automated buoy, sounding every ten seconds a 1.5-second blast that can be heard six miles at sea. Each foghorn and lighthouse has its own individual signal, as distinctive as fingerprints, enabling mariners to identify their position and avoid deadly shoals. Often I hear the horn while I am working in the garden, when the land is clear, and I must remind myself that the ocean may be soupy and dangerous.

The rhythmic pulsations of the horn could be the voice of the fog itself. The fog never lasts long. It gathers in the hollows to the east, among the hills, as lingering gossamer floating islands of mist. Then the islands gradually vanish and the sun strikes the evergreens which are refreshed by the morning dampness. Finally even the foghorn is silent. The garden is liberated from the overcast and I no longer can avoid the chores that await me.

It is a glorious day to collect thatch, clear and cold. Even early in the day the sun has a feel of coming spring although winter is not officially here yet. The marsh sparkles in the brilliant morning light, its blue-blue water riffled by a stiff breeze.

Gulls wheel about and complain, probably expressing their grievances and discussing the day's prospects as they search for shellfish to carry to a nearby parking lot where they drop them on the hard surface to break the shell. I have the marsh to myself, except for the gulls. There is the smell of the sea and a ripe aroma from a pile of clam shells to be returned to the water for oyster spat to set on.

We had a high tide last week, driven by vigorous winds, so I am hoping to find a good supply of thatch washed in. Thatch is primarily a salt-tolerant broad-leaf grass called spartina (alterniflora), or coardgrass. It grows along the edges of tidal marshes and creeks, reaching more than six feet tall, waving gracefully in the rising tides. In the fall the stalks die, turn brittle, and are broken by winds and ice and washed in on the tides.

Thatch grows by a spreading underground root system and has no seeds like hay, making it ideal as mulch. It breaks down slowly, adding valuable mineral-rich organic matter to sea or soil. It has much the consistency of hay or straw but tends to collect in long, tangled windrows that are sometimes difficult to separate and heavy when water soaked. Like seaweed, it is often washed in on one tide and taken away on the next, and is better left unused for a while so rains can wash out much of the salt.

When we moved to Cape Cod I could get all the thatch I could use. Now it is scarce as more people recognize its value as a mulch. Mulching, like compost, is an article of faith among organic gardeners. Soil is prevented from drying out by covering it with straw, hay, leaves, grass clippings, or any vegetable matter that will decompose. Mulch is especially effective in protecting the upper few inches of soil where most plants have their roots, keeping soil uniformly cool in hot weather and protected during prolonged cold spells; it prevents wind erosion, discourages weeds, and eventually breaks down to improve soil texture and provide food for growing plants.

Most important of all, perhaps, mulch provides a stable and uniform climate that enables soil microbes to do their vital job of digesting organic matter, according to T. Bedford Franklin in *Climates in Miniature*. He believes these organisms work best at a temperature of about 100 degrees, stopping work when it climbs to 130 or drops below 41. Mulch, he says, is the most efficient means to keep temperatures in this critical range.

Even a light two-inch mulch has been found to keep soil 7 degrees cooler in summer and as many degrees warmer in winter, we are told. In my sandy soil I could not do without it. Mulching is, after all, an ancient method, invented by nature millions of years ago. Bare ground rarely exists in nature. Mulch is one of her more important life-sustaining tools.

In the fall, winds blow leaves and dead matter against plants to blanket them against winter's icy blasts, then they gradually break down to add new layers of humus. This is nature's own method of building soil and providing food for plants which, in turn, feed animals. Mulch, the forerunner of compost and humus, provides the primary fuel for life itself. It is the great synthesizer, helping persuade nature to accept the artifice of a garden as part of her scheme. Mulch, like compost, is vital to those of us who do not use chemicals and are more dependent on natural processes.

Luck is not with me today. If thatch washed in, the sea or more alert competitors beat me to it. The area is bare, only a few dry shreds clinging to the ripe clam shells awaiting return to the water. I should have come sooner. Optimism is often my undoing. A bit of pessimism seems to serve me better, at least avoiding disappointment and keeping me on my toes.

Havelock Ellis recommended having a little of each if we would "walk sanely amid the opposing perils in the path of life," although he also noted that "the place where optimism most flourishes is the lunatic asylum."

Undaunted, I recall another possibility. At the head of the bay, where it is fed by a river that runs through the adjoining marsh, is a dike where thatch sometimes collects. The dike supports the road and has a clapper valve that permits the river to flow into the bay while limiting the tidal flow back into the marsh. Incoming water is restricted to protect an adjacent golf course. Much of the marsh has dried up for want of enough tidal flow; golf courses usually seem to come out ahead in conflicts with nature.

This time I am in luck. A deep bed of thatch has washed up on the rocks that form the bayside of the dike. It is always the last to be taken because the wet, heavy stuff must be carried up several concrete steps to the road. My old Jeep pickup is parked at the top of the steps and I must climb over a guardrail to dump the pails of thatch into the bed.

It is hard going but occasionally I take time to admire the magnificent scenery, the dunes, bay, and horizon, all melding into one, and watch the antics of the gulls. The wind blows harder here on the elevated dike, swooping off the bay and across the marsh. Each time I fill the galvanized pail, climb the stairs, struggle over the metal guardrail, and dump the thatch, much of it blows across the road or back into my face. Repeatedly I must climb up on the truck bed to stomp down the thatch before it takes off. Nature is reluctant to let me cart off these sea nutrients.

I am stomping furiously and removing loose thatch from my hair, ears, and mouth when I notice a car full of people parked across the road. Visitors frequently come here to admire the vista of marsh and bay, and particularly the spectacular sunsets.

But it is not the view that attracts these visitors today. They are watching me, laughing at my frustration. My task must appear as pointless as I look ridiculous. I wave to them and continue my exertions. They return the greeting and drive off, still laughing, leaving me to struggle with the unruly thatch and my old adversary the relentless wind, and trying to figure how to factor absurdity into the cost of food production.

That grand old poem called winter.
—Henry David Thoreau

Snow fell all day yesterday, through the night, and into this morning. It is a blizzard, the first of the season, with winds at almost 45 miles per hour. That merry choreographer, the north wind, has the flakes dancing a lively jig, molding them into exquisite designs and delicate shapes. The temperature is below 20 degrees.

This ends the suspense. Only a week ago the thermometer hit 70, breaking the record 64 set for the date in 1912, according to the paper. There should be something solemn and processional about such an event but the weather seems quite blasé, as if records mean nothing to it.

Just four days after hitting 70 degrees the temperature plunged and a light snow fell as winter finally threw aside all inhibitions and pretensions. The early dusting of snow left the garden white except for a few green shoots of frozen lettuce, several heads of cabbage that never got picked, the steadfast kale, and a row of bedraggled parsley.

The blizzard leaves no remaining trace of green. There is only unbroken white, drifts mounded against the fence and atop banked mulch on the carrots and leeks. Snow is nature's own winter mulch, protecting soil from excessive cold and drying winds. As it melts, the moisture helps break down organic matter and replenishes groundwater. I am also indebted to it as a source of cheap fertilizer, as it gathers nitrogen and minerals from the air in its journey to earth. The snow on the ground appears lifeless but fairly teems with enterprise. Mice and other small creatures tunnel through it on their rounds while transacting business as usual. If the chill has not penetrated too deeply, soil microorganisms remain active under the insulating blanket.

The garden demands nothing of me now except to admire its new garment of white. But I do have to clear snow from in front of the beehives so air can circulate through the reduced entrances and, should the weather turn warm, the bees can get out for a "cleansing flight."

For the moment I do not bestir myself. I am immobilized by the beauty of the snow. I watch the falling flakes through windows decorated by the master artist with frost flowers. The wind flings the tumbling snowflakes about, sculpting them into ethereal shapes, the final act in nature's most stirring winter drama.

Thoreau, as poet and overseer of snowstorms, did not overlook snowflakes: "A divinity must have stirred within them before the crystals did thus shoot and set . . . myriads of these little disks . . . glorious spangles, the sweepings of heaven's floor. And they all sing, melting as they sing of the mysteries of the number six—six, six, six."

Modern science is fascinated with snow crystals in their myriad individual shapes but as early as the second century B.C. the Chinese recognized the hexagonal character of snow crystals. A Chinese poet in 157 B.C. observed that most flowers have five petals but snow flowers have six.

Each flake is an individual story, each a separate miracle that begins in the atmosphere as a tiny speck of dust that enlarges itself with condensed moisture, freezing, ever increasing in size and complexity but always retaining the magic six-sided figure of Thoreau's lyric. Why did nature decide on the hexagon?

The ice crystals are indifferent to my wonder and admiration as they stick together to form the dancing snowflakes buffeted about by the wind.

The delicate snow crystals have only a short life, barely surviving the earthward trip, their distinctive crystalline shape soon lost on the ground as the flakes melt or merge in a formless assemblage of ice granules.

Science long marveled that no two snow crystals were ever exactly alike but recently I read that a researcher claimed to have found two that were identical. Is this a gain for science or a loss for poetic mystery? Nature is given no respite in the ceaseless pursuit of her secrets.

Four days after the blizzard we are suddenly back to summer. The temperature is 60 degrees, the snow already melted by the stillwarm earth and unseasonable temperature. The bees were out even before the snow vanished, leaving the white blanket spotted with their droppings. Flying in this weather is risky for bees. The sun beats on the hives, building up the inside temperature. If the weather is cold, below the critical 55 degrees, they may be deceived into thinking it is warm outside, and those who venture out may perish. The bees flying today appear tentative, as if saying to one another, "Can you believe it? Is it true? Is it to be trusted?"

Carrots and leeks under their mounds of mulch must wonder what is going on with this erratic weather. I pull back just enough thatch to dig out a supply of carrots. The exposed earth is wet and cold but not frozen; there are even worms. The carrots are unbelievably crisp and sweet; they never taste as delicious as when rescued from their soil haven on a winter day.

It seems as strange to remove the result of summer's planting of carrots as it does to think about getting ready for spring and summer. Gardening always anticipates the future. We live with one eye on the calendar and the other on the weather. In the spring we plant for summer and fall. In late summer we put in winter crops. In the fall the soil is prepared for spring. In the winter seeds are ordered, gardening strategies are planned, and flats started for the harvest far ahead. Gardening must be one of the more optimistic of all endeavors.

To tend a garden makes one acutely aware of the sun and seasons. We speak of a garden as if it were an entity of summer, but there are, in fact, four separate gardens, one for each season, each different in mood, needs, and the way it produces. Our primary reference points are the first and last frost dates, October 23 and April 23, respectively, in these parts. Both are approximates. Frost may come earlier or later. We have had snow in June and summer's heat in February.

Rarely does the weather follow an expected course, but behaves as if proving it has a mind of its own and refuses to be taken for granted. Despite the variations, caprices, and treacheries of weather, we accept certain fixed guidelines and plot our garden lives accordingly. We take for granted that the seasons will follow some kind of reasonable progression and we can expect broad conformity to "seasonal variations." Experience supports this optimism.

A garden is, above all, an act of faith. We assume that certain things will happen in a certain sequence, and usually they do within the parameters of expectations we live by. Despite the planning and anticipation that go into a garden, how much we live in the future or dwell on the past, there is only one reality: today, while keeping a wary eye on tomorrow.

Once more, after another week of summer's lingering grace, winter has returned in earnest, this time probably to remain. The temperature is 16°F. The weather bureau reports that cold weather is expected to stay through the end of the year. The lettuce in the cold frame is finally frozen solid, its "salad days" behind it. Now we look forward to the January thaw and spring. Winter, officially, is barely under way and already I am weary of it, eager for spring and the new garden to come.

I ask not for a larger garden,
But for finer seeds.
—Russell Herman Conwell

The last act of the gardening season is under way. Or is it the first? Does nature consider seeds beginning, end, or both? Words like *beginning* and *end* are human terms, part of our fragmented thinking and terminal mentality. They have no place in nature. She deals only in cycles, or regeneration, as it now seems to be called.

Each year Peggy and I go through much the same ritual ordering seeds for the coming garden. Invariably it seems to be a Sunday afternoon in January. The sun is deceptively warm through the southern window behind the couch. I like to think the sun's heat or some deep atavistic urge prompts us to think about providing our food supply for the coming year. A more likely reason is that we are already late; it is almost time to put in flats of vegetables.

In front of us are the new catalogues and a box of leftover seeds. First we must decide which of the old seeds are usable. The rules call for putting a few seeds between wet sheets of paper and enclosing them in a plastic bag for several days. If only 50 percent germinate, out they go. A 75 percent rate calls for sowing thicker than usual. New seeds usually have a 90 percent or better germination figure stamped on the packet.

I do not bother to test seeds. This is another act of faith on my part, assuming that most are viable for up to five years. Exceptions are onions, parsley, and parsnips, which are good for only one year. The others I usually keep for up to three years, a bit of tempered optimism that seems to work out fairly well.

The soil itself is my primary testing ground. If seeds fail to sprout within a reasonable time, I reseed. The season is still early so little time is lost and I save myself some trouble. Maturity is not delayed substantially because the chilled earth delays germination anyway. Plants start moving, I have found, when they are ready. Not before.

Seed catalogues started arriving several weeks ago, even before Christmas. Each year, it seems, they come earlier, in greater volume, thicker, more colorful, and offering more items for sale with more breathless descriptions and adjectives designed to get winter's tired blood racing. The catalogues, like gardeners, are reaching toward the sun and the promise of coming spring.

I have read that there are now over two hundred seed catalogues. We get more than two dozen, unsolicited and most of them new to me. Our name was bought from some other company's mailing list and once on it is impossible to get off or stop the avalanche of direct-mail offerings.

I have no real objection to these catalogue offerings, other than the extra burden they impose on the local landfill. They are harmless enough otherwise. Some are even helpful, providing seed viability charts, planting schedules, tables, folksy messages, and gardening tips. Often the material is identical from one catalogue to another. Most offer much the same items for sale and probably feature seeds from the same wholesalers. Few companies grow their own seeds nowadays; most seeds are grown by large corporations, often foreign owned. The only real competition, generally, is in the price and claims made by hired copywriters who often seem to draw on the same research.

Each new generation of catalogues appears to be more

extravagant. Piled one atop another, year by year, they would give a kind of evolutionary record of gardening, like fossils found in rocks. Some of the newer models promote specials, bargains, and once-in-a-lifetime opportunities. One of this year's crop had over two hundred pages. Offerings include everything even indirectly related to gardening, from seeds, fertilizers, and pesticides through cherry pitters, yard furniture, and plastic owls to frighten away birds. Gardening has become big business.

Vegetable seeds are deeply rooted in American history. Originally they were brought here by early colonists and added to those procured or stolen from the Indians. Most colonists saved their own seeds but imports could be had. The earliest ads for seeds appeared in a Boston paper about 1870. Poor mail service made possible only local distribution at first but when the Pony Express began to deliver mail the business took off on a large scale. A trade association was formed in 1883 to certify seeds for trueness of variety and freedom from disease.

Most of the old, traditional seed companies either no longer exist or have been bought by huge conglomerates, for diversification, and given a corporate image. Their catalogues are usually slick, an explosion of colors and graphics. I try, in vain, to picture Farmer Bagley confronted by one of these glossy publications.

A few seed companies have avoided extreme commercialization. One is Johnny's Selected Seeds in Albion, Maine. Privately owned and operated, it grows some of its own seeds but tests all, uses few pesticides, and puts out a modest catalogue containing personalized but factual information and valuable growing advice. Another is Shepherd's Garden Seeds of Felton, California, which specializes in European seeds not ordinarily found here. One that I learned about only recently is Pinetree Garden Seeds in Gloucester, Maine. Founded in 1979, its catalogue is a refreshing black and white, simple, informative, and forthright; the seeds are tested, reasonably priced, and primarily geared for the Northeast. There are others that still emphasize quality without slickness. A growing number of small firms, often individually owned, deal in so-called heritage seeds, old varieties no longer available in mass markets.

Most commercial catalogues emphasize new varieties that are bred to be bigger, earlier, more productive, or more resistant to this or that. Generally they are hybrids, products of genetic manipulation or cross-breeding. I occasionally use hybrids but prefer open-pollinated strains so I can keep my own seeds for the following year. Hybrids do not breed true after the first generation.

Most catalogues feature tomatoes as garden superstars, coming up with something new each year. Tomatoes won this acclaim only after a slow start. They were once regarded as ornamentals and known as "cancer apples," which were thought to cause disease. The French later embraced them as "love apples" *(pomme d'amour)*, considering them an aphrodisiac.

Tomatoes were popular in Europe long before they were accepted here. For many years Americans thought them poisonous. An oft-told story holds that one Robert Gibbon Johnson boldly announced in 1820 that he would publicly eat a tomato in Salem, New Jersey. Doctors protested, preachers prayed, women fainted, so goes the story. Johnson ate not only one tomato but several without ill effect and the tomato was on its way to garden glory. A skeptic noted that had Johnson eaten a modern supermarket tomato he might have had second thoughts.

Catalogues, when I started to garden, offered only a few of the more commonly known vegetables. Now there are scores of vegetables and varieties. There are said to be 72 vegetables commonly listed in seed catalogues, at least 17 of them originally from the Americas. But the number of varieties can be almost overwhelming; there are 350 varieties of tomatoes alone, embodying every known tomato technology. What would Farmer Bagley have made of this state of affairs?

Most new vegetable strains are not developed for taste or nutrition but for some commercial advantage. An eternal shelf life and "pretty face" represent commercial Nirvana. Cosmetic values and longevity almost invariably rate higher than intrinsic quality in the marketplace.

Seed catalogues, regardless how skillfully composed, cannot change the basic truth of gardening: Scratch the earth, plant a seed, water it, and wait for the warmth of sunlight to nurture it into a food-bearing plant.

Failure has no place in seed catalogues. But not even the most adroit copywriter can change the fact that gardens are ruled by a direct cause-and-effect relationship. Misdeeds are generally punished and the well-done rewarded. If all conditions for success are met—the soil is right, the seeds not too old or unsuited to the climate and correctly planted, and the weather reasonable—there is the probability but not the certainty that the seeds will prosper and produce food.

The actual ordering of seeds does not take long but the ritual is drawn out because we both enjoy the discussion and debate. Peggy, in the end, selects most of the varieties, just as she does most of the harvesting and canning, the beginning and end of the garden year, and I do most of the in-between tasks. This has evolved as our division of labor, although we give one another a hand in time of need or crisis.

Even while we prepare the order, my thoughts are largely on soil preparation and what will go where this year. Account must be taken of the shade cast and tolerated by various plants, individual soil requirements, time of maturity, spacing, crop rotation, and other such matters. An invaluable aid in planning a garden is a reliable memory or, better, old calendars with records of plantings. I rely on old calendars.

Peggy generally likes to order only the amount of seeds she thinks we will need. I am more comfortable with margin for error. This is something of a role reversal for us. Usually I am the frugal one. But here personality dominates economics. She assumes that almost every seed will grow into a bearing plant, reflecting her view of life. I am less optimistic but do not know if this is my innate skepticism, a lack of confidence in nature, or, as a friend said, some abiding distrust of the universe itself. A garden is full of unsettling self-insights, most of which I could do without.

The cardboard seed box on the coffee table in front of us is full of my past margins for error: soiled packets torn open and taped shut (opened seeds should properly be stored in airtight jars) and some that were never opened. Margin for error can fill cardboard boxes and clutter lives.

Despite new seed varieties and technological breakthroughs, specials, bargains, savings, discounts, and once-in-a-lifetime opportunities, we generally order the same varieties in most years, the majority coming from Johnny's. Occasionally we follow the advice of garden writers and "try something new." But usually we revert to old favorites that have served us well in the past. We specify untreated seeds, not doused with fungicides to prevent rotting in cold soils, taking our chances with nature and her idiosyncrasies.

The order is finally completed, a check written, the envelope stamped and mailed. Almost immediately I start looking for a notice in our post office box that a package awaits us. Anticipation is part of the pleasure of gardening, and waiting for the seeds to arrive seems to make winter pass a little faster.

The seeds finally do arrive. I hand Jack, the postmaster, the slip advising that a package awaits us. I feel elated, even excited, but Jack perfunctorily pushes the box across the counter, unaware of the high drama of this transaction, my expectations and eagerness to get started. He cheerfully bids me to "have a nice day" and resumes sorting the mail.

> *Come, gentle Spring! Ethereal Mildness! Come.*
> —James Thomson

Snow still covers the garden. The weather remains cold. Birds come to the feeder. There is the occasional warm day when bees take a cleansing flight. The sun's ascending arc casts new shadows. Crows caucus out of sight and complain about lingering winter.

February is a difficult month. It seems to hang somewhere between hope and despair. Everyone is impatient for warm weather to arrive. Many year-round residents who can afford it have gone south or abroad for the month. The town and those of us left behind seem to be hibernating.

I have already started flats of onions, leeks, and celery in a commercial mix. Sterilizing garden soil in the oven does not appeal to me, although I have complete directions. The sterile mix helps prevent "damping off," a fungal disease said to be caused by forty different organisms, and leading to fatal wilting of young plants; the vectors of other disagreeable ailments also may lurk in unsterilized soil. The seeds were germinated by covering the flats with plastic wrap to retain moisture, and then kept warm in the kitchen.

Onions and leeks germinate first, like fine blades of grass. Then incipient celery leaves finally poke through the mix. I must remove the plastic covering immediately or mold will form and kill the young plants. After a few days the seedlings go under lights in the basement, a half-dozen workbench-type fluorescent fixtures suspended from chains so they can be raised or lowered on S hooks.

The flats rest on a sheet of plywood supported by high sawhorses. The lights at first are only a couple of inches above the plants but are raised gradually as the foliage reaches for the light. An automatic timer turns the lights on in the morning and off at night. Otherwise I would never remember one or the other, and the alternating periods of darkness and rest are as important as those of light and growth; most plants require at least five hours of darkness daily to convert stored carbohydrates into a usable form for their expanding tissues.

The earliest seedlings remain in flats. But tomatoes, peppers, and squash, after developing their true leaves, are transplanted to individual pots, usually old Styrofoam or yogurt containers with holes punched in the bottom for drainage. Some must be transplanted again if the roots outgrow the space; plants can be permanently damaged if rootbound. The potting soil is a homemade mixture of screened garden soil and compost, sphagnum moss, and vermiculite. Sowbugs, millipedes, worms, and other small creatures in the soil appear dazed, their biological time clocks betrayed by the unnatural basement warmth.

Transplanting tender young seedlings is one of my favorite spring tasks. By now the days are getting longer and warmer. The potting soil has a pungent fragrance that merges with the aroma of the plants. The stems have deep green leaves and their roots are often longer than the growth aboveground.

A hole is poked in the soil with a pencil-like dibble, an elegant little instrument brought to me from England by Bill and Helen; the fragile roots are carefully eased into the hole and the earth is firmed for solid contact. Enriched with seaweed fertilizer and drawn by the artificial lights, the plants succeed at an astonishing rate. Already the new tomatoes release their special aroma when touched; the entire basement smells like a greenhouse.

Each year brings its own adventures. Once I failed to mark two varieties of peppers and could never tell one from the other until the fruit appeared. Another year Lily leaped up on a tray of tomato flats balanced precariously on the arms of a chair in the dining room. Tray and flats shot into the air to crash to the rug in a glorious tangle of dirt and mangled plants; Lily had disappeared before they landed. I salvaged several of the tomatoes but had to plant them as mystery plants. That was a great year for cherry tomatoes. Still another time white flies migrated to the flats from infected houseplants and wiped out all of the tomato and pepper seedlings.

When all goes well, the plants are removed from the lights before they get too "leggy" or rootbound and are taken to the garden cold frame to become accustomed to the sun and night-time temperatures. After a week or so they are "hardened off," ready to be transplanted into the garden itself, embarked on their life work. Early plants, including onions, leeks, and pars-ley, go in "as soon as the ground can be worked." Tomatoes, peppers, eggplant, and other tender crops do not go in until Memorial Day weekend. That is local wisdom which I follow.

But all of that remains ahead. We are still in February. Most of the seeds are not yet in flats. Winter has not yielded. The pile of manure gathered in the fall is frozen. Usually manure generates enough heat to prevent freezing, but this severe win-ter has subdued the microorganisms now waiting for spring to reclaim them to duty.

I, too, feel subdued and weary of winter. I long for the sun's heat on my body, the feel of earth on my fingers. It rejuvenates me and returns a bit of spring to my autumnal bones. I am cheered by the thought that spring is moving north from the Everglades at 15 miles per day, or so I read, although it advances up mountains at only 100 feet a day, without regard to those of us who eagerly await it and would like to speed things up a bit.

On this cold but sunny February day I must content myself preparing the new garden calendar, copying planting dates from previous calendars smudged with dirt and bearing cryptic scrawls. One notation demands particular attention. It is in bold print, followed by three exclamation points: SQUASH BUG ALERT!!!

I put the entry in the new calendar, proclaiming lethal intent with a jotting down of a date months away while the squash bugs sleep, unmindful and undisturbed in their winter shelters, not yet ready to produce the offspring that will attack plants from seeds still in sealed packets. Even now, in the frozen solemnity of late winter, next summer's bloody engagement for the zucchini is already in the making.

The seeds are arranged in plastic bags with paper slips denoting planting dates for the various crops. This year I have resolved to be more vigilant and efficient. I may even get around to painting the cold frame, reglazing the glass, and repairing the sagging gate. I have wonderful intentions to reform and improve my character and have the finest garden ever, if the weather and gods of chance cooperate.

I contemplate the unopened packets of seed before me. They, like the catalogues announcing them, are my harbingers of spring. I hear squirrel raiding the feeder at the kitchen window again but do not rouse myself to scare him into one of his daring leaps into the nearby oak so the birds can eat in peace. Nature is on its own for the moment.

I muse on what was primitive man's harbinger of spring. Did he observe the angle of the sun from his cave and depend on its increasing warmth to alert him that spring was coming? Or was he, like the wild creatures and plants about him, more attuned to nature, knowing in his bones and juices that the vernal equinox was almost at hand?

An older man, a native, I met in the post office today commented that the weather is changeable this time of year. "This morning," he said, "it's so cold that I put on my long drawers, but by noon it's so warm I have to change."

With the sun gaining strength, the seeds here, the last snow melted, potatoes and onions from last year sprouting in the root cellar, and long johns being shed by noon, can spring be far behind? Soon it will be time to plant the peas, that annual rite of the new growing season, calling the garden back to life in answer to the invisible and silent summons that bestirs the blood and continues the ancient cycle of birth, death, and renewal.

This we know. The earth does not belong to man; man belongs to the earth. This we know. All things are connected like the blood which unites one family. All things are connected. Whatever befalls the earth befalls the sons of the earth. Man did not weave the web of life, he is merely a strand in it. Whatever he does to the web, he does to himself.

—Chief Seattle